Skeena STEELHEAD

Unknown Past, Uncertain Future

R.S. Hooton

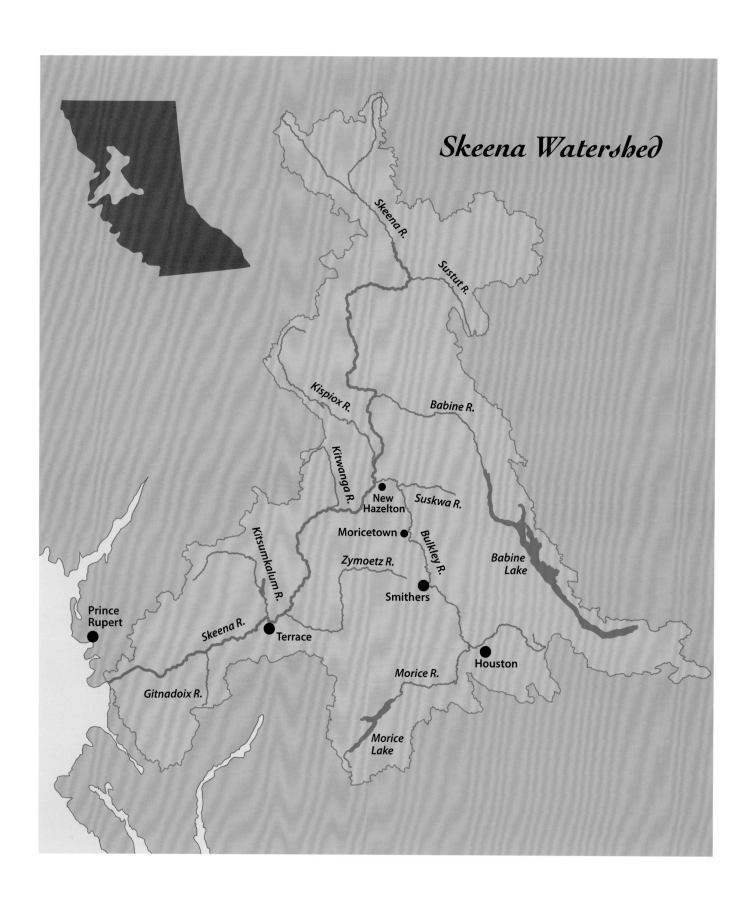

Skeena Watershed

Skeena STEELHEAD

Unknown Past, Uncertain Future

R.S. Hooton

Frank Amato Publications

ACKNOWLEDGEMENTS

Steelhead anglers who never took from the resource but gave so much back to it deserve recogniton for inspiring me over my life as a steelhead advocate. Without them I would never have reached the point of preparing this book. Topping my list are original Steelhead Society of British Columbia members Cal Woods, Lee Straight, Pete Broomhall and Bob Taylor. Later there was John Brockley. Unfortunately, among those fine gentlemen, only Pete is still with us. Jim Culp has carried the Skeena steelhead torch longer and more relentlessly than any angler I have ever known. Too few of those who fancy themselves as the top guns of the day will ever know what he has done for them. Champions of fish and fish habitat Rob Brown and Bruce Hill are hall of famers as well. Keith Douglas, the pit bull of the Skeena steelhead warriors, holds feet to fires as never before. Departed anglers Bob York, Carl Mauser and Faye Davis provided diaries and accounts of yesteryear that helped me understand much about the culture and philosophy that created the reputation of the Skeena and its treasures. Ed Neal was extremely helpful and generous in recounting details of the early days on Babine and Sustut. My mentors and professional colleagues in a life in the fisheries management business were more influential than they might ever appreciate. Among them are Ron Thomas, Zeke Withler, Hugh Sparrow, Gerry Taylor, Charlie Lyons, George Reid, Mike Whatley, Dave Narver, Harvey Andrusak and Al Martin. In a class by himself is my personal hero and friend Art Tautz. No one on the planet ever did as much for Skeena steelhead. Provincial staff of the Smithers office, past and present, most notably Mark Beere, Dana Atagi, Jeff Lough, George Schultze, Colin Spence, Reid White and Jim Yardley, made life in the trenches worth the struggle. George deserves full credit for the idea of the Steelhead Run Status newsletter. Whether they knew it or not the passion and conviction of some of the pioneers of the guiding and lodge businesses was always a source of inspiration. Honorable mention goes to Olga Walker, Ken and Alice Belford, Bob Wickwire. George Pattern of the Pacific Biological Station library was a tremendous help in searching out historic Federal Government publications that added greatly to my understanding of the history of fisheries management interventions. Mariusz Wroblewsky and Analisa Fenix of Ecotrust were wonderfully supportive of this work throughout. Analisa's GIS skills are out there in a different universe. Lastly, above all others, my wife Lori deserves as much credit as I for the existence of these pages. She was the rock that kept our home happy and healthy in spite of all the passion and politics that pervaded the Skeena steelhead scene for all those years in Smithers and since. To her and our three children, Raylene, Carmen and Brock I dedicate this book.

Ecotrust's mission is to inspire fresh thinking that creates economic opportunity, social equity and environmental well-being.

All inquiries should be addressed to:
Frank Amato Publications, Inc. • P.O. Box 82112 • Portland, Oregon 97282
503-653-8108 • www.AmatoBooks.com

Book and Cover Design by Mariah Hinds
Cover Photography by Adam Tavender
Photography by: Art Lingren: page 8, 9, 18, 28, 38, 44,
Bill McMillan: page 59, 76, 113, 133, 145, 149, 151,
All Other Photographs by Author
Maps by Ecotrust: page 12, 20, 22, 32, 65

Limited	Softbound	Hardbound
ISBN-13: 978-1-57188-476-3	ISBN-13: 978-1-57188-474-9	ISBN-13: 978-1-57188-475-6
UPC: 0-81127-00318-1	UPC: 0-81127-00316-7	UPC: 0-81127-00317-4

Printed in China

1 3 5 7 9 10 8 6 4 2

To order more copies, please call (800) 541-9498

TABLE OF CONTENTS

PREFACE

Measured by abundance, diversity of species and life histories, as well as integrity of the habitat, the Skeena is one of the most important remaining wild Pacific salmon and steelhead systems in the world. It has the highest population of wild steelhead of any river drainage anywhere. That a watershed this size is still relatively intact at the start of the 21st Century is simply remarkable. That it remains biologically productive, persistently defying the northward progression of systemic collapses witnessed on the continent's other great salmon producing rivers, seems nothing short of miraculous. That such productivity continues to support the evolution of diverse ecological, economic, and cultural relationships/wealth is practically an abstraction, especially to someone who knows such wealth/relationships exclusively in the context of a lament for its passing, and nostalgia for its return.

But the protections so far afforded the Skeena by a combination of its geographical isolation, biological resilience, and effective defense by advocates are temporary and incomplete. Pollution, extraction by the logging, commercial fishing, and mining industries, and the development of rail lines and roads have already left their mark on the ecology of the watershed. Reduced salmon returns have heightened tensions between stakeholders concerned about fish and access to their harvest. Consolidation of that access, to an increasingly commoditized resource, has concentrated economic and political power. Patterns from other rivers foreshadow other familiar trends – towards a gradual transfer of accountability for management from specific individuals within the community to the more ambiguous framework of government and its proxy agencies, and the parallel transfer of the voices of protest to large coalitions of institutional advocacy organizations.

Fortunately, there are several critically important variables that challenge the relevance of such comparison. First, the suite of imminent threats to the Skeena's integrity is arriving at the same time as unequivocal results of a century of experimentation on rivers like the Columbia: there is no apparent way to subordinate the integrity of the system and retain its resilience as reflected in complex, abundant, diverse and dynamic natural and human communities. This understanding creates the opportunity to discuss choices in their historical and bioregional context.

Second, the scale of the watershed is big enough to be internationally significant but small enough to accommodate direct discussions between residents.

Third, Skeena residents remain extremely connected to their surrounding environments and engaged in deliberations affecting their future. Responsibility has not been completely divested to institutions outside the watershed; people still look to each other to supply and share information. Resources, and their management, have not become placeless – and neither has advocacy on their behalf. All of this suggests a powerful potential for self-determinism that is preciously rare. By communicating the patterns of loss and its consequences we can help ensure everyone knows what we've got here, certainly before its gone but perhaps without it ever going at all.

Ecotrust is honored to help the distinguished author and the publisher in producing this book.

We gratefully acknowledge The Charles Engelhard Foundation, Deborah J. and Peter A. Magowan Family Foundation, William H. and Sally Neukom, Foster Reed, Yvon Chouinard, and Tim and Karen Hixon.

—Spencer B. Beebe
Founder and President, Ecotrust

FOREWORD

In the 80's and 90's while I was covering environmental issues for big daily newspapers in British Columbia I learned that were only a handful of government employees who you could count on to tell the truth. Bob Hooton was one of them. He put steelhead first, was fearless in defense of the environment, and never ducked tough questions—even when the answers could add up to career suicide. He didn't know it then and he probably still doesn't, but he was an inspiration. As long as there are Bob Hootons in the world there is the chance that the truth will come out and the right things will get done.

In this brilliant historical analysis of what has gone wrong with steelhead and salmon management on B.C.'s magnificent Skeena River, he paints a bleak and at times depressing picture. When you read how badly, how corruptly, things have been managed, you might tend to think, as I do at times, that we don't deserve to have wild salmon in wild rivers. Maybe it's over. Maybe all we really deserve is hatchery trout in lakes surrounded by luxury recreational homes, where the water is crowded with power boats.

But then, as the author leads you through the sorry history of the Skeena you are reminded of how great things once were—and you find yourself asking, why can't it be that way again? The fact is, if enough people care, if enough people get informed, get mad and get motivated, it can be. Yes, we can have a river with 100,000 steelhead. Just think about that for a moment.

Bob Hooton tried to change the world when the provincial government put him in charge of steelhead management on the Skeena. And he did. He fought back. He fought like hell for steelhead, and he was a pivotal agent of change. He argues passionately in these pages that he failed because he fell short of his goal, but I disagree. He moved steelhead way up the agenda in government offices in Victoria and Ottawa. And with this book he is giving the species another big push into the light by keeping the focus on steelhead management and on the need for reform.

It should be obvious to all of us that no one person, no isolated group, can force the government to alter a mindset that has become ingrained through 100 years of repetition. The salmon rivers of the West are managed now, as they have always been, to maximize commercial harvests, even if it means driving weaker stocks into extinction. The federal government's Wild Salmon Policy (drafted years ago but still not fully implemented) would change that dramatically, but federal Department of Fisheries and Oceans bureaucrats have been doing their best to sabotage it, in the same way they always tried to derail Bob's effort to save steelhead. They create the institutional equivalent of a tar pit, through endless consultations, report drafts, communication strategies and budget strangulations— then they let good ideas and good people go there to die.

But some people just won't quit, just like some ideas, like the idea wild steelhead are worth saving, won't go away. In this polemic Bob worries about society's loss of collective memory. He was driven in his career by his love for wild fish and wild rivers. I am sure he was often alone on the water, as we must be at times, if we are really going to get, bone deep, what fishing is all about. He caught fish that took his breath away. Stunning, cold, hard fish shaped by the incredible perfection of 10,000 years of evolution, and he knew he just couldn't let them go down. He wonders if his grandchildren, faced with crowded rivers and diminished returns, will ever experience what he did. He worries that if they don't they won't care as much about it all, because they just won't know. I share those worries for my own kids. In 'Big Yellow Taxi', Joni Mitchell warns about the destruction of paradise by singing "you don't know what you've got 'til it's gone." The sad reality is that once it is gone, you don't know what you had because it is forgotten. The collective will to restore paradise can erode to nothing in a single generation. The truth is forgotten and society becomes mindless. But I think Bob has made sure with this book, through his detailed, painstaking research into the shameful record of mismanagement, that the truth about Skeena steelhead—which is that they aren't lost, but are willfully destroyed—will never be forgotten. Not only that, but he has set down in black and white an unequivocal argument for how we can, and must as a society, change directions. The Skeena's remarkable steelhead runs can not only be saved, but with tough decision making and resolve, and a bit of luck, they can be restored. The tragedy of gill net and gaff can be undone.

To paraphrase Edmond Burke, all it takes for evil to triumph is for good men to remain silent. Bob Hooton has never been one of those silent men, and he is raising his voice loud in *Skeena Steelhead*, he's railing against all the fisheries managers and politicians who would do nothing. He's raising his fist against power and saying to all of us, don't forget, and don't ever, ever, give up the fight.

—Mark Hume
Vancouver, 2011

INTRODUCTION

One of the great things about history is you don't have to make it up.[1*]

The world is replete with examples of fisheries that once were. Whether it be bluefin tuna, coral reef fishes of southeast Asia, the northern cod of eastern Canada, Atlantic salmon throughout most of their range or the chinook and steelhead runs of California's Central Valley and northern coast and the Columbia, to name but a few, the story has been the same. The human animal has consistently placed a lower value on fish than the economies that have grown to compete for them and, eventually, against them. The end result – each generation of us lowers the bar and re-defines a benchmark for the next. Regrettably, succeeding generations rarely understand or appreciate where the bar once stood.

Some isolated opportunities still exist to savor what little remains globally of the once abundant premiere river sportfishing opportunities for iconic species like steelhead and Atlantic salmon. Kamchatka is the last frontier for steelhead, albeit inaccessible for most of us. Across the vastness of Russia, at its opposite corner, the Kola Peninsula supports the best of what remains of Atlantic salmon fishing. Some might place the rivers of Iceland on equal footing. In North America the single remaining opportunity to reach out and touch a piece of past glory rests with the Skeena watershed in northwestern British Columbia. Alaska may boast more pristine environments than modern-day Skeena and it undoubtedly reflects abundances of anadromous fish no longer found outside its borders but it does not support the world record class wild summer steelhead of the fabled Skeena.

The Skeena steelhead fishery story began to unfold with the arrival of commercial fishing in the late 1870s. By the turn of the 20th century the commercial fishery and its inevitable proliferation of canneries had assumed ownership of fish and fishing. No one will ever know with certainty how many fish of any species, especially steelhead, once occupied the waters of the Skeena. Regulations governing fishing and catch recording lagged the blossoming fishery by several decades and "fisheries science" took even longer to develop, let alone be applied. Aboriginal people sustained themselves on the strength of Skeena fish for countless generations before the commercial fishery began but their numbers, distribution and technology were never a threat to fish, at least not until the European-descendent entrepreneurs arrived. There is no record of any description to suggest the era prior to the arrival of commercial fishing saw fish abundance influenced measurably by those who preceded it.

---

*See Endnotes, page 152

Sport fishing as a detectable element of the Skeena fishery mosaic did not materialize until more than a half century after the first gill nets were deployed in the path of Skeena-bound salmon. Not until the early economies worked through the succession from fur trading to canneries to mining and logging did a railroad and highway allow access to rivers and fish that had never been subjected to angling. Float planes and helicopters followed and jet boats were not far behind. Now we have the worldwide web and an unprecedented proliferation of fish porn. Some perceive it as the best thing that ever happened for fishing. I view it as the worst possible thing for fish.

At any time in recent history the harvesting capacity of any of the three sectors involved in the Skeena fishery, if unconstrained, exceeded the capacity of the resource to sustain it. Conservation imperatives restricted fishing effort progressively but rarely prospectively. Fishing effort restrictions always lag behind fishing efficiency improvements. Perceptions among fishing-sector spokespersons hardened as they saw their "rights" and lifestyles being compromised. The debate of the day around steelhead became conservation versus allocation. Amicable resolution of that issue is as likely as peace in the Middle East. Nonetheless, governments of the day have contributed resources thought not to exist toward the process of resolution. The investment in interpretation and application of policies and unanswerable questions has spawned a growth industry whose output is measured in everything but the status of fish and fishing.

So, how long will Skeena steelhead and the sport fishery as it has come to be known last? How did we get to where we are? What will it take to see an outcome different from everywhere south where the obvious inverse relationship between the abundance of people and the abundance of fish has relegated fishery after fishery to photo albums? Will lessons learned elsewhere ever be applied?

Much has been written about particular aspects of the history of the Skeena watershed. Richard Geddes Large's 1957 piece "Skeena, River of Destiny" is an intricate and wonderfully readable description of early developments stemming from the first fur traders and missionaries through two world wars and the economies that developed thereafter. Cicely Lyons' milestone, *Salmon Our Heritage*, published in 1969 is an excellent account of the history of the commercial fishing industry in British Columbia as seen from the corporate boardroom. Geoff Meggs' 1995 book, *Salmon: The Decline of the BC Fishery*, sharply contrasts the boardroom accounts. Between Lyons' encyclopedic documentation and Meggs' take on exploitation of workers is K. Mack Campbell's warm personal reminisces of the rise and fall of the outlying canneries along the BC coast (Campbell, 2004). More recently Allan Gottesfeld and Ken Rabnett's 2008 publication *Skeena River Fish and Their Habitat* documents and knits together into a highly instructive reference a huge volume of technically focused background material originating from sources unknown or unavailable to most. Hundreds of references embedded in a half century's worth of scientific literature on fish and fisheries include Skeena-related material. The explosion of records and reports emanating from the golden age of process, from 1990 to the present, add to the mix. Foremost among references on sport fishing in the Skeena is John Fennelly's 1963 classic *Steelhead Paradise*. Paralleling the proliferation of scientific literature has been the steadily increasing volume of sportfishing-related publications in magazines, journals, hard cover and, of course, the worldwide web. Nowhere, however, is there anything that documents the steelhead sportfishery development and the struggle of successive generations of advocates to preserve what too few know as an international treasure. It's a story worth telling.

I contemplated two approaches for the story. One was a chronological account that attempted to knit together, step by step, the history and interaction between the Indian fishery, the commercial fishery and the sport fishery. The other was to treat each one of those separately and leave the bulk of the knitting until all three were described. I chose the latter, not in the least because I think it makes for a more readable product. Prefacing everything though is the need to understand something about the fish themselves, the geography of the area and the governing bodies involved.

Part 1: The Preliminaries

Chapter 1

FIRST, THE FISH

M y years in meeting halls and boardrooms, on boats and in fishing lodges and from remote villages in the Skeena outback through Vancouver and the provincial capital, Victoria, instruct me that many of the people who influence Skeena River steelhead lack a basic understanding of what a steelhead is and how it differs markedly from those other five salmon species. Commercial fishers tend to look upon them as the bane of their existence. First Nations fishers view them as food, not to be played with. The sportfishing fraternity often refers to Skeena steelhead as the province's ultimate freshwater game fish and one that should be exempt from harvest. Even some who label themselves professionals in the fisheries field sometimes reveal their lack of knowledge. Regardless of persuasion it seems a primer on basic steelhead biology and life history, Skeena focused, would be useful.

For perspective consider that the Skeena's watershed is less than one-tenth that of the Columbia and only one-quarter of the Fraser's. It is less than one-third as long as the Columbia, about two-fifths as long as the Fraser and its mean annual flow is about one-quarter of the Columbia's and three-fifths of the Fraser's. Most of the Skeena watershed lies north of the 54th parallel of latitude. Winters are long and growing seasons short, especially in many of the higher elevation summer steelhead-producing tributaries in the interior of the drainage. The Skeena is not productive fish territory by any classic biological metric. Yes, it is the home of world-record-size steelhead and yes, those fish can still be found in some of the most splendid waters and surrounding uplands one could ever hope to visit. But, the waters are often nutrient limited, the temperatures less than optimal and growing seasons short. If one wants to see high volumes of timber per acre of forest land per unit time one doesn't look to Skeena country. The same applies to fish. A host of streams in Washington, Oregon and Northern California easily eclipse the Skeena's productivity. What sustains Skeena's place in the angling mythology of the planet is not some unique capacity of its steelhead to withstand the same levels of human incursion found virtually everywhere to the south but simply the fact the northern creep of that influence has not arrived in similar magnitude, at least not yet.

There are two distinct groups of steelhead within the Skeena system—summer and winter fish. By definition summer fish leave the ocean in a sexually immature state in the summer and early fall of the calendar year before they spawn.

Six inches and one more winter to go before heading to sea.

Winter steelhead stay at sea until late in the winter or spring of the same year in which they spawn. They are relatively mature on arrival. Summer fish overwinter and mature in fresh water. Both groups spawn at roughly the same time in the spring. Summer steelhead are, by far, the most renowned and are the only group that will be discussed in the pages that follow. They originate in the interior tributaries of the system, mostly 100 miles or more from the coast. The Skeena tributaries most commonly associated with the summer fish are the Copper or Zymoetz near Terrace, the Bulkley/Morice system which enters at Hazelton, the Kispiox slightly upstream and opposite and then beyond to the Babine and Sustut (Fig. 1, page 12). There are more than a dozen other summer steelhead tributaries of the Skeena that are less well known due to their remoteness and/or their small stock sizes they now support. Winter steelhead originate in the Skeena tributaries downstream from Terrace. Transitional between the "pure" summer and winter stocks are the Kitsumkalum and Lakelse rivers at Terrace. Both support summer and winter fish. I remain unconvinced the Copper supports steelhead that fit the accepted definition of a winter stock but locals are adamant the fish they catch in the lower river in winter and even into early spring are not fish that left the ocean the previous summer or early fall. Within each of the major summer steelhead producing tributaries and in numerous other smaller tributaries of the Skeena there are many individual stocks of varying abundance that, collectively, contribute to a broad diversity of inheritable

characteristics such as run timing and age (and therefore size) at first spawning.

In contrast to salmon, all steelhead are multi-year river residents prior to emigration and life at sea. Evolution has pre-determined that steelhead smolts (the term applied to seaward-migrating juvenile steelhead) achieve a size of approximately six to eight inches before they undergo the physiological transformation that equips them for survival in a water environment fundamentally different from that in which they were born. Yes, there are exceptions that someone will be quick to point out but the discussion here is a primer, not an exhaustive reporting of stock by stock and year by year variations on a theme.

The circumstances that dominate how many steelhead can be produced from the streams in which they originate are the amount of suitable space, the water temperature regime and the supply and ratio of dissolved nutrients, principally nitrogen and phosphorus. In the Skeena waters, temperatures are well below growth-sustaining levels for up to half the year. Given that water temperature dictates growth it follows that it takes much longer to grow a Skeena steelhead smolt than one from warmer climates elsewhere to the south. Not unrelated is the fact that at Skeena latitudes water temperatures that catalyze spawning among steelhead that have remained semi-dormant over a long winter don't arrive until deep into spring. Distance inland from the moderating influence of the coast and elevation operate together to govern when the 5°C or 40°F threshold that generally triggers the transformation from overwinter dormancy to the push to

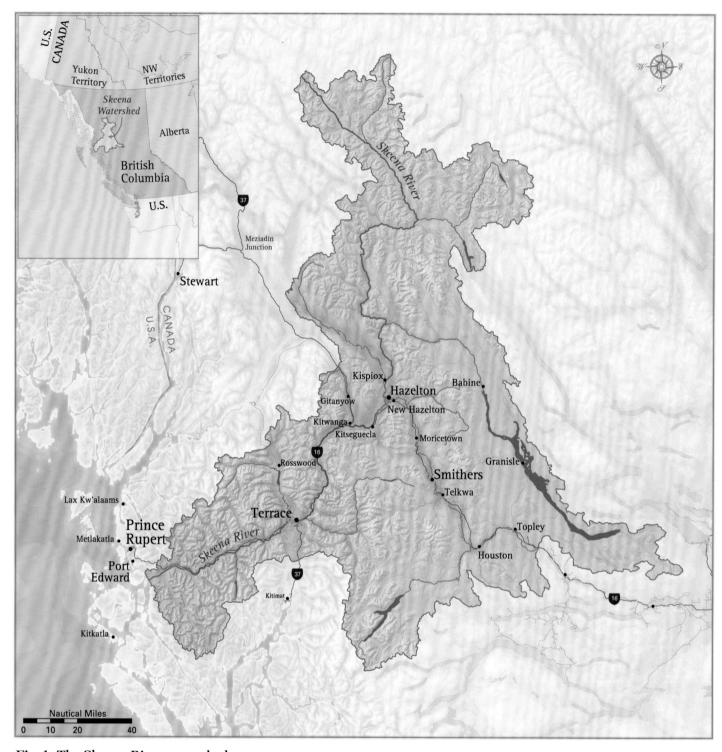

Fig. 1: The Skeena River watershed

spawning areas will occur. In a lower Kispiox tributary it might be as early as mid-April. Two hundred miles to the interior and 3,000 feet higher at the outlet of Sustut Lake it might not be until two months later. The later the spawning date, the later the eggs will hatch and the shorter the period of time available for newly emerged fry to grow before they take refuge in stream substrates to endure a long, growth-retarding winter. Steelhead smolts head seaward at about the same time as the adults of a former generation are spawning. Snowmelt-swollen rivers speed them along under a cover of turbidity that all but eliminates predation.

At the historic center of abundance of steelhead, the Columbia basin, the interrelationships between water temperature, nutrients and growing season are far more conducive to high growth rates among juvenile steelhead than can be found with increasing distance north or south. In the best of all circumstances a wild-steelhead smolt can be produced in a single year. The more common time is two, however, rising steadily with increasing distance northward. Skeena steelhead smolts are dominated by three-, four- and five-year-old fish with six year olds not unknown. In several of the high-elevation upper Skeena tributaries where spawning occurs in late May or early June steelhead eggs do not hatch early enough for the fry that emerge to grow large enough to produce scales in their first year of life. Scale readings from older juveniles and adults that were once relied on to determine freshwater ages had to be adjusted upward by one year when this phenomenon was finally documented.

Steelhead juveniles are not gregarious like other salmon. They are territorial. More space and resources are required to sustain each individual fish as it progresses through annual cycles to achieve smolt size. The natural mortality that occurs from year to year while juvenile steelhead grow to seaward-migrating size progressively reduces the number of recruits (smolts) produced by each spawning pair. The number is always far less than the number of recruits per spawning pair of any salmon species. All else being equal that is the primary reason there are never as many steelhead as there are of any of the other species that cohabit their river of origin.

Once at sea the sharply contrasting productivity of rivers versus oceans manifests itself. After three to five years a Skeena steelhead smolt might have grown to a length of eight inches and weigh in at perhaps seven or eight fish to the pound. Two or three growing seasons at sea will see that same fish between three and four times as long and fifty to one hundred times as heavy. Time spent at sea is the primary determinant of size at return and that time is genetically determined. Some stocks such as the Morice are comprised of a relatively high proportion of fish that return after only one winter at sea while others such as Sustut and Babine will rarely produce fish that spend less than two full winters in ocean pastures. Summer steelhead that reach the mid-twenty, thirty- and even forty-pound mark have

remained at sea for three to five winters before their maiden return. That said it is not uncommon to see fish of similar ocean age but widely divergent size, especially between years. "Good" years at sea are evidenced by higher weights for a given length (high condition factor) whereas poor years will generally see the reverse. The interrelationship between growth and survival shows up here as well. Years of fish exhibiting high condition factor tend to be years of high abundance. Just as the pounds of beef that can be produced per unit of pasture in a season depends on the quality and quantity of food, so too does the number and average size of fish relate directly to the availability and abundance of food organisms in the central north Pacific.

The ocean life history of steelhead is neither more nor less understood than that of any other salmon. We know the smolts are not estuary dwellers and move quickly away from the coast in a general northwesterly pattern. The ocean distribution is defined by ocean temperature boundaries which can vary in their north-south locations between years. Skeena steelhead are likely better off than many southern stocks in that they enter the ocean sufficiently far north they escape the relatively warmer coastal waters that have been more of a feature in the southern half of the North American steelhead's ocean range over the past decade or two. Steelhead in general move considerably further west than other salmon. Researchers from the North Pacific Anadromous Fish Commission who have documented high-seas catches and distribution of North American-origin steelhead since 1981 have noted an annual counter-clockwise circuit that concentrates fish between longitudes 175°W and 165°E and latitudes 42°N and 52°N for the prime growing months of the year. The specific distribution of Skeena fish is unknown but likely to be included within this broader quadrant. The center of the quadrant is about 2500 miles from the mouth of the Skeena River. At least five known North American-origin steelhead have been captured off the southern tip of Kamchatka, well over 3100 miles from their home river.

Adults that have reached maturity and are returning to North American rivers apparently spin off from their annual North Pacific circuit and travel quickly toward the coast. A pattern than is now well understood for Skeena steelhead is their tendency to landfall in Southeast Alaska as they exit the North Pacific on their homeward journey. There they encounter the first of a succession of commercial net fisheries that plague them all the way to the Skeena. The Skeena's summer steelhead approach the river estuary between late June and September, peaking in late July or early August. Their return timing overlaps all the other and more abundant salmon species and subjects them to the same commercial net fisheries that target sockeye and pink salmon. Winter steelhead from Skeena and elsewhere in British Columbia do not approach the coast at times when the commercial net fisheries operate and are therefore largely exempt from

One of those larger Skeena (Babine) steelhead that could have spent as few as three, as many as five, but most likely four winters at sea before returning. (Approximately 40")

harvest by that sector. The majority of the Skeena winter steelhead ascend lower Skeena tributaries between late March and early May with immigration closely linked to the commencement of the spring thaw and freshet.

The life history feature of steelhead that distinguishes them from all other salmon species is that they don't die following spawning. The incidence of multiple spawning by steelhead is not high, however, especially among the summer fish. Males linger in spawning areas fighting off other males to spawn with as many females as they can. Females spawn and emigrate immediately, riding freshet flows back to sea in as little as a few days. The protracted occupation of spawning areas and the aggressiveness of males reduces their chance of survival markedly. Repeat spawning is always highest among females but generally less than 10% of the number of their cohort that spawned the first time. Males do well to achieve one third of that level. Summer steelhead, whether from Skeena or elsewhere, do not repeat spawn in successive years. They remain at sea for a full calendar year following their re-entry in the spring that followed their first spawning migration. Repeat-spawning winter steelhead return in successive years. One must appreciate that even if the repeat-spawning frequency is as high as 10%, the number of fish returning a third time is only 1% of the original population and any such fish would be adding four years to their total age. Depending on how many years an individual fish took to achieve smolt size and considering that longevity for the species rarely exceeds ten or eleven years, it follows there is an upper limit on how many times a Skeena summer steelhead can spawn. Repeat-spawning summer steelhead are seldom the largest fish because they spend so much of their adult life in unproductive rivers and lose considerable weight prior to spawning. Whereas that loss is replaced quickly upon return to sea, a fish that remains at sea feeding and growing and spawning only once at the end of its life expectancy has the greatest potential to achieve the largest size.

One fine point of steelhead repeat-spawning frequency that is rarely explained in the technical literature, let alone the popular material in circulation, is the proper expression of the rates that people assume when interpreting scales. Assigning a repeat-spawning rate for a sample of scales taken from adult steelhead in a given year is inappropriate unless the population of fish from which the scales were taken is broken down into cohorts or groups of fish that originated from the same brood year or at least the same ocean-entry year. An example might help. I once looked at scale data that had been recorded for a large sample of steelhead captured by at the Skeena River test fishery in 1988 (that fishery is discussed in detail later). There was an unexpectedly high incidence of repeat spawners that piqued my curiosity. On analysis I discovered the number of repeat-spawning fish observed in 1988 was large relative to the number of first-time spawners that entered the Skeena that year. The repeat spawners originated from strong

The two 40-pound-plus plus steelhead caught at the Skeena River test fishery on Aug. 1, 1998. This diorama, now located at the Smithers Airport lobby, originally resided in the Ministry of Environment office in downtown Smithers where this picture was taken.

returns in both 1984 and 1986. The repeat-spawning rate cited in 1988 was highly inflated because it considered only the number of fish exhibiting one or more previous spawnings relative to the total number of fish scales sampled that year. The proper analysis would have been to assign the repeat-spawning rate on the basis of the number of multiple spawners relative to the number of first-time spawners they originated from two and four years earlier.

Allow me to wander a bit here and refer to some examples of Skeena steelhead life history that are out there in the public domain already. The two behemoths that grace the Smithers Airport lobby will be familiar to some. I'll speak to them in a different context later. The life history designations that accompany the display were interpreted from scales removed from those fish. I'm personally very familiar with the scale impressions and I appreciate what they seem to be telling us. Caution is suggested though. The likelihood of the larger of those fish being as old (in its 14th year) and spawning as many times as the scales imply (on its fourth time around) is exceedingly remote. It isn't impossible but it is out there in the realm of the odds on winning a $50M lottery. The other example of longevity and multiple repeat spawning among Skeena steelhead involved a large tagged female one of my colleagues caught in the Babine River on November 7, 1994 while we were engaged in a radio telemetry program. We recorded the tag color and number, photographed the fish and went about our business. Recapturing a tagged steelhead was nothing out of the ordinary. However, on return to our offices and checking archived tagging records it was discovered the tag had been placed on the fish in October, 1987 (at almost the exact location where she was recaptured). Light bulbs!

The 1987 tagging record said this fish's weight was estimated at ten pounds. If accurate the most likely interpretation of the ocean life history of the fish would be that it spent two winters out there. Putting all the pieces together the total age of this fish would have been between 12 and 14 by the time it spawned in the spring of 1995. The spread relates to the potential smolt age.

Methuselah. Babine River approximately 2.5 miles upstream from the Shelagyote confluence, November 7, 1994.

In this case it was likely between two and four. Again, total age 14 is not impossible but it is definitely pushing the boundary, especially if multiple spawnings are involved. Had any of us present when she was caught ever thought there was the slightest chance the tag had been on that fish for seven years we would have taken a scale sample to test the accuracy of the ocean life history interpretation from scale reading with the known life history features revealed by the tag data.

Methuselah was unique in another respect. Her repeat-spawning behavior was out of sync with the alternate year pattern expected. We can reasonably assume she was a maiden fish in the fall of 1987, spawned in 1988 and returned to sea that spring. Theory says she would have returned to the Babine again during the 1989, 1991 and 1993 seasons and spawned a second, third and fourth time in the spring months of 1990, 1992 and 1994 respectively. If the theoretical repeat-spawning pattern had prevailed she should have been at sea when she was caught in November, 1994. So much for theory.

A last point: the weight of this fish at capture was close to 24 pounds on my field scale. This was an impressive female to be sure but she would have been very much larger at the same total age if she had not sacrificed so much of her potential adult growth period (roughly 30%) in maintenance mode in the river while enduring long winters prior to spawning. That statement is corroborated by another tagged fish that returned to the upper Sustut River on a third spawning migration in 2004. Data for that fish indicated it had grown from about 27.5 inches to about 32 inches (7.5-12 pounds) in the four years between its first and third spawning migration. To me this is more evidence in support of the scale interpretation for the airport-lobby fish being inaccurate. It just isn't plausible that Skeena summer steelhead could grow that large if they spent almost a third of their adult life starving in a river.

Repeat spawning may be infrequent and impacted heavily by fisheries that harvest them intentionally or otherwise but it can be a major factor in sustaining steelhead populations. Repeating females are consistently more fecund and supply larger eggs with higher energy reserves that give their fry an advantage not seen among the offspring of first or maiden spawners. Repeat spawners make a disproportionately valuable contribution to a river's population, especially in years when the abundance of maiden spawners is diminished.

Between repeat spawning and the multiplicity of fresh water and ocean age combinations displayed both within and between Skeena steelhead stocks, compensation for excessive mortality in a given year, whatever the source, is maximized. Among Skeena fish we can count at least 20 different combinations of freshwater and ocean ages and repeat spawning patterns. Any given tributary will support most of these every year. Add to that the occasional incidence of the offspring of non-migrant or resident rainbow trout adopting the migrant or steelhead mode and/or the offspring of steelhead choosing to remain as river residents and the complexity of life history strategies is magnified. Such diversity smoothes out peaks and valleys in abundance that are observed frequently among pink, coho and sockeye salmon whose populations are dominated by fish of only one or two age combinations. Steelhead will never be as abundant as salmon for all the reasons described previously but their remarkably complex and diverse life history is a large part of the reason they are still around to be considering in 2010.

Diversity is a concept that deserves a bit more than passing mention. It is what defines the Skeena's summer steelhead. To a scientist the term might best be expressed by defining the full genetic spectrum contained within the aggregate Skeena steelhead population. To those with little understanding of such complexities diversity is better understood by observing the broad range of characteristics evident among steelhead as opposed to, for example, sockeye. Steelhead may weigh anywhere from three pounds to more than forty. Some are programmed to return in late June or early July, some not until September, and still others somewhere in between. They may be five years old or ten and spawning for the first time or the second or even third. Each river and even its individual small tributaries supports fish with heritable characteristics uniquely adapted to the habitat from whence it came. Adults that return to their natal stream do so at the same time generation after generation. They spawn in the same places at the same time and produce offspring of similar freshwater and ocean ages. Juveniles of a particular stock have been shown to exhibit unique physical characteristics that distinguish them from all others. Stock-specific differences, if lost, will not be replaced by other steelhead, at least not on a time scale that any of us will observe. Some stocks or populations will produce more offspring per adult than others and are better able to withstand harvest. Unproductive stocks are at a distinct disadvantage under a similar harvest regime. No one can say with certainty how much of the diversity that existed among Skeena steelhead prior to human intervention has since been removed but no one can argue credibly that 130 years of commercial-fishing harvest has not had its effect, especially on the smaller and less productive stocks. Skeena sockeye are replete with examples. The first rule of tinkering is worth thinking about. Keep all the parts.

An excellent illustration of diversity is the contrast between the (historic) returns of Morice River steelhead relative to those of the Kispiox. Morice fish were once sufficiently abundant to support excellent fishing at the outlet of Morice Lake by late August. Those fish were represented heavily by fish that had spent only one winter at sea. Kispiox fish were also available, though in lesser numbers, by late August but those fish were comparative giants, having spent multiple winters at sea. Each river also supported other fish that displayed less pronounced differences in time of return and size but the extremes are what defined those individual populations. To some a steelhead is a steelhead is a steelhead. Nature doesn't see it that way.

The ultimate question, and the one most asked, is how many Skeena steelhead are there? This will never be answered conclusively but we can put some boundaries around past and present. Historic catch information from the earliest of the commercial-fishing records will be dealt with in some detail later but, suffice to say here, there were many more fish before the net fisheries descended. Since 1956 the number of summer steelhead entering the Skeena between June and August each year (and part of September in some recent years) has been estimated by a test-fishing vessel operated in the intertidal zone of the Skeena River slightly upstream from the commercial-fishing limit. The "Tyee Test Fishery" as it is known operates under contract to the federal government's Department of Fisheries and Oceans. The test fishery is another subject I'll have more to say about in a later chapter.

The only material available that gives some appreciation of historic abundance of Skeena steelhead (or other salmon) is derived from the number of cases of canned fish put up by the industry in its early years. Two sets of numbers are available to shed light on the question. These are dealt with along with some considerations of what was occurring coincidentally in Southeast Alaska in a later chapter. The point to be made here is that a conservative estimate based on the available fish-processing records places the number of summer steelhead Skeena bound from the central north Pacific at more than 100,000 annually in years before commercial harvesting began. The highest total run estimated to have reached the river in any year since the test fishery began was 70,000 in 1998. That return probably represented the optimal combination of events — high smolt production from the brood years contributing to it, high ocean survival of those smolts and relatively little commercial fishery along the return corridors. In most years since 1956 the number did not reach half the 1998 high. For perspective consider the much maligned and wild-fish impoverished Columbia system where the number of summer steelhead swimming past Bonneville Dam has averaged about 400,000 annually over the past ten years. Roughly 40% of those fish did not begin life in a hatchery.

Another approach to questions of steelhead abundance involves estimating the capability of the Skeena's steelhead habitat to grow them. Much effort was put into that exercise in the late 1980s and early 1990s. Habitat quantity was determined according to documented spatial requirements for various life stages (fry and parr) and the cumulative total amount of those habitats available in all known steelhead-producing areas in the watershed. Habitat quality was assessed according to water temperature regimes that govern annual growth periods and nutrient availability that interacts strongly with the growth period to determine how many years of freshwater residence are required to produce a smolt. Then the average female size and fecundity was used along with expected survivals from egg through smolt life stages. Experts in sophisticated computer modeling of these variables predicted that if the available habitat was seeded to capacity by spawners the Skeena system could be expected to produce about 575,000 smolts annually. If that capacity was achieved and if the longer-term average-smolt to adult survival thought to exist at the time (about 14%) prevailed, 80,500 steelhead would return to the river. The difference between that total and historic numbers alluded to previously and discussed again later is most likely related to reduced quantity and quality of habitat over the past many decades. It should also be recognized that smolt-to-adult survival is anything but constant. A given smolt supply surviving at the high end of the observed range (20%) would produce ten times more adults than it would if those same smolts experienced survivals at the low end. Unfortunately the recent trend over most of the steelhead range has been toward the low end of the range.

The next point of interest on the subject of abundance is the number of spawners it takes to utilize the full productive potential of the steelhead habitat as it is presently understood and described. That question was addressed through a rigorous technical review process known at the time (early 1990s) as PSARC (Pacific Stock Assessment Review Committee). Think of it as the Federal Government hoop the Province was required to jump through to establish a scientifically defensible number for the steelhead escapement that would achieve freshwater habitat saturation. Remember, juvenile steelhead are territorial and require a certain amount of rearing space to reach smolt size. In the traditional fishery management approach that translates to a ceiling on the number of adults necessary to achieve full production. Anything beyond that number is "surplus" and harvestable. In the lexicon of the commercial-fishing industry surplus translates to waste.

The PSARC process endorsed 26,500 as the number of steelhead required to fully seed the Skeena summer-run

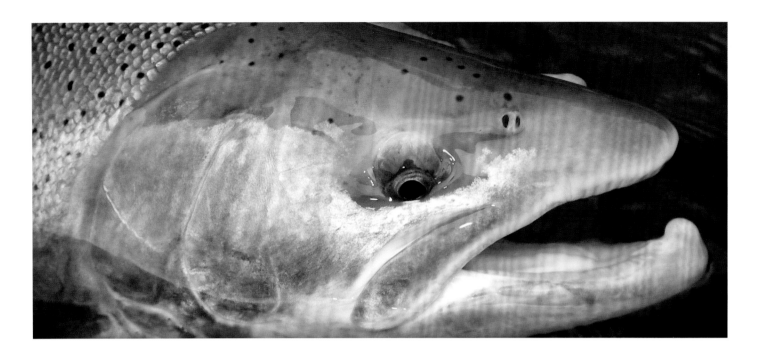

steelhead habitat (Spence and Hooton, 1991). Inherent in that number were some huge assumptions. First, the number of males and females had to be evenly divided. Second, the number of fish destined for each Skeena tributary had to match the scientist's prescription. Third, the fish in each tributary had to be perfectly distributed throughout to ensure no habitat went unseeded. Finally, the number didn't accommodate any losses likely to occur between the time the steelhead entered the lower Skeena River and spawning time many months later. Those losses could result from one or more of angler-related mortality, First Nations harvest, disease and predation. Eventually these additional factors were considered and accommodated by adding 8500 more steelhead to the escapement target. In the end the prescribed steelhead escapement sufficient to achieve full habitat seeding while accommodating all other sources of post commercial-fishery mortality, sex ratio and distribution influences settled at 35,000. That figure was partitioned into river-or-stock-specific escapement targets although that exercise was purely academic because there has never been any method employed in managing any of the commercial or in-river First Nations fisheries that could address such a precise objective.

More needs to be said on the abundance of fish from individual Skeena tributaries. Over time a range of investigations and techniques has addressed that subject. They involved everything from sophisticated scale pattern analyses, morphometry examinations (comparison of select scale and body measurements), catch data analyses, habitat productivity analyses, radio telemetry and, most recently, DNA analyses. The cumulative outputs from them are not surprising, at least not to anyone who has spent any time on the various Skeena tributaries. The Bulkley/Morice system is the dominant producer followed by Babine, Kispiox, Zymoetz, Kalum, Lakelse and so on down the list. The general pattern is diminishing numbers of fish originating from the smaller, colder, nutrient-poor streams. The pattern becomes more pronounced with increasing distance upstream along the Skeena. Once again the point to emphasize is all of this research came far too long after the development of the Skeena commercial fishery to consider it the historical benchmark. By the last couple of decades of the 20th century, when most of the steelhead work was finally underway, the contribution of steelhead from numerous Skeena tributaries that very likely once produced them was impossible to determine and wouldn't have been included in any modern management context even if it could.

The last issue deserving mention in this steelhead primer is hatcheries. In Skeena there are none. The reasons are simple. The water temperatures required to grow smolts in the one-year period that operation of a cost-effective hatchery program demands are not available at such northern latitudes. Options such as heating water or adding a second year onto the smolt growth period are even less attractive both economically and biologically. Add to that the machinations around collection of brood stock that adequately represents the desired end product, the inordinate costs of collecting and holding adults through maturation, the costs of transporting and releasing smolts at the appropriate times and places and the folly of steelhead hatcheries in remote northern environments ought to be abundantly evident. If that isn't enough one could consider the plethora of science emerging from the Pacific Northwest United States which points ever more strongly to the fact hatcheries accelerate the loss of diversity in favor of concentrated and competitive feast or famine fisheries that will persist only as long as public agencies are willing to subsidize them. A recent proposal to eliminate hatchery steelhead programs in most or all of Washington State's Puget Sound streams is a compelling lesson in this regard.

Chapter 2
GEOGRAPHY AND NETS

One can hardly begin to talk about the history of Skeena steelhead in the absence of repeated reference to the commercial fisheries that have prevailed over the years of written record. An appreciation of where the fisheries occur is fundamental to much of the rest of this book. I'll begin with reiterating that the migration route for homeward-bound Skeena fish is clockwise out of the North Pacific until they landfall along the north coast and then parallel it to the river itself. Landfall commonly occurs in Alaskan waters at Noyes Island (Fig. 2, Page 20). Call it the entrance to the funnel. There is a long history of commercial fishing in that area, now known as District 104, initially with traps but eventually with seine nets. That too will be discussed later. For now all we need to know is the interception of Skeena-bound fish begins at Noyes Island about 200 miles from the Skeena itself. The next significant area of encounter is Cape Fox or District 101 as it is labeled today (Fig. 2). That one is a gill-net fishery. Cape Fox is 150 miles from the Skeena's mouth but only about 4 miles from the Canada/US boundary and the first point of contact of Skeena fish with the northern BC net fleets off the north face of Dundas Island. In the BC fisheries repertoire Dundas Island is mostly in Statistical Area 3 (Fig. 3, page 21). The migration route for Skeena steelhead splits at that point with some fish choosing the eastern or inside route through Chatham Sound and others moving south down the outside on the west coast of Dundas. The pattern of seine boat distribution around Dundas suggests more Skeena-bound salmon and steelhead choose the western route. The inside route from Dundas to the innermost boundary of the Skeena commercial-fishing areas is about 52 miles. The outside adds another ten or eleven.

Note that Dundas Island bisects Statistical Areas 3 & 4 (Figs. 3 & 4). The boundary lines between those areas are highly significant in the context of commercial fishery catches of Skeena-bound fish. As drawn, the entire northern and western shores and about one-third of the eastern shore of Dundas are labeled Area 3. Some like to pretend the Area 3 catches are not part of the Skeena story because that area is dominated by fish homing to other areas such as the Nass River. For the present I'll ignore the lines and simply state the net fleets that operate on either side of Dundas Island, from the extreme northern tip to its southernmost end, are fishing in the neck of the funnel leading to the Skeena (above).

The tip of the migration funnel is the next area of special attention. It is known as Statistical Area 4-15 in the commercial-fishery management lexicon of today but more commonly referred to by fishermen as River/Gap/Slough[2] (Fig. 5, page 22). Smith Island is the real estate that divides the two long-known migration corridors

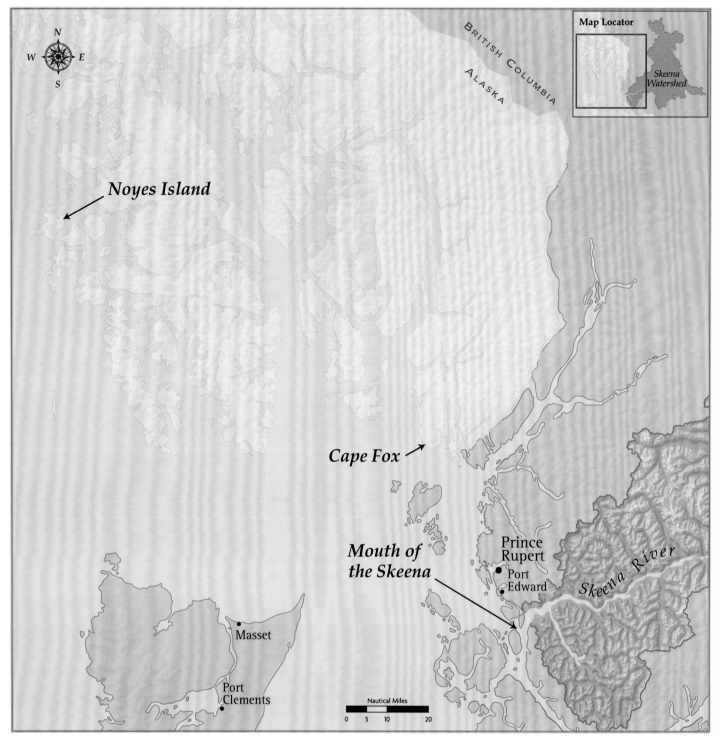

Fig. 2: The commercial-fishing territory through which Skeena-bound steelhead must pass. Noyes Island is in the northwest corner at about 11 o'clock and Cape Fox is in the center of the image.

from the outside waters through the last gauntlet where nets are deployed before today's commercial fishing boundary is reached (Fig. 5, page 22). Around the southern shore of Smith Island and through "the Gap" the distance from the outer boundary of R/G/S to the fishing boundary is about ten miles. Around the northern route and through Inverness Pass (i.e. "the Slough") the boundary to boundary distance is about two miles longer. "The River" is the area between the innermost extent of the other two and the fishing boundary upstream. Both routes have long been known to be the principle migration corridors for all Skeena fish. R/G/S was the historic epicenter of the commercial fishery and remained so until gasoline engines replaced sails and oars. The shortest distance across the Skeena at the commercial fishing boundary is 1.6 miles but that is the full wetted width of the channel, not the more restricted migration corridor, especially at low tide.

The final point of interest in terms of the Skeena approaches and the entry to the river proper is the location of the Tyee Test Fishery approximately six miles upstream from the commercial-fishing boundary (Fig. 5, page 22).

A Google Earth image of the Tyee Test Fishery.

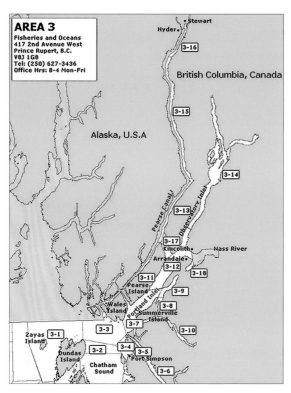

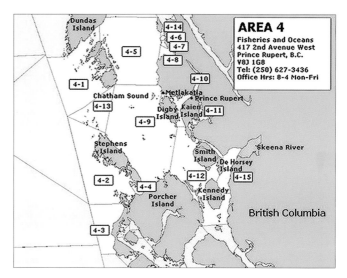

Figs. 3 & 4: The northern British Columbia fishing areas referred to as Statistical Areas 3 and 4 by the Federal Government's Department of Fisheries and Oceans.

Part of the gill-net fleet at dockside on the Prince Rupert waterfront between commercial-fishing openings.

The seine fleet in operation in the boundary waters of Statistical Areas 3 and 4 on July 28, 1995.

The origin and purpose of that fishery is dealt with in subsequent chapters. The Google Earth imagery reveals quite clearly how restricted the actual migration corridor can be at low tide. The imagery date was July 1, 2005 at which time the Skeena River discharge was near its long-term average for that time of year. (The river flow declines steadily from its peak runoff in early June through the entire commercial-fishing season.) The precise hour of the photo is not known but the tidal stage is obviously on the low side and the channel therefore more confined than it would be on high tide. The major steelhead movements tend to occur on the start of the flood tide immediately following the low slack (i.e. when the river channel is smallest). The annual summer-steelhead run was barely underway at the time of the photo. The shortest distance across the only migration corridor available was about 1,500 feet. The gill nets employed by commercial fishermen are 1,200 feet long. In the early days of the fishery the upstream boundary of the commercial-fishing area was well upstream from its present location at which point the low tide channel width and migration corridor was considerably less. Tidal influence on the Skeena extends many miles upstream from the present and historic fishing boundaries.

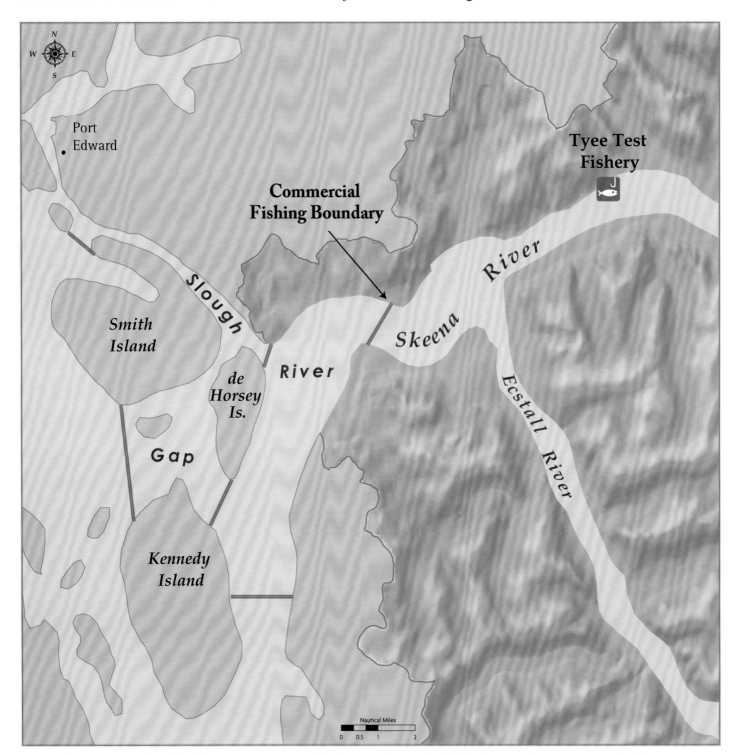

Fig. 5: "River/Gap/Slough" (the innermost part of Sub-Area 4-12 and all of Sub-Area 4-15 in Figure 4), the innermost commercial-fishing area at the mouth of the Skeena River. Note the proximity to the Tyee test fishing location.

Chapter 3
GOVERNANCE

The Random House Dictionary defines governance as a method or system of government or management. The distinction between governance and management is easily blurred. I'm not going to try and split hairs and define precisely where each one applies. Whether one chooses to define governance as the framework of regulations and policies administered by the agency in charge or the day to day, season to season application of those regulations and policies or a combination of the two is of no consequence to the fish. In order to appreciate what governance/management means and how it manifests itself in the world of Skeena steelhead it is useful to have a basic understanding of how we arrived. This is one of many aspects of fisheries management that most normal people find less than exciting. Rather than wearing anyone down with excessive detail I'll try to hit the historically significant points and minimize the legal speak. Bear with me.

It is a given that long before the arrival of Europeans on the shores of North America there were healthy rivers and an abundant supply of fish. The original inhabitants of the Skeena tell us compelling stories about how they managed their fisheries for hundreds and even thousands of years before then. Whether it was careful and precise administration of salmon harvest or a small and sparsely distributed population with relatively primitive harvest technology and finite capacity to process, preserve and transport a final product, or some combination of these, the balance that once existed began to erode relatively soon after the whites invaded.

The beginning of Euro-Canadian control of the British Columbia fisheries, once the exclusive domain of Indians, came with the fish-canning industry in the late 19th century. Canneries were owned by the industrial leaders of the era, none of whom acknowledged any ownership or entitlement on the part of the original inhabitants of the land. Government brought with it British law which suited its purpose in orchestrating its vision of development of the western extremities of the Dominion. (For details see Harris, 2001, page 155.) There was no real separation between the views and policies of industrial and political leaders in terms of how they approached the exploitation of the seemingly unlimited salmon resources. Federal government legislation known as the Dominion Fisheries Act of 1868 had been developed and applied to inland fisheries in eastern Canada when the first cannery began operating on the Skeena in 1876. The Act provided a framework to do such things as appoint fisheries officers, issue fishing licenses, establish basic rules around how and when fish might be caught and set out fines for non-compliance.

Having a framework for governance and making regulations to administer it were two very different features of the early Skeena commercial-fishing period. Every regulatory measure that was developed for the west coast salmon industry emerged on the Fraser River first and all of them were driven by conflict among competing cannery owners and between them and Indians who historically harvested large quantities of Fraser sockeye. The Skeena was remote in comparison and restrictions there were actively opposed by some high-ranking government officials on grounds that they would discourage immigration of the labor required to service and develop a fishing industry with enormous potential. Cannery owners were equally sensitive to anything that might negatively impact their ability to secure the only labor force available—Indian men to row the cannery-owned boats and Indian women and their older children to populate the canning lines. In combination these issues left the Skeena far behind the readily visible world to the south. After all, what value were regulations when the primary objective of government was to facilitate commercial exploitation of the resource and the industrial leaders sought only to maximize profit? It wasn't until 1894 that the provisions of the Dominion Fisheries Act manifested themselves in regulations specific to the BC fishery. Eighteen years of cannery owners having exclusive control of the openings and closures and gear specifications had already passed.

The neglect of the BC salmon fishery is difficult to comprehend given the fact that by 1905 it was the most lucrative in Canada, outstripping in volume and value the combined output of lobsters, cod and herring (Newell, 1989). Examples of the significance the central government of Canada attached to the west coast salmon fishery in the early years include the whopping $635.00 budget allocation in 1877 (Harris, 2001) and the fact it took more than 75 years for a British Columbian to be named to the position of Minister of Fisheries. We'll ignore the fact he was born in Ontario.

In 1904, more than a quarter century after the first cannery began operation at the mouth of the Skeena, the first fisheries official of the federal government took up residence on the north coast. Known as the Fisheries Inspector for District 2 (approximately the northern two thirds of the BC coast) he set up shop at Port Essington, the hub of transportation to and from the Skeena as well as the center for a dozen canneries clustered around the mouth of the river. That same year the Inspector sent an officer to the Babine Lake country to address complaints from cannery owners that Indians were overharvesting sockeye salmon to the detriment of the flourishing commercial-fishing industry. That visit initiated a series of events over the next three years that culminated in what became known as "The Barricades Agreement". The specifics of that situation are dealt with in a later chapter. The point to be made here is the Barricades Agreement was the first time the federal government used its

self-imposed power to attempt to regulate the Indian fishery in the Skeena system.

The nation's capital in far off Ottawa remained the decision-making center for the west coast fishery for more than fifty years following the arrival of the canneries at the Skeena. Fisheries came under the jurisdiction of a dual portfolio Department of Marine and Fisheries. The west coast fishery remained the poor cousin of this arrangement. Finally, in the late 1920s, the distant bureaucrats bowed to pressure from cannery owners, fishermen's organizations and senior Provincial Government representatives and created a separate Department of Fisheries. Ultimate control remained in Ottawa, a problem that plagues fisheries management even today, but at least fisheries had its own identity.

From the turn of the 20th century until the 1940s management of the Skeena fishery consisted of progressive restrictions on commercial fishing. The BC Fishery Regulations enacted in 1894 were the vehicle for addressing high exploitation rates resulting from unlimited expansion of canning capacity and perceived competition by Indian fishing. The two principle measures applied were reduction in fishing time and area. Throughout this period the sale of fish by Indians was mentioned frequently and regulations were in place to deal with that. However there is no evidence of any significant application of law in that respect. The Indian fishery was altered and, arguably, constrained in terms of the gear employed and there were efforts to require Indians to obtain permits to fish. In essence, however, there was no real change in how the Indians themselves went about the business of managing their use of the resource. They continued to harvest as many fish for food as they wished. Sale of fish was simply an application of the white man's money economy to the pre-contact trade and barter system. Of special note was the seasonal and even permanent migration of a large proportion of the total Indian population of the Skeena watershed to the coast-based commercial fishery to take advantage of the economic opportunities it provided.

In the mid-1940s the Department of Fisheries finally took steps to document something other than the number of cases of individual species canned at the mouth of the Skeena River. It sent members of its southern-based Fisheries Research Board (FRB) to undertake a program known as the Skeena River Salmon Investigation. This was significant in that it marked the first time people trained as scientists had a role to play in the Skeena fishery. The FRB intervention came in the aftermath of chronic overfishing and more complaints from cannery owners who, by then, were struggling to survive. The primary objective of the Investigation was to determine what escapements were required to provide the greatest return to the commercial fishery and how the fishery should be regulated to achieve those escapements. In pursuit of that the FRB conducted the first-ever exploration of all the significant sockeye-producing

The Babine River weir or counting fence. The aerial photo was taken in August 1987,
the ground level photo in September, 1985. The latter view is from river right on the upstream
side of the weir. The original wooden superstructure was completely replaced with concrete
and steel in early 1993 and two concrete boat launches were built on river left immediately
above and below the weir. The Department of Fisheries and Oceans camp is on river right upstream.

systems and estimated the number of spawners. The FRB also examined in detail the historic and current harvest of Skeena salmon by the commercial fishery, the extent of the Indian harvest of fish and the influence of obstructions to salmon migration. Think about this. The second largest commercial fishery in the entire Province of British Columbia had been in operation for almost three quarters of a century before the basic information necessary to manage it began to be collected. For all of that time the Skeena commercial fishery had been largely under the control of cannery owners bent on maximizing profits. Furthermore it wasn't until 1978, fully a century after the cannery era began, that there were Federal staff in Prince Rupert permanently. Prior to that there was only a seasonal presence of government overseers in the heartland of the industry.

The FRB scientists at least had influence if not control of management of the Skeena commercial fishery through the mid-1940s. The results of their investigations became the basis for new measures to regulate fishing effort and provide more reliable estimates of catches in the commercial and Indian fisheries. Perhaps the most significant individual product of their presence was the construction in 1946 of the fish-counting weir at the head of the Babine River. The actual in-season administration of the Skeena fishery remained with the Prince Rupert offices of the Department of Fisheries while the FRB staff continued to operate from the same agency's relatively isolated research facility in Nanaimo, far to the south.

The next stage of governance, or management if you will, came as a result of a rock slide in the remote canyon reaches of the lower Babine River in 1951. The slide seriously reduced the number of sockeye getting to Babine Lake that year and in 1952 before it could be cleared sufficiently to restore normal fish passage. In anticipation of the inevitable consequences of the poor escapements in 1951 and 1952 the Federal Minister of Fisheries appointed the Skeena Salmon Management Committee (SSMC). It consisted of the Director of the FRB's Biological Station at Nanaimo and the Vancouver-based Chief Supervisor for the Department of Fisheries' Pacific Coast. Their mandate was to assess the condition of the Skeena River salmon stocks, improve their management and increase the yields. Rehabilitation of the Babine sockeye stock was to be given special attention. The Minister also appointed an Advisory Board to work with the Committee. The Board was comprised of nine members. Six of them were cannery owners and/or managers. The remaining three were gill-net fishermen representing the three prominent fishermen's organizations of the period (United Fishermen's and Allied Workers Union, Prince Rupert Fishermen's Cooperative and Native Brotherhood). It is interesting to note here that Committee meetings were open to the public. Those held in Prince Rupert were frequently attended by a large contingent of Indian fishermen with long service as gill-netters.

In terms of the original mandate of the SSMC the three major outcomes were the establishment of the test fishery at the mouth of the Skeena, the commencement of annual sockeye smolt enumeration at the outlet of Babine (Nilkitkwa) Lake and the commencement of the limnological investigations that led eventually to the construction of the now famous spawning channels on two of the largest tributaries to Babine Lake. The smolt counts provided the basis for predicting adult returns, the test fishery the basis for managing harvest in-season and the counting weir the tool for evaluating the accuracy of the test fishery estimates and the consequences of fishery management actions.

By the early 1970s the management oversight provided by the FRB was transferred to the stock-management sector of the Department of Fisheries (Wood, 2001). That placed responsibility for all aspects of Skeena salmon management (e.g. the Babine spawning channels, the Babine adult and smolt counts, and regulation of the commercial fishery) in the hands of Prince Rupert-based staff (Sprout and Kadowaki, 1987). Participation of the FRB staff on what had evolved from the original SSMC was also de-emphasized. In essence the long-overdue and short-lived influence of trained professionals in decision making for the Skeena fishery was trumped by a new group of staff whose professional credentials fell well short of those of their predecessors. At about the same time the political influence of an Indian community increasingly dispossessed of its historic fishery was beginning to emerge. Looking back the impression one derives from the on again, off again inclusion of science is that it was crisis oriented. When the imported scientists had addressed the immediate problems to the satisfaction of the industry leaders it was back to business as usual.

So far steelhead have been conspicuously absent from the discussion of governance or management. Originally that was purely the result of the abundance of steelhead relative to salmon and their lack of commercial significance. Eventually, however, steelhead found its way into the equation as a result of the jurisdictional split between the Federal and Provincial governments. The roots of the split go back to 1867 when the Fathers of Confederation delegated sea coast and inland fisheries to the jurisdiction of the Federal Government under terms of the British North America Act. In 1938, by agreement with the Federal Government, non-tidal fisheries management was turned over to the Province. All things salmon (i.e. those five species traditionally called salmon but not including steelhead which were only relatively recently included in the same genus as the rest of the Pacific salmon) remained under Federal jurisdiction. Included are First Nations fisheries, commercial and recreational fisheries in tidal waters and salmon fisheries in non-tidal waters. Federal jurisdiction is also paramount in relation to fish habitat. The Province got steelhead but only once they were past tidal boundaries.

If Skeena salmon management started from a position of compromise three quarters of a century late, steelhead were much worse off. The transfer of freshwater fishing jurisdiction to the Province in 1938 brought steelhead under the responsibility of a group known as the Game Commission. Functionally that was meaningless. There was no such thing as a fisheries biologist until 1957 when a first ever Provincial Government agency (Department of Recreation and Conservation) was established to deal with rapidly expanding interest in outdoor recreation and habitat protection. Before then fish and game management in British Columbia consisted of enforcement of hunting regulations and predator control. That fell to either Game Wardens or officers of the BC Provincial Police, both of whom had been on the landscape since 1905. The catch-up process was painfully slow for those first biologists. There was one for the northern half of British Columbia from 1957 until 1973. His office was in Prince George, almost 200 miles east of the nearest Skeena tributary, except between 1966 and 1968 when the biologist of the day resided in Smithers. The biologist had a technical assistant that moved back and forth between Terrace and Smithers but not until 1967. A permanent Provincial Government fisheries biologist presence in the Skeena watershed didn't happen until 1974.

Things began to change in 1975 with the signing of a memorandum of understanding between the Federal and Provincial governments that initiated planning for a comprehensive Salmonid Enhancement Program (SEP). That program's objective was to double the coast-wide catch of salmon over a ten- to fifteen-year period. Doubling was supposed to amount to restoration of the longer term average catch. An astute Provincial Government participant in the backroom processes leading to implementation of the program drew a line in the sand, pointing out that doubling salmon catch would double steelhead catch and that had to be "considered". God bless him for that. There was never any specific interpretation of what "considered" meant but it was good enough to get a provincial foot in the salmon-management door and keep it there. By the time SEP was contemplated sport fishing for steelhead in Skeena tributaries was well advanced and concern among anglers over the impact of gill nets at the mouth of the Skeena was starting to be heard. The Provincial Government steelhead equivalent of the FRB salmon investigations of the mid 1940s was soon underway. The commercial fishery was a century of history at that point though and no one could ever know what was missing when the camera came out to try and take a latter-day snapshot.

There was a second Provincial agency that also factored in the Pacific fisheries scene. It was formed in 1932 in the aftermath of a court decision that saw jurisdiction for fish-processing plants given to the Province. The Fisheries Branch, as it was known, was folded into the new Department of Recreation and Conservation in 1957. The successor of that Branch lives on in Victoria. Its influence on Skeena steelhead will be discussed later.

For the remainder of the 20th century and into the next governance of the Skeena fishery or fisheries entered an era of convolution and complexity that would require volumes to recount in full. The fisheries lexicon soon became dominated by terms such as consultation, consensus, stakeholders, and facilitation. Policies, procedures and process topped the agenda. Underlying all of them was a newly minted Constitution Act (1982) that recognized and affirmed existing aboriginal and treaty rights of all Canada's aboriginal people. Treaty rights then defined or those to come from subsequent processes added to the complexity. Historic treaties that gave signatories the right "to carry on fisheries as formerly" continue to consume inordinate resources in legal interpretation of what that means in a modern context. Food, social and ceremonial needs of aboriginal fishers were constitutionally protected. Provided conservation requirements are met, those fisheries take precedence over commercial and recreational fisheries. The FSC fisheries as they have come to be known are essentially unlimited in any situation where a commercial and/or recreational fishery on the stocks affected has been sanctioned. Aboriginal rights to fish for "livelihood" are over and above the FSC provisions. High-court rulings demanding consultation with First Nations in any situation where an aboriginal right has been asserted (assertions do not have to be proven legally) spawned a growth industry. A new era of "co-management" of salmon by Federal and First Nations representatives began. Instead of two governments and three fishing advocacy groups debating allocations there are now three governments at the table (as well as the original advocacy groups).

While all this was evolving the production of documents thought to be critical to guiding the good ship governance through the thickening fog accelerated. An abbreviated list includes several United Nations agreements wholly endorsed by Canada's Federal Government: Convention on Biological Diversity (1992), Agreement on Straddling Fish Stocks and Highly Migratory Fish Stocks (1995), Precautionary Approach to Capture Fisheries and Species Introductions (FAO 1996) and the 2002 Johannesburg Commitment to Achieve Maximum Sustained Yield by 2015. Domestically we have A New Direction for Canada's Pacific Salmon Fisheries (1998), Allocation Policy for Pacific Salmon (1999), Policy Governing Public Participation in the Pacific Scientific Advice Review Committee (1999)[3], A Framework for Improved Decision Making in the Pacific Salmon Fishery (2000), Policy for Selective Fishing in Canada's Pacific Fisheries (2001), Recreational Fisheries in Canada – An Operational Policy Framework (2003), Strengthening Our Relationship – The Aboriginal Fisheries Strategy and Beyond (2003), Treaties and Transition – Towards a Sustainable Fishery on Canada's Pacific Coast (2004), Wild Salmon Policy (2005), Pacific Fisheries Reform (2005), Pacific Integrated Commercial Fishing Initiative (2007), An Integrated Aboriginal Policy Framework (2007), A Vision for Recreational Fisheries in British Columbia 2009 – 2013 (2010), Strategic Framework for Fishery Monitoring and Catch Reporting in the Pacific Fisheries (2010). . . Enough!

Today the groups formally recognized as "the stakeholders" and those who Federal and Provincial governments must consult and involve directly in any decisions that influence management of Skeena salmon (and therefore steelhead) include a composite advisory group representing the commercial fishing sector (North Coast Advisory Board or NCAB), a multi-tiered group from the recreational fishing sector (Sport Fishing Advisory Board or SFAB), umbrella First Nations groups such as the Skeena Fisheries Commission and the Gitxsan Wet'suwet'en Watershed Authority and individual First Nations Tribal Councils, elected and hereditary chiefs, Clans, Houses and/or Bands. On the perimeter of the consultative obligations are local governments, tourism association representatives, chambers of commerce, prominent business interests, conservation organizations, fishing-guide associations and so on. Connecting all the pieces and players and orchestrating effective governance or management according to law and continually shifting policy is an unenviable task. The uncertainties imposed by an increasingly unfriendly natural environment only add to the difficulty. And, I haven't even mentioned the fisheries that impact Skeena fish outside Canadian waters. For those seeking the ultimate experience in fisheries management futility try selling Skeena steelhead concerns to any of the players in the Pacific Salmon Treaty arena. The Canadian Government is plenty interested in keeping Alaska net interception of Skeena, Nass and Fraser sockeye and Alaskan troll interception of Canadian origin chinook and coho on that agenda but it could care less about Skeena (and Nass and Stikine and Taku) steelhead.

One should pay particular attention to the distinction between policy-driven consultation that both Federal and Provincial governments have obligated themselves to and court-driven consultation to which both governments are now legally bound. The cumulative effect of the various Supreme Court of Canada decisions pursuant to the Constitution Act of 1982 has been establishment of a firm foundation for direct participation by First Nations in the protection, management, allocation and benefits of fisheries resources within their territories. That has created a drastically different governance model than anything experienced in the history of British Columbia fisheries. The model is best termed a work in progress. Add to that the ongoing treaty negotiations certain to produce formal treaties sooner or later and it is obvious First Nations influence will dominate the future of fisheries governance. I'll touch on this again later. How quick the evolution; it wasn't until 1960 that Indians were even allowed to vote in federal elections!

Before I leave the subject of governance I should clarify my use of the labels I've attached to the fisheries agencies central to the management history of the

Skeena and confirm their organizational hierarchy and geographic distribution.

Both the Federal and Provincial government agencies responsible for fisheries management have undergone a number of re-organizations and name changes over the history of the Skeena fisheries. For about the last 30 years the Federal agency has been known as the Department of Fisheries and Oceans or DFO. The comparable Provincial agency for most of that time has been the Ministry of Environment or MOE. I'll try and stick to those two acronyms, at least in the modern era. Alternate labels such as Federal or Provincial managers that I use at various points are functionally the same. The status of fish and fishing has never borne any relationship to any of the labels.

Prince Rupert has been the North Coast District headquarters for the Federal Government's fisheries management staff for almost all of the Skeena commercial-fishery history (albeit seasonally until 1978). Vancouver is the Pacific Region Headquarters and Ottawa the national headquarters. A Federal Government fisheries research capability lives on at the Pacific Biological Station in Nanaimo but that group has been effectively removed from any direct fisheries management role since the 1970s. Smithers is the Regional headquarters for the Provincial Government staff responsible for Skeena steelhead management. Victoria is the Provincial headquarters. First Nations fishery managers are probably best characterized as decentralized and somewhat less hierarchical relative to either DFO or MOE. Individual communities tend to take greater responsibility for managing local fisheries although the two umbrella groups mentioned previously are intimately involved in the overarching issues affecting the various traditional territories along the Skeena. Those two are the Gitksan Wet'suwet'en Watershed Authority and the Skeena Fisheries Commission. The latter represents all First Nations within the Skeena watershed while the former speaks for the two First Nations in its center. Both are headquartered in Hazelton. For what its worth, some sense of the governance playing field can be taken from the relative sizes of the DFO and MOE staff complements and budgets dedicated to the Skeena fishery. I go from personal association and memory here rather than a forensic audit but I doubt I'm far off in suggesting DFO staff outnumber MOE by a factor between 10 and 15. The comparative budgets are even further apart.

Part 2: Original Owners

Chapter 4

INDIANS AND EARLY EURO-CANADIANS

O f the three fisheries that have bearing on Skeena steelhead none is more complex or difficult to recount than that of the original occupants of the watershed. It is a delicate task to try and piece together fragments of history into a mosaic that reasonably describes life in the Skeena country in the 18th and early 19th centuries and what part a particular species of fish might have played. Respected Royal British Columbia Museum official Richard Inglis in the Foreword to Wilson Duff's "Indian History of British Columbia, The Impact of the White Man" said it best:

"It is important to recognize that aboriginal peoples are becoming increasingly critical of studies by non-aboriginal academics. In their views, outsiders cannot adequately understand their cultures and, therefore, do not represent First Nations perspectives of history."

That said, the material that follows is intended purely as a best attempt to describe the nature and extent of the interaction between First Nations people and steelhead. Historic use and allocation of salmon, typically sockeye and chinook, has attracted far more interest and documentation. Those species are central to the ongoing debates around rights and privileges that will ultimately be sorted out by treaty negotiators, lawyers and judges. Steelhead, always the non-target casualty of any fishery focused on the much valued Skeena sockeye, will not escape the outcome. In the meantime there is instruction in an overview of the historic use of steelhead by First Nations people of the Skeena.

The terms used to describe the original inhabitants of British Columbia vary over time. In the earliest material from government archives "Indian" was most common. That term dominated until deep into the 20th century. Today it is considered outdated by many people. "Natives" and "Aboriginal people" also appeared with increasing frequency as the decades unfolded. "First Nations" has been the most prominent descriptor for British Columbia's first citizens in recent years and will be applied where it fits the history of the day. However, where historical records are available and make specific reference to Indians, Natives or Aboriginal People those terms are used.

The names and affiliations of First Nations of the Skeena watershed have also changed frequently over recorded history. So too have the names and spellings of most of the communities they inhabit. In some cases even the locations have changed.

This has added to the confusion around the accepted names and affiliations that should be referenced today. I have done my best to address these complexities by citing sources and cross referencing information that might otherwise be misinterpreted. I remind readers that my primary purpose is not to regurgitate every detail of the ethnographic history of the First Nations of the Skeena but to reasonably assess the likely influence on steelhead by those who knew them first.

Broadly speaking there are four First Nations recognized within the Skeena watershed today. These include the Tsimshian of the coastal islands around the Skeena estuary and its approaches plus the main-stem river and tributaries upstream to Kitselas, the Gitxsan whose traditional territory extended from there up the Skeena to its headwaters, the Wet'suwet'en of the Bulkley drainage and the Ned'u'ten who claim the Babine system upstream from Shannagh Creek and all the watersheds that drain into Babine Lake. Considerable overlap exists between individual First Nations (or Bands) and politically affiliated groups of First Nations who assert aboriginal rights and title to different pieces of the Skeena watershed. Regardless of the often conflicting and confusing historical interpretations of who claims which rivers and responsibility for which fisheries the end game is the influence of First Nations collectively.

The absence of any comprehensive record of First Nations populations and distribution throughout the Skeena drainage prior to contact with the first Europeans who visited the area leaves one with best guesses at those parameters. The earliest available material comes from the journals of explorers and fur traders. The former arrived by sea in the period 1786-1790 and quickly established a trade in sea otter pelts. The first reported land-based contact between Europeans and Skeena First Nations people occurred in 1812 when principles of the fur trading post at Fort McLeod on Stuart Lake, east of the Skeena drainage in the Fraser system, accompanied two Indians from Babine Lake on their return journey (Large, 1957). The first attempt at census of the Indian population came via Hudson Bay Company officials in 1835. According to Wilson Duff, author of "The Indian History of British Columbia – The Impact of the White Man", first published in 1964, those records and others suggest a provincial population of about 80,000. Of this total 8500 were estimated to occupy Tsimshian territory, including all the settlements in the Nass watershed north of Skeena. No estimate was given of the populations of the Bulkley and Babine areas.

Of importance in the years following the first attempt at census was the influence of smallpox. Duff noted the Tsimshian population estimate of 1835 dwindled to 4550 by 1885 and 3550 by 1895. Some communities apparently suffered much higher losses than others, especially along the coast. Inland where contact was sporadic and less frequent the influence of the dreaded smallpox may not have been as severe. One must remember that by 1835 the Tsimshian had been in contact with Europeans for up to 45 years. The full influence of that contact on First Nations populations of the period will never be known.

Figures not dissimilar to those of Duff are cited in the work of Douglas Harris (2008) regarding a census undertaken in 1881. At that time it was reported there were 3086 people living in the lower Skeena and Nass region. Of these 2893 were Indians. Vastly different estimates of the Indian population of the region show up in a variety of less well documented sources. One relatively recent piece stated the area around present-day Prince Rupert Harbor and the mouth of the Skeena once supported 8,000 people and was one of the most densely populated areas of pre-contact North America. One wonders how such impressive populations could have left so little evidence of their presence and diminished so dramatically in number by the time the first Europeans arrived.

A popular misconception is that there were numerous permanent Indian villages, settlements or communities scattered throughout the watershed prior to European contact and for a considerable period thereafter. After researching much of the written record I'm led to believe that any evidence (often referenced as oral history) of use or occupation of any site by Indian fishers, however brief, sporadic or seasonal, led to listing of such locations as permanent settlements. For example, Fort Babine, which became the focus of a highly controversial and much publicized weir fishery in the early 1900s, was established by the Hudson Bay Company traders in 1871. It followed from neighboring Old Fort (or Fort Kilmaur as it was originally known), also established by the Hudson Bay Company in 1822. The archived records of the Fort McLeod based white men who first travelled to Babine Lake in 1812 noted four villages along the lake. These were later confirmed to be seasonal fishing encampments rather than permanent settlements. The only other settlement in the upper Skeena referred to by the fur traders of the era was Fort Connolly, built near a small Indian village on Bear Lake in 1827. Kisgegas (now often spelled Gisgagaas) and Kuldo, on the lower Babine and upper Skeena respectively, are referenced a number of times in various sources. Sufficient evidence is available to accept they were once occupied continuously. However, at some point, presumably before Europeans became a feature of the area, they were abandoned. If not, the detailed written records of the Hudson Bay Company officials of the period were woefully inaccurate.

None of the earliest known settlements described in writing supported large numbers of people. Hudson Bay Company archives pertaining to the establishment of Fort Kilmaur noted a population of 250 Indians in the vicinity of the Fort in the 1822-23 period. In 1891 the Indian Reserve Land Commissioner of the day, Peter O'Reilly, in notes made while meticulously delineating Indian Reserves in the Babine area, recorded 83 people residing in 28 houses adjoining Fort Babine. Fort Connolly supported far fewer people. Later records involving the infamous Babine weirs and the "barricades agreement" (discussed later) never speak to more than perhaps 300 people in the areas surrounding the two Babine Lake fur-trading communities. It should be recognized the fur trade records are limited by the fact they focused only on site specific areas and do not necessarily reflect the complete demography of a region. That said there is a large body of evidence to indicate that most of the Indians of the day gravitated to the new white man's communities to take advantage of tools, traps, guns and numerous other materials heretofore unknown. All of this was, of course, designed to increase the flow of valuable furs through the Hudson Bay Company outposts to European markets.

Downstream along the Skeena the villages of Kispiox and Gitanmaax were clearly established long before the arrival of Europeans. Modern-day Hazelton, New Hazelton and South Hazelton came well afterward, as did Glen Vowell (now Sik-edakh). Further downriver one encountered the villages of Gitsegukla (Kitseguecla) and Gitwangak (Kitwanga). Up the Kitwanga River was the village of Gitanyow (Kitwancool). Once again, all of these communities were relatively small with no records to substantiate populations of more than a few hundred in any of them. The population of Kispiox, likely as large as any Indian community in the middle Skeena area at the time, was estimated at 400 in 1888 (Large, 1957). In the Terrace vicinity there were historic villages at Kitselas Canyon and on the Kalum River. There too the populations were small. A small village once existed at the mouth of the Lakelse River. It was already in decay when first described in 1879 and virtually abandoned at its next mention in records of the day in 1891. The principle First Nations communities as they are known today are shown in Fig. 6, page 32.

Hagwilget and Moricetown on the Bulkley River are an instructive example of the conflicting interpretations around the history of the Skeena country and its fisheries. Kennedy (2007), in an exhaustive review of literature and archival material relating to settlements and land use patterns of the Wet'suwet'en, cites references indicating that by 1800 the primary settlement along the Bulkley River was "Kyah Wiget", now known as Moricetown. About 1820 (some say 1824) a rock slide almost blocked the Bulkley River in Hagwilget Canyon and prevented most of the salmon from passing upriver to the traditional fishing area at Moricetown. The people from Moricetown then moved downriver *en masse* and built a new summer village on a narrow shelf adjacent to the newly created river constriction below. The new village was known as "Tse Kya" (also referred to in some early accounts as Rocher Tombe and Roche DeBoules). It was abandoned about 80 years later when its occupants moved either up onto the terrace above to establish the village known today as Hagwilget or back to Moricetown. Presumably fish-passage difficulties created by the earlier slide had naturally diminished by that time thus facilitating easier passage through to Moricetown where harvest of salmon

was, once again, more productive. The material covered by Kennedy included records of 18 houses at Hagwilget and 28 at the Moricetown *summer* village in the early 1800s. The population occupying the latter was estimated at 1092. That assemblage included people from distant areas within and even beyond the Skeena watershed.

Another point of departure among some relatively recent references to Hagwilget and Moricetown concerns alleged actions by fisheries officials. Morrell (1985) transcribed conversations with Wet'suwet'en elders who spoke of the blasting undertaken by the Department of Fisheries in Hagwilget Canyon in 1959 and how it totally disrupted the major Indian fishery. In fact the blasting targeted the remnants of the rock slide that occurred in the 1820s. Whereas those actions clearly affected fishing sites that came into use after the slide there is nothing in the historical literature to indicate there was any fishery at the site before then. Even the Moricetown Band website acknowledged there was no village or fishery at Hagwilget prior to the rock slide. The Department of Fisheries records of the Skeena and Bulkley Indian fisheries of the 1940 through mid 1960s period are relatively extensive. The only references to Hagwilget were in the context of fish-passage delays that were considered to be contributing to steady declines in abundance of the Nanika bound sockeye, historically the largest stock of any species in the Bulkley system. The fish harvesting at Hagwilget did not warrant any special consideration. Moricetown was the center of that universe. Given the historical facts it is quite remarkable that the 1959 blasting became the subject of court proceedings that commenced in 1985 and concluded with a $21.5M out-of-court settlement in April 2009 on grounds that a fishery Gitxsan and Wet'suwet'en people were dependent on continuously since before European contact was deliberately destroyed by government officials.

The point to be made regarding Hagwilget and Moricetown is the discrepancies which exist between carefully recorded written history and the oral-history material that frequently dominates discussions and proceedings. In researching a plethora of material pertinent to this book I find numerous similar examples of transformation of unsubstantiated oral accounts to fervent beliefs about historical circumstances and events. Too often these have gone unchallenged and made the task of knitting together past and present unenviable. No one wants to be reminded the foundation of their passion and purpose is sometimes unrealistic.

At the coast where the winter climate was less hostile and food resources more readily available continuously the historic communities were scattered. Modern-day Prince Rupert was not one of them. It was carved out of rock and scrub timber commencing in 1906. Metlakatla was the winter home of many of the Tsimshian. The much-referenced community of Port Simpson (now referred to as Laxkw'alaams but originally known as Fort Simpson) was established by the Hudson Bay

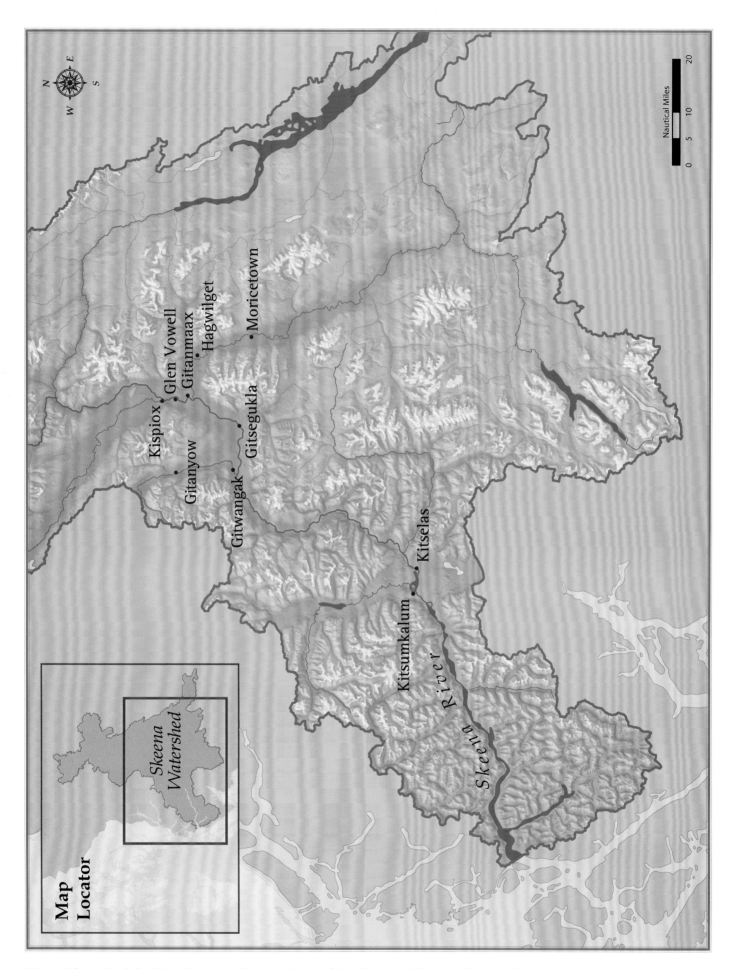

Fig. 6: The principle First Nations Communities of the Skeena River as they are known today.

Company in 1834. It was an important camping site for the Tsimshian prior to arrival of the fur traders but it was not a permanent village. Early records did, however, make note of large Indian settlements located five miles south of Port Simpson at Lakou Creek and a further 15 miles south near what eventually became Prince Rupert harbor (this was probably Metlakatla). The Tsimshian population of Port Simpson was estimated at 2300 in 1857 but only about 1100 in 1879 in the aftermath of smallpox and the exodus of about one-third of the original population who followed religious zealot William Duncan to Metlakatla (Duff, 1997). Duncan's followers apparently left Port Simpson just in time to escape the ravages of smallpox that devastated it and other coastal Indian populations in years following. Port Essington (see map) which became a flourishing community during the early days of the Gold Rush and the commercial fishery that followed was once another important seasonal encampment for the Tsimshian but never a historic village site. Its permanent Indian population even at the peak of activity there and in the surrounding area probably never exceeded a few hundred. Nature has reduced visible evidence of Port Essington today to a few rotting pilings and decaying bits of buildings and machinery.

Contrasting the information gleaned from the journals and records of the first Europeans to penetrate the Skeena is that taken from the 2008 book by Gottesfeld and Rabnett, *Skeena River Fish and Their Habitat*. Their work implies a much greater First Nations presence. They refer to numerous fishing villages in places never mentioned in early written records. William Henry Pierce, himself born of a Tsimshian mother and raised in Port Simpson, gave a markedly different perspective on late 19th and early 20th century Indian settlements in Skeena country in his 1933 memoir From Potlatch to Pulpit. Suffice to say Indian life was hard and far less attractive or comfortable than that enjoyed by contemporary whites. The historic material reviewed by Kennedy (2007) concluded that social organization of First Nations involved two types those family aggregations that concentrated at salmon fishing locations seasonally but dispersed into smaller groups in the winter and those who occupied large cedar-plank houses at salmon-fishing sites and made a series of seasonal movements to annually occupied resource camps. Whatever the case, the list of Gottesfeld and Rabnett included "villages" on the Skeena near the Gitnadoix confluence, at the mouth of the Lakelse River and three other sites upstream on Lakelse, three sites on the Kitsumkalum River, throughout the Zymoetz drainage, on the upper Kitseguecla River, throughout the Kispiox, two sites in the Slamgeesh drainage, at the outlet of Motase Lake, at least two sites on the Sustut River and at several other tributary confluences along the Skeena upstream from Sustut. "Kisgegas Canyon was the heartland of many adjacent Gitxsan villages and was likely the largest aboriginal settlement in the Skeena

watershed"[4]. How that conclusion was reached given the absence of any detection of a significant settlement by the early fur traders who scoured the country or the census takers who followed remains a mystery, to me at least.

Morrell's lengthy 1985 report in the Gitxsan and Wet'suwet'en fisheries of the Skeena system referenced extensive interviews conducted with elders from various bands. Once again, the oral-history accounts create a different impression than can be gleaned from any written records. According to Morrell's information the permanent settlements at Kuldo and Kisgegas were present until well into the 20th century but were abandoned because the Department of Indian Affairs pressured inhabitants to re-locate near a few non-Indian service centers. I recall my own visit to historic Kisgegas in the late 1980s. The story given me by an Indian encountered along the Babine downstream from the old bridge crossing to the village was that Kisgegas had been wiped out by smallpox many years before and was considered a forbidden place thereafter. Nature had reclaimed any obvious evidence of a major settlement long before I was there. Intensive fish harvest at Kisgegas today is facilitated by the road built originally to reach the rock slide that nearly eliminated the 1951 sockeye return to the Babine (more on this later). The road was upgraded decades later by the forest harvesters and a spur was constructed from it to the river to accommodate large refrigeration trucks used to transport fish to the point of sale. How or why large quantities of salmon would have been moved from that area to settlements elsewhere historically has never been revealed as far as I can determine.

The prevalence of weirs is another subject replete with differing perspectives. Gottesfeld and Rabnett stated there were numerous fish-weir operations on Skeena tributaries, and even multiple weirs on some. Sites included the upper Zymoetz, Kitseguecla, Kitwanga, Suskwa, Bear and Slamgeesh rivers, near Kisgegas on Babine River, at the Motase Lake outlet (headwaters of Squingula River) and on the Bulkley River approximately one mile upstream from the Suskwa confluence. Those authors quote the Hudson Bay Company Summary Report for New Calendonia for 1822-23 as mentioning a weir across the Babine River at an undisclosed location in the lower canyon. I went to the trouble of obtaining a copy of the referenced report from the Hudson Bay Company archives in Winnipeg, Manitoba. I found no mention of weirs of any description at any location in that report. Morrell stated there were weirs completely across the Kitwanga, Bulkley, Kispiox and Babine rivers and on the Skeena above Kuldo. The interview-based material he presented stated the Kispiox supported a major weir fishery well into the 20th century. To quote Morrell:

"The Kispiox and Kitwanga rivers supported major weir fisheries well into this century; these traditional fisheries have been suppressed and replaced with intensive sport fisheries. Today, the

The remnants of the abandoned settlement at Kisgegas, September 1993.

limited Indian fishing in these and other tributaries is carried out clandestinely in defiance of government regulations."

He also referenced "adaawks" or family histories that spoke of a weir across the Skeena below Hazelton. Given that the written history of the country extends back at least 200 years one can only assume such impressive engineering feats and labor-intensive devices could not have gone unnoticed or unacknowledged if they had been utilized since that time. The Babine weirs which attracted so much attention and set the precedent for Indian fisheries forever after in the Skeena drainage were the only such fisheries other than on Kitwanga River that ever assumed any prominence in numerous other publications I researched on the Indian fisheries of the time.

The establishment of Indian reserves by government officials, primarily Indian Reserve Commissioners, in the period when such efforts were critical to the identification of areas of importance to First Nations utilization of fish resources gives more insight into the history of the Skeena fisheries. Most of this work was undertaken in the 1890s but it continued through 1925. Reserves obviously surrounded the significant First Nations communities but also included numerous sites that First Nations members identified as fishing stations, fishing places, sites used en route to fishing grounds, drying grounds and even sites that contributed wood or other materials used in the processing of fish. In total there were approximately 55 reserves established from the coastal islands and mainland near the mouth of the Skeena and along the Skeena and its tributaries. Douglas Harris (2008), who thoroughly documented the recorded history around the Indian fisheries, claimed the Indian Reserve Commissioners responsible for most of the reserves that exist in the province today acted liberally by standards of the era. The contrast between

the number of sites of import to Skeena First Nations as identified in Harris' book and the substantially greater but less thoroughly referenced number that show up in other works adds to the difficulty in interpreting the influence of historic fisheries on Skeena fish populations. Nonetheless there is instruction available from the earliest records.

The importance of salmon as a food commodity prior to European influence cannot be overstated. However, there is nothing to suggest the exploitation of salmon was significant relative to levels that developed progressively thereafter. There was no such thing as selling fish because there was no one to buy them. That all changed with the arrival of the fur traders whose supply and commerce conduits originated far to the east. They needed meat to sustain their western outposts. Supplying sufficient meat from the east was logistically impossible. Locally caught salmon therefore became the staple. It was far easier and more cost effective to buy salmon from local Indians anxious to avail themselves of items only Europeans could offer than to catch it themselves. That didn't happen overnight. The report of the Hudson Bay Company for New Caledonia in 1822-23 was referenced above. That report included an instructive piece about the quality of the dried fish that were the dominant food item of Indians. The fish were described as being of such low food value they would allegedly ruin the constitution of even the most robust of the Company employees within two or three years. Years later, after the introduction of salt, the quality of the fish preserved improved markedly.

An indication of the emerging demand placed on salmon is taken from Hudson Bay Company archives for 1836-37. The New Caledonia District (which included Fort Connolly as well as much territory to the east in the Fraser River drainage) accounts for that year listed 67,318 dried salmon and 30 "winter fresh" fish as having been supplied to the entire District, presumably all by Indians. A similar figure (67,500) was used in Large's 1957 history of the area and was alleged to have been the number of fish "consumed" at Fort Connolly. The archives would indicate otherwise. Unfortunately specific records of fish originating within the Skeena system and traded through the Hudson Bay Company are almost non-existent and add little instruction to accurate depiction of the times. Data limitations aside the Hudson Bay Company forts at Babine Lake were the focus of a highly significant and precedent setting trade in salmon that ultimately influenced steelhead. For that reason the Babine circumstances command more thorough discussion.

There can be no doubt the Indian population that occupied the Babine Lake area prior to the arrival of the fur traders was isolated and small. It is equally clear significant numbers of Babine salmon were harvested by Indians. How many were harvested and how many of those were shared and/or traded among Indians from both the Fraser River system to the east and the Skeena system downstream from Babine Lake is pure speculation. Given the size of the Fraser sockeye populations in the pre-contact era it seems unlikely trade with other Indians to the east would serve any purpose. If and when shortages of Fraser sockeye did occur post contact, the common practice of the Carrier Indians from Stuart Lake was to move across the Fraser/Skeena divide and harvest Babine sockeye in that lake's southern basin tributaries such as the Beaver River (now known as Sutherland). They didn't need to trade for them. The downstream Indians within the Skeena always harvested Babine sockeye as well as numerous other Skeena salmon stocks in their traditional fishing areas in tributaries or along the middle reaches of the Skeena and up to Kisgegas on Babine itself. Clearly there was no shortage of salmon, thus implying little advantage in transporting Babine Lake caught fish downstream for trade. As Lyons (1969) pointed out, there was trade between sparsely populated settlements at the coast and the interior for products available only in specific locales (e.g. eulachon oil, dried herring roe, dried caribou meat, bear grease) but the ubiquitous salmon were generally of no value for trade among Indians. However, with the expansion of commerce catalyzed by fur trading, a Babine fishery that for uncounted generations had been a localized sustenance fishery grew almost overnight to become what could only be described as a commercial fishery.

The earliest available records of trade in fish at Babine Lake are from Fort Kilmaur where 44,000 salmon were delivered by Indians by the end of October in 1825 (Harris, 2001). This creates yet another perspective on the emerging level of salmon harvest that came with European presence and commerce. It is not clear if or how much trade in Babine salmon escalated over the last half of the 19th century but two things are known. First, fur trading was in decline by the middle of the century and had ceased to become a major industry by 1870. Second, fish were replacing furs as the primary trade commodity.

Harris (2001) notes that trade in fish associated with large influxes of gold rush traffic to the Omineca in the 1870s and the Klondike in the 1890s, together with servicing a growing agricultural community in the Bulkley Valley, became the only real source of livelihood for the Babine people.

By the turn of the century a commercial fishery was well underway at the mouth of the Skeena River. With that began the competition for Babine sockeye. It must be kept in mind here that the Babine system supported, by far, the largest component (about 70%) of the highly desired Skeena sockeye runs that were the primary focus of the burgeoning commercial fishery. In 1904 the fisheries authorities, at the behest of cannery owners in Prince Rupert, sent an officer named Hans Helgesen from Hazelton to remove the Indians' weirs at Babine Lake and curtail the sockeye harvest the cannery men contended would ruin the resource. Of course the contemporary fleet of more than 700 gill net vessels choking the mouth of the river to service eleven canneries in operation at the time was not a problem!

The details of the events surrounding the 1904 and subsequent visits leading to the infamous "Barricades Agreement" of 1907 are well documented elsewhere and won't be repeated here. What isn't generally appreciated, however, was the incestuous relationship between fisheries management authorities and commercial industry kingpins of the day and how pervasive that relationship became for most (some would say all) of the history of the Skeena commercial fishery. In fact the cannery owners sent a letter to the Fisheries Minister of the day (Louis Prefontaine) stating that if he ignored their requests for action at Babine they would no longer support him. By today's standards such measures would be considered less than seismic. At the time, however, this was serious stuff. The other standard of the day worth noting was that fisheries guardians and officers were appointees of the local Liberal associations. Two other features of the 1904 confrontation also molded the future, namely the mythology that persisted about the scale of the fishery and the legacy of the terms of the agreement that saw the weirs removed.

Helgesen's estimate of the harvest of sockeye at the Babine weirs in 1904 was 750,000. How that figure was derived was never clarified. The only figures offered by the officer at the time were that 500 to 600 fish per day were being removed by two weirs and 16 smokehouses were in operation. The 750,000 total would require harvest of more than 20 times the 600 figure every day for 60 consecutive days. The logistics of cleaning, preparing, processing and storing that many fish given the cumulative total population of 278 Indians (including children of all ages) residing in Old Fort and Fort Babine that year (Harris, 2001) rendered such an estimate absurd. Considering that it took 700+ gillnets and 2500 shore workers with the best technology of the time to harvest and process about 1.25 million sockeye in the Skeena commercial fishery that same year it is remarkable such a figure would never be challenged, much less become pivotal in the longer term scheme of things. A quote from the 1904 Fisheries Inspector's report illustrates the mythology and attitudes of the day and how they influenced the years that followed.

"The Indians do not only catch and cure salmon for their own use, but hoard it up for sale and barter. It is a sort of legal tender amongst them, 10 salmon for a dollar and so many for a blanket. They sell salmon to packers, miners, to all those that haul with dog sleights, in every part of the upper country during the winter and to Merchants. Every storekeeper that I asked told me that they handle more or less salmon every year. The Babine post had an order from Stuart Lake for 9,000 salmon.

As I mentioned before there are about 3,000 Indians in the Skeena district, and we can reckon safely on three to a family which makes one thousand families, and I have it on good authority that with dried and fresh salmon it takes one million fish to supply the Indians in that district every year, besides what they sell, to say nothing of the multitude of dogs that number nearly as many, and are continually fed on dried salmon, and every fish, almost without exception, is killed before it is spawned, and when we take into considerations that nearly every salmon stream in the country is barricaded and this has gone on for years and years, it is not then a great wonder that there are any fish left at all?" [5]

The consequence of allowing the catch estimates to go unchallenged can be judged by information in circulation today. The web site of the First Nation presently involved in treaty negotiations at Babine Lake states:

"Prior to 1906 the Babine people harvested salmon using barricades and fish traps where the present Department of Fisheries and Oceans fence is. It was estimated that at that time the people harvested upwards of 750,000 salmon there each year."

The harvest figure was a gross overestimate but 100 years later it is obviously being used to advantage in dealing with treaty processes, historic rights and contemporary fish allocation. Contrary to popular belief the site of the Department of Fisheries and Oceans weir, originally constructed in 1946 and operated continuously ever since, is not one of the historic weir sites. The two weirs which became the subject of the Barricades agreement were located well upstream and had only been operated for perhaps four or five years at the time of Fisheries Officer Helgesen's visit in 1904. Maps of all the weir sites in use in1871 and eventually designated as Indian Reserves in 1891 are available in Harris (2001). The present DFO weir site was not one of them. Fort Babine itself, ten miles upstream, was well documented to have been constructed where it was to take advantage of the supply of sockeye traditionally harvested by weirs at Smokehouse Island immediately adjacent to the Fort. Finally, the "Barricades Agreement" as it was known

at the time is now commonly referred to as a "treaty", despite the fact evidence in support of the existence of any written agreement has never been produced. None of these historic facts appear to be germane to ongoing treaty negotiations.

From a steelhead perspective the early Babine scenario and the Barricades Agreement were highly significant in terms of their ultimate influence elsewhere in the Skeena. What the agreement did was force First Nations to substitute gill nets for their traditional weirs. Government committed to supply every family or independent, self supporting man or woman with 100 ft of net every second year. It took until 1909 but gill nets became the norm for First Nations harvest at Babine from that point forward. Also by 1909 came threats by the Gitxsans at Hazelton to build their own weirs if that is what it took to receive nets from Fisheries (Harris, 2001). Government continued to supply nets at Babine for the next 50 years. The upper Babine area itself never mattered to endemic steelhead because they rarely, if ever, progress beyond the outlet of Nilkitkwa Lake to the areas where the provisions of the agreement were first implemented. Elsewhere, however, the stage was set to replace what were once actively managed site specific fisheries targeting seasonal abundances of prolific salmon runs ("terminal fisheries") with a completely decentralized passive fishery operable any time and place that suitable flow conditions prevailed ("mixed stock fisheries"). The transition didn't happen overnight by any means but the longer term result was the gill nets frequently characterized today as indiscriminate walls of death became the First Nations' principle tool for harvesting Skeena fish. Steelhead, whose run timing and protracted pre-spawning freshwater residence frequently made them the only fresh fish available outside salmon migration periods, could now be targeted.

The inescapable conclusion after reviewing all the materials referenced above, and more, is the First Nations populations within the Skeena drainage were relatively small, dispersed and highly unlikely to have had any significant influence on the dynamics of any salmon, but especially steelhead, in the pre-contact era. In fact reference to steelhead in any early literature or records is virtually non-existent. Why would one expect otherwise? Steelhead were the least abundant of the Skeena "salmon" and their presence during the summer fishing seasons was always masked by preferred species. Steelhead were obviously the only anadromous fish present after the salmon spawning season but by then the Indians had generally dispersed to other seasonal residences to pursue other food gathering activities. Occasional latter day references to utilization of steelhead as fresh fish in the winter and spring no doubt have some foundation but one cannot overlook that rivers of the Skeena country are commonly sealed by ice for the winter. Harvesting fish as scarce and elusive as steelhead with spears and primitive hooks through holes in thick ice or after ice-out in the spring could not have

been a productive pursuit. The fresh fish argument now becoming a political club is not supported by tangible historic evidence.

Interestingly, Large (1957), in listing early Indian communities in the Skeena watershed, notes that the name Gitenmax (now Gitanmaax) was derived from the custom of natives thereabouts to fish for steelhead salmon by spearing the fish in torch light. Nowhere else in the now considerable material surrounding the history of Gitanmaax was any similar reference uncovered. The Large reference appears to have originated with William Henry Pierce's prior book From Potlatch to Pulpit. Pierce recounted much the same story but referred only to salmon, not steelhead. Underscoring the negligible role of steelhead in the early history of the Skeena was Douglas Harris' work around the legal underpinnings of the Babine and other early Indian fishery scenarios. Harris exhaustively reviewed a tremendous amount of material and in the foreword to his "Fish, Law and Colonialism, The Legal Capture of Salmon in British Columbia, he made detailed reference to the five Pacific salmon. Steelhead did not warrant mention until deep into his book and only in the context of unique late 19th and early 20th century circumstances on the Cowichan River on Vancouver Island. The literature surrounding the early commercial fishery on the Skeena is similarly lacking in mention of steelhead. Even the many publications of the Federal Government's various fisheries agencies that addressed the Indian fisheries of the times rarely made mention of steelhead.

It comes as no surprise that evidence of Skeena steelhead being used to any substantial degree prior to European contact is absent. Economy and efficiency were undoubtedly hallmarks of the early Indian fishermen. When one considers that steelhead have always been far less abundant than other co-migrating salmon species and never concentrated enough to support catch rates that would justify the effort required to target them with the primitive harvesting tools of the day it is only logical that the focus would have been on sockeye and chinook. Regardless of what significance First Nations may attach to steelhead today there is no case to be made that the Indian fishery affected their recruitment or, for that matter, the recruitment of any other salmon species in the thousands of years archaeologists tell us predated the arrival of the white man.

As a postscript on the historic Indian fisheries that have been talked about by others as harvesting steelhead I'll say only this. If they are all accurate there must have been vastly more steelhead present than anything imaginable from piecing together all the fur trader records, the commercial fishery catch records, the fisheries agencies' fish distribution accounts and the fish habitat capability assessments. They must also have been far more widely distributed than anything seen in more than a century.

Chapter 5
RAPID CHANGE

The commercial fishing industry arrived at the mouth of the Skeena River in 1876 and the first pack of canned fish was put up in 1877. By that time the white entrepreneurs had already established two communities in the area. "Skeenamouth" on the north side of the river and Port Essington across from it on the south were a decade old when the first cannery went into operation. Inverness Cannery, the first of many to follow, was located at Skeenamouth. Both of the original communities developed as hubs to facilitate the movement of men and supplies arriving by sea from the south inland to "the forks" (Hazelton) and the telegraph line and gold fields beyond. Keep in mind this was still a remote land quite unlike the lower Fraser River and Columbia River regions far to the south. The only modes of transportation prior to the arrival of the first steam powered riverboat in 1891 were foot and canoes. Between winter ice, spring freshet and major rainfall events that occurred periodically in fall, flow conditions precluded navigation by canoe for at least half of any given year. The trip from the coast to Hazelton could take anywhere from one to two weeks.

Commercial fishing and canneries quickly replaced the remnant fur trade and the emerging inland fish sales economy as the primary opportunity for Indians to adapt to the new order descending all around them. In the beginning the cannery men and the Indians needed each other. The remoteness of the country and its meager white population left the Indians as the sole source of labor, at least in the early going. Indian men quickly filled the demand for oarsmen and net pullers while women and even children served to construct and mend the nets and populate the canning lines. It was commonplace for cannery owners to hire native fishers so they could secure the labor of wives and daughters on the canning lines. The owners didn't have to pay to get the labor to the site, provide anything other than the most primitive accommodation, or return anyone to their point of origin after the season. Geoff Meggs' description (in Salmon: The Decline of the British Columbia Fishery) of those early times is graphic:

"If working conditions were primitive for fishermen, they were doubly so for cannery workers, who differed from slaves only in the fact that they were laid off at the end of the season."

The extent of Indian participation in the rapidly expanding commercial fishery in the closing decades of the 19th century was such that the interior communities of the Skeena watershed were largely vacated by able bodied men and women from late spring until late summer. Well in advance of season start up the cannery owners sent their agents to all the villages as far upstream as Kispiox to contract the labor required to harvest and process fish. Notes from the Provincial Archives of British Columbia are ample evidence of how life changed. These recount a conversation with Chief Henry Johnson of the Gitxsan village near Hazelton who was speaking about the earliest period of fishing activity on the lower Skeena (Anon., 1976).

"They travel by canoe from up river. Four or five families to one canoe, and came down here early in spring…..And the women work in the cannery and so on like that."

"These women at the cannery in the spring, they're knittin' the sockeye net…..There's a carton of twine. I think women get two and a half to make a net."

"And during the summer when the canning was on, the women got three cents a tray, filling the cans; 150 trays to a rack. That's a lot of money for them because it's an awful lot of fish in those times."

"And fishermen they went out. They don't sell fish by each fish the same as we do today. They only get paid by the month - $30 for a captain and $25 for a boat puller. And it's only two months in a year they fish. They fish day and night for that $30 a month.

"And they use the flat-bottom skiff with no shelter, just open skiff with two pieces across to sit on. You know how much wind and how much rain are here! And these people would sit out there, and the rain and the wind blowing. They didn't have enough money to buy slickers……..In those days a lot of people died."

"They don't care how many die."

"And there's nobody else besides our native people doing the fishing in those days. No other race of people before Japs and whites."

The traditional food fisheries that had, for as long as anyone knew, sustained Indian people didn't disappear but they certainly diminished in scale with the seasonal exodus of labor to the coast. So too did the harvest of fish for trade and barter, at least during the peak salmon migration times when those who previously attended to those pursuits were employed at the coast. Whereas the Babine fishery and a few others such as Kitwanga and Moricetown remained as significant fisheries into the 20th century they were something less than a sole source of livelihood when so many of the providers from those communities moved elsewhere for at least part of the year to avail themselves of the relatively lucrative opportunities that had emerged in the non-Indian world.

Other features of the evolving Skeena environment that influenced Indian fishing included the fact that food other than fish was becoming readily available. The Indians who left traditional settlements to partake of commercial fishing or logging soon developed eating habits different from anything they had known previously. Also, dogs which were once a dominant feature of all Indian settlements and which were fed largely on salmon or their carcasses became increasingly less important.

What remained of any need for fish to sustain dogs used to pull sleds or pack loads diminished further with the steady modernization of transportation. In the relatively remote Babine Lake country the arrival of moose around 1920 quickly resulted in carcass remains replacing fish as the dog food of choice.

Racial discrimination was a hallmark of the commercial fishing industry through its early evolution. In a matter of a few decades the industry went from actively soliciting and embracing Indian participation to replacing them with immigrant workers even more susceptible to exploitation. Indians had to adjust to growing competition from various European maritime nation fishers and Americans from the Columbia and Sacramento rivers and, soon after them, the Chinese and Japanese. The latter quickly filled the void created by white fishers who left the coast in search of gold in the interior of the Province and in the Yukon. Rapid technological change and labor disputes deeply rooted in ethnic partitioning of fishermen became the norm. Pivotal events are well documented, especially by Geoff Meggs. In the canneries the women faced similar issues – competition with whites and Asians, racial animosity and discrimination, rapid technological changes and even displacement by organized workers with pre-emptive agreements with the cannery owners. The outcome was that in a single working lifetime Indians saw their domination of the commercial fishery labor force progressively eroded, leaving most of them with no other employment option. Ultimately many whose grandparents had been the sole occupants of the land were now dispossessed of the fish that were the cornerstone of their culture and sustenance. Some Indian fishermen and cannery workers remained however and became the base for future generations whose attachment to fish was spawned of the white man's economy rather than any historic roots with their own.

As the 20th century progressed the inland or food fishery slowly began to exert new influence on steelhead. Gill nets replaced weirs (what few there may have been), dip nets, spears and basket traps as the primary fish harvesting method. To reiterate, the shift was driven by the Babine weir controversy and the oft mentioned Barricades Agreement that resulted. Sockeye and chinook remained the targets but with the majority of both originating well upstream of the major Indian communities scattered along the main stem Skeena the fishing activity was increasingly focused on the migration corridor rather than the spawning tributaries. Contributing to the changes was the absence of many villagers from their traditional fishing areas during the peak salmon migration times. Food fish needs that were not met by sockeye and chinook due to forced relocation of fisheries and fishing methods meant that the main stem gill net fishery began to operate in non-traditional times and places. Over time the 100-foot lengths of net originally prescribed by Fisheries Department officials and provided by the

Indian Department became 200-foot lengths and later still were replaced by longer, deeper and much more effective commercial fishing nets brought up from the coast. This could hardly have come as any surprise considering the government only supplied web and twine, not the ready to fish commercial nets already equipped with lead lines and floats. With the appearance of these more effective nets the Indian Department apparently ceased supplying nets as per the original Barricades Agreement. Precisely when is unclear but it must have been sometime after 1947 given that Indian Department records indicated between 22 and 47 nets were given out each year from 1941 to 1947. What proportion of the total nets in use these figures represented could not be determined from information available.

Gillnets held many advantages over the traditional fishing methods employed by Indians. They eliminated the labor associated with all the other capture techniques, they didn't require concentrations of fish to be effective and they could be employed any time suitable flow conditions prevailed. They were just as effective at catching coho and steelhead in August and September as they were catching chinook and sockeye in June and July. What problem could there possibly be if no one knew anything about steelhead or ever bothered to record any information on effort and catch? As with the commercial fisheries influence on steelhead at the coast, no data = no problem. In retrospect all that can be said is steelhead were beginning to absorb harvest pressure previously unknown. The single greatest exception to the trend toward main stem gill nets was the Moricetown fishery although a similar but much smaller scale fishery persisted at Hagwilget. Even Kisgegas on the lower Babine, touted as a major dip net and trap fishery that had existed for hundreds or thousands of years, was abandoned in favor of gill netting in the mainstem Skeena. Moricetown is a special case deserving of its own discussion in pages that follow.

Quantifying the influence of the Indian fishery on Skeena steelhead is anything but straightforward. For at least the first third of the 20th century there are only scattered records regarding the size of the Indian population, its spatial distribution and its catch of fish. What transpired in the half century before when Fisheries Inspector accounts are the only retrievable records is obviously uncertain. Most of what credible information can be found regarding the Indian fishery deals with the period from the mid-1940s onward following the arrival of fisheries scientists from the Federal Government's Fisheries Research Board (FRB). Between 1944 and 1948 they undertook the aforementioned program, The Skeena River Salmon Investigation. It was initiated in response to the painfully obvious declines in sockeye salmon abundance that had followed decades of commercial fishing at the river mouth. In pursuit of their assignment they compiled, among other things, all available information on the Indian fishery (Milne, 1948).

From that and numerous other scientific publications that followed a better understanding of that fishery emerges.

On the number of Indians who lived in the various reserves along the Skeena and relied on the fishery for sustenance Milne quoted records of the Indian Department. Their figures documented the number of individual families living in each village and/or reserve throughout the entire Skeena. The 1944 totals were 660 families and 2,223 individuals. A comparable exercise in 1934 arrived at a figure of 2,130. Those figures were up slightly from the 1900 Indians Milne quoted from another estimate prepared in 1900. The proportional distribution of the Indian population in 1944 appeared to be similar to what had existed for at least several decades before. The Babine Lake vicinity (principally Old Fort and Fort Babine) supported 18%, Moricetown about 13%, the Kispiox through Hazelton area, including Hagwilget, about 40%, Kitwanga, Kitseguecla and Kitwancool combined about 23% and the lower Skeena roughly 5%. Less than 2% of the Indian population of the Skeena watershed (i.e. less than 45 people) lived anywhere upstream from the Babine confluence in the mid-1940s. Villages which, according to other authors, once existed at Kitselas, Lakelse, Kitsumkalum and elsewhere along the lower Skeena were not mentioned in any of the Indian Department population accounts from those years.

The dearth of information on annual harvests of salmon and steelhead by Indians before the inception of the Skeena River Salmon Investigation can be traced to several factors. First and foremost there was no one monitoring or reporting on Indian catches on any consistent basis. Second, there was tacit agreement between the Indian Department and the Fisheries Department not to invoke the full force of regulations originally designed to control the Indian fishery. The Skeena was still a very remote country in the closing decades of the 19th century and the first several of the 20th. A heavy hand on people who relied on fish for sustenance would only create more hardship and greater demands on the Indian Department whose task had become providing for those who couldn't do it themselves. The Oblate Missionaries of the time were openly supportive of leaving the Indians to do as they had for generations. This position was generally upheld by the public at large and fostered something less than rigorous application of the law. Finally, after decades of no surveillance and no consistent application or enforcement of regulations there developed a scenario whereby Indians believed they were completely free to do as they wished. The situation that greeted Milne and his cohorts is well illustrated by two quotes from their 1948 report. The first is in relation to the broader Skeena fishery, the second specific to weir fishing on the Kitwanga River.

"Undoubtedly the whole question of the Indian fishery on the Skeena is now, by accident or design, rather clouded and indefinite. The oft-mentioned treaty (Author's note: the Barricades

Agreement) *under which the natives gave up certain privileges and practices in return for other privileges does not seem to be available. From the present uncertainty, it would appear that it must have contained many very loose promises for which local interpretations have been given throughout the system. These rulings have come to be accepted as law through application. The resulting confusion leaves no alternative but to recommend a complete and thorough re-examination and revision of the plan by representatives of the Dominion Department of Indian Affairs, the Dominion Department of Fisheries and the Fisheries Research Board of Canada to solve the difficulties and evolve a new design more favourable to salmon conservation.*"

"*Under the present agreement, however, it would seem that this behaviour should not be permitted. If the practices are not deemed injurious, they should be legalized. Half-way measures in enforcement have a tendency to build up at least a disrespect for, if not a complete disregard of responsibility and discipline. When the revised terms become law, they should be publicized and explained in complete detail both to the Indians and within the protective agency. The penalties for bartering, selling and illegal catching should be made perfectly clear. Only after this understanding, will it be possible to enforce anything approaching sound regulation*".

So, against a backdrop of a consistently small Indian population, the trend toward abandonment of traditional fishing sites and methods by able bodied fishers during traditional fishing times, limited vigilance with respect to catch monitoring, and replacement of traditional fishing methods with less selective gear, what observations are actually available that allow reasonable conclusions about Indian catches of steelhead through the first half of the 20th century?

The first government records originated with fisheries guardians who were deployed at Woodcock, Hazelton, Moricetown, Fort Babine and Donald's Landing (Babine Lake) by 1935. From their annual reports Milne (1948) noted the catch of steelhead by all Indians fishing upstream from Terrace between 1935 and 1947 ranged from 660 to 3,345 fish and averaged 1,800 annually. These figures were dominated by catches from the Skeena around Hazelton and Kitwanga and from the Bulkley at Moricetown. The steelhead catch downstream of Terrace was not recorded but assumed to be insignificant given that the average annual catch of salmon by the eight families present was only 3,000 fish. Steelhead would also have been taken in areas not monitored by guardians (e.g. Bear/Sustut system and perhaps elsewhere in the uppermost reaches of the Skeena) but the Indian population in these areas was clearly small and steelhead harvest would likely have added only a small increment to that which occurred downstream. Separate estimates of the catch of steelhead at Moricetown between 1930 and 1945 averaged 449 annually. The Babine system fishery that gave rise to the Barricades Agreement near the turn of the century continued as a major fishery but one prosecuted exclusively with gill nets deployed in times and places where steelhead were not present (i.e.

Nilkitkwa Lake in August and September).

The Skeena River Salmon Investigation participants suggested the Indian catches were constant from year to year and predicated on food requirements. The observed pattern of able bodied Indians, especially from the Kispiox through Kitwanga areas, moving to the coast to partake of the commercial fishery and return to their home villages after the season began to emerge as a steelhead issue in years when food fish requirements were not fulfilled by the preferred earlier timed chinook and sockeye. Shortfalls were met by coho and steelhead, both readily available in the main stem Skeena and at Moricetown after the return of the fishermen. Of course the harvest method in the Skeena was gill nets.

All things considered the picture that emerges up until deep into the 20th century is one where the Indians of the Skeena were not major players in the dynamics of steelhead. Reasonable estimates of the number of steelhead harvested by Indians from the mid-1930s to at least the late 1960s show relatively little variation in the annual catch. When considered on a per capita basis the number was relatively constant at about one fish per person per year over this extended period. The obvious conclusion to be drawn here is that steelhead was never a significant food item for Indians. Further, no evidence can be found there was ever any social or cultural significance attached to Skeena steelhead by Indians.

In the latter half of the century some different trends emerged. First and foremost the Indian population that had remained stable for at least 75 years increased dramatically in the next 50. It started slowly. Wilson Duff's 1964 publication The Indian History of British Columbia – The Impact of the White Man noted the combined population of all the aboriginal people occupying the various Tsimshian and Gitxsan communities up and down the Skeena in 1963 was 3,391. This included 1094 at Port Simpson and 187 at Metlakatla. Duff's figure was only slightly higher than at any time in the previous century. Statistics Canada census data for 2006 revealed there were about 12,000 First Nations people belonging to various Bands within the Skeena drainage and living within its boundaries. There were about 9,000 more members of the same bands residing elsewhere in British Columbia. Of the 12,000 Skeena residents, most lived in communities outside their Reserves. About 7,000 of them lived in either Prince Rupert or Terrace. There were 8,344 members of the five Gitxsan plus two Wet'suwet'en Bands at the center of the present in-river fishery (i.e. between Gitsegukla and Kispiox on the Skeena and up to Moricetown on the Bulkley). Only one-third of them, call it 2800, lived in those communities. No single community had a population of more than 700. Indian and Northern Affairs Canada (IANC) data complete to January 2010 indicated the cumulative total number of "Registered Indians"[6] belonging to the Bands and living in those same communities had increased more than three fold to 8,710.

Determining how many Registered Indians there are today with a recognized claim to Skeena River fish is another difficult task. Along the coast north and south of the Skeena estuary there are Bands who traditionally travelled to the Skeena but also to many other areas of the north coast. The most obvious example is Lax-kw'alaams or Port Simpson as it was once known. Indian and Northern Affairs Canada data complete to January 2010 reports 3,265 Band members, only 825 of which live on the reserve there or on "other reserves". We know Port Simpson supported many Tsimshian in the mid-1800s but most of these were affiliated more strongly with the Nass River than the Skeena. To the east and south are Bands that were primarily focused on the Fraser River watershed but moved back and forth between there and the Skeena seasonally. Today's Lake Babine Band would be an example there. Referring to current IANC data again, there were 2,275 Band members reported. Almost 1500 of them live on reserves, but in or around Burns Lake, not Babine Lake. Adding to the confusion is the influx of Metis people who, from a statistical perspective, are lumped with the "aboriginal identity" population. "Other North American Indians" is another, albeit small, inclusion in the population agglomeration data. Then there is the uncertainty regarding the number of people who lived in unorganized areas rather than designated communities. Some data are compiled for specific communities only and some for much broader geographic areas. Different data sets apply to different census periods and some of the sets include figures others exclude.

The remarkable feature of Skeena First Nations demographics in recent times is the age distribution. In 2006 70% of the population was under age 30. The population growth rate in the preceding decade was 39%. In contrast, the non-First Nations population of Prince Rupert, Terrace and Smithers, the largest communities in the Skeena watershed, all declined steadily over the same period. This was due primarily to economic downturns in the forest industry. That trend is expected to continue. The total population of the Skeena watershed as of 2006 was 51,120. British Columbia's population at the same time was 4,113,487. The proportion of registered Indians among the total population of the Skeena (24%) is dramatically different from their proportion provincially (3%). If we use the January 2010 IANC data on the number of registered Indians belonging to the various Bands likely to lay claim to Skeena fishery resources the proportion of them relative to the total regional population rises to 32%. The combination of a growing First Nations population, a declining non-First Nations population and gravitation of First Nations band members to the larger population centers in the region will have significant bearing on attitudes and perceptions in the Skeena area in future

It warrants mention that part of the increase in the First Nations population in recent years resulted from amendments to the federal government's Indian Act in 1985. Those amendments, among other things, restored the status and Band membership of Indian women who had married non-status men. It is unclear from figures readily available through Indian and Northern Affairs Canada how many Indians from the Skeena region were involved but for the province as a whole the number whose status was restored between 1985 and 2007 was 19,500. If the proportion of the status Indian population growth attributed to restored status provincially (16%) is applicable to the Skeena area we could assume about 1,900 Indians were involved. Applying provincial figures again, a reasonable estimate of the number of those 1900 living in traditional villages or on crown land within the Skeena watershed would be 400.

Now, just to recap – the Indian population at the time of first contact with whites was small and dispersed. That situation remained for more than a century that followed. There is no evidence that utilization of steelhead by Indians any time during that period could have been a factor in the status of that species. As the commercial fishery started and flourished through the late19th century and on into the 20th there were progressively less fish of all species making their way past the river mouth gillnets. Most of the able bodied Indians from the villages that were the dominant fishing sites up-river opted for seasonal employment in the commercial fishing industry. Between the absence of labor during the peak of the salmon migration season and replacement of abundance dependent traditional harvesting methods with gill nets that could be effective any time and anywhere progressively more attention focused on fishing later in the summer and fall when steelhead were more prevalent in the catch. If there ever were any rules that applied to gill net fishing in the Skeena they were never enforced. Fishing could be prosecuted 365 days of the year, fish could be sold openly and no one blinked.

Entering the fish abundance equation slowly but steadily all through the 20th century were the inevitable changes in the watershed brought about by cattle ranchers, loggers, miners and railroad and road construction activity. Fish habitat once untouched by human hands was eroding steadily. There were no rules for road location, drainage structures or stream crossings. Land clearing to tame the wilderness and supply sawmills or produce cattle feed was widely promoted. Waste management from mines or any other industrial pursuit, fish canneries included, was unheard of. Environmental standards came long after the fact and had about as much weight as the paper they appeared on. With each passing decade the commercial fishing industry increased its efficiency. Much diminished fish populations had no hope of recovery in the absence of Draconian measures industry leaders refused to accept. There were more people on the landscape than ever before. Virtually all of them believed the Skeena country was still the grass beyond the mountains. The patterns so clearly established

in watershed after watershed all along the Pacific coast from San Francisco to Vancouver were being repeated.

Where did things change to the point where the Indian fishery emerged as something more than a negligible factor with respect to steelhead? The first comprehensive work done by the Indian community itself to document its past and present use of Skeena salmon and steelhead was undertaken by Morrell and published in 1985. He estimated the Gitxsan and Wet'suwet'en set and drift net fishery in the main stem Skeena removed between 1,400 and 3,300 steelhead annually in the early 1980s. The Moricetown fishery added another 200 to 700. The Department of Fisheries estimate of Indian harvest of steelhead remained at 1,200 or less through 1979 but rose sharply thereafter. For the 1980 -1988 period catches ranged from 3,900 to 15,195 and averaged 8,180. These figures likely included the tidal waters catch in addition to the harvest in the traditional food fishing areas inland. Beyond the late 1980s the reliability of steelhead catch estimates is highly suspect for all the same reasons that will be discussed later in the context of commercial fishery catch reporting. In fact the Indian community itself was anything but cohesive in terms of administration of its own inland fishery. A headline article in the Prince Rupert Daily News in January 1995 reported on a federal government review board hearing in

which members of the Gitxsan community spoke out about fear and intimidation tactics employed by the Gitxsan Wet'suwet'en Watershed Authority which supposedly represented the chiefs and band members of the area. There were serious allegations of lack of accountability with respect to budget expenditures. Worse still was the revelation that the federal managers had adopted a hands off approach concerning anything to do with overseeing the inland commercial fishery that, by then, had become a highly significant feature of the overall harvest of Skeena fish.

Earlier on I said the level of steelhead harvest by Indians appears to have been relatively constant through most of the 20th century. There just wasn't anything to suggest the Indian fishery had ever been a problem and little attention was paid to it. But, when 15,000 fish didn't make it to the rivers where another user group full of expectations awaited, rumblings of discontent began. They got a lot louder in the early 1990s when, for the first time since estimates of steelhead returns began in 1956, the run size escaping the commercial fishery approached historic low levels in three successive years and steelhead conservation came to the forefront. The insoluble debate about the size of the steelhead pie and who should get the pieces was on.

Chapter 6
LESSONS FROM MORICETOWN

Why should the recorded history of the Moricetown fishery command special attention? This seems a logical question given the diversity of food fishing sites in the Skeena and the number of Indian fishers using that site relative to others any time in the past 100 or more years. We know the Babine fishery attracted more interest from Fisheries Department officials than any other in the earliest years of the department's existence. Equally understood is the fallout from the Babine scenario (gill nets) and how it influenced the main stem Skeena fishery. At Moricetown, however, we have the Indian fishery that dominated the records for most of the post Barricades Agreement history. It was instrumental in shaping the attitudes, regulations and policies that have had the greatest bearing on steelhead if not on all the other salmon species since the mid-point of the last century. The mere fact the fishery occurs in plain view of the major transportation and communication corridor for the region has served to keep it in the forefront for a good part of the last century and all of the present. The significance of Moricetown is underscored by the fact the Bulkley system supports the largest stock grouping of Skeena summer steelhead.[7] Most of those fish must pass the gauntlet to get to their final destination. Understanding the Moricetown history is central to appreciating how steelhead have been influenced and how they will continue to be influenced.

The first references to the Moricetown fishery by government officials came from the same Fisheries Officer who led the cannery owner inspired assault on the Babine weirs. A quote from his 1904 report is another of the examples of the perceptions and attitudes of the time.

"On examining the canyon I found it about 250 yards long, the narrowest part 18 feet wide, and from the numerous paths, staging, ladders, etc., I could judge that the canyon during the fishing season was lined with Indians, hooking and catching salmon by every conceivable contrivance. They even shove out a long pole with a rope through the end of it from one side of a crevice in the other side, bend on a trap or basket, haul it to the other side, lower it down, and when a sufficient quantity of salmon enter they haul it back. Every salmon that comes up that foaming, boiling cauldron goes into little eddies for rest, and every eddy is filled with contrivances for his capture but if indeed some of the fish are lucky enough to escape the multitude of hooks and traps in the canyon, a worse fate awaits them at the falls immediately above; where the falls at low water during the fishing season is by all accounts 14 feet, behind the falls is an array of various kinds of traps and baskets; the salmon keep on jumping incessantly to get up and fall back into the basket. Thus only a few fish get up the river to the lakes, and I could see no

other way to remedy the evil in that narrow place where the salmon is entirely at the mercy of the Indians: so by the authority under Sub sec. 16, clause 5, Chp. 51 and other section of the Fishery Act, I placed a notice above the Falls, and another at the lower end of the canyon, which strictly forbids fishing on any kind for a distance of 300 yards. I might have excluded surface fly fishing but there are no sports in the vicinity."

In Milne's 1948 Skeena River Salmon Investigation report, no doubt driven by another generation of self serving commercial fishery interests at the coast, he referred to this passage and concluded "Unfortunately the no fishing regulation mentioned above was never enforced". The fact that the Moricetown fishery had been in operation for generations before the first gill net was ever deployed at the mouth of the Skeena, without diminishing the supply of fish returning to the Bulkley River system, shows no evidence of ever being acknowledged by anyone in the Fisheries Department.

By 1935 the Department guardian stationed at Moricetown was actively administering the regulations of the day and monitoring catches on a consistent basis. Regulations to address Indians fishing in non-tidal waters had been in place for decades by that time but they were never applied as those who created them would seem to have intended. To reiterate, the soft approach to enforcement originally came from cannery owners sensitive to upsetting their access to the only ready source of cheap labor. Clergymen of the day were also strongly supportive of hands off regarding Indian fishing. Then there was the constant tug of war between the two Federal Government agencies, one that served the commercial industry, the other the inland victims of it. Finally, the absence of any proof of the terms of the Barricades Agreement created lingering uncertainty around the measures applicable to Indian fisheries in general. Collectively these factors resulted in localized interpretation and application of the laws that did exist. The lack of consistency and continuity was readily exploitable in the longer term. In the shorter term, however, there were some interesting measures applied at Moricetown. They provide useful insight into power and influence of government fisheries officials in bygone days.

The most significant restriction ever imposed at Moricetown and the one that has been ignored in virtually all the modern day references to the history of that fishery concerns the use of gaffs. The basket traps and dip nets that prevailed from the time of first observation until the arrival of a guardian were outlawed by the Department of Fisheries in 1935. The name or position of the individual within the Department who was responsible for this decision never appeared in any of the published records but Department members themselves made repeated references to the measure being of their own making. Gaffs were imposed at least in part due to quarrels over ownership of the one main basket trap and division of the catch. The common belief that gaffs were

the method of choice at Moricetown or anywhere else long before the arrival of whites and their rules is just one more example of selective interpretation of facts. Accounts of Moricetown fishery history prepared by Indians themselves frequently err in their reporting of the historical sequence of fishing methods and related events. Virtually none of those reports ever cite published material.

In retrospect the introduction of gaffs was the second very bad decision by the Department. Replacement of weirs with nets at Babine was round one of new and lasting implications for steelhead throughout the Skeena. Gaffs and all that followed on the Bulkley was round two. Elimination of weirs and traps buried any potential for selectively harvesting target stocks and species for decades afterward.

Ironically, a mere ten years after gaffs were forced upon the Moricetown fishermen, the researchers from the same agency that mandated them were recommending repeatedly their use should be eliminated. Those recommendations followed detailed studies of the number of fish that were hooked by gaffs but escaped. Another element of the waste associated with gaffing was the amount of gaff damaged flesh that was carved out of landed fish and discarded before processing The loss to the spawning population was confirmed repeatedly by the total absence of gaff injured fish of any species among thousands of spawned out fish examined at regularly surveyed prime sites upstream from Moricetown. The replacement of veteran fishermen by young, inexperienced, part time fishermen whose hooked to landed ratio was consistently higher aggravated the waste scenario. Many veterans were reported to have left the fishery to gain employment in the forest industry or with the railroad (Milne, 1948).

One can easily become lost in the details of two decades worth of published reports on the Moricetown fishery. That makes for rather tedious reading. Those interested in the scientific reports can look them up readily enough (See, for example Milne, 1948A & B; Palmer, 1964, 1965, 1966, 1986; Harding, 1968). What would seem valuable here is a simple distillation of the salmon focused results that eventually spill over onto steelhead. The story goes like this.

Fish populations arriving at the falls were already in decline when the first serious observations were undertaken by Fisheries Research Board scientists. No factor other than the commercial fishery could possibly be held responsible for diminished returns. The situation worsened steadily and prompted studies aimed specifically at assessing the impact of the falls and the fishery. Sockeye from the Nanika system, far upstream in the Morice headwaters, had been a mainstay of the falls fishery for generations. Now their status was sounding conservation alarms. The scientist quickly demonstrated the consequences of gaffing. Not only did gaffs catch a higher proportion of the available fish than previously

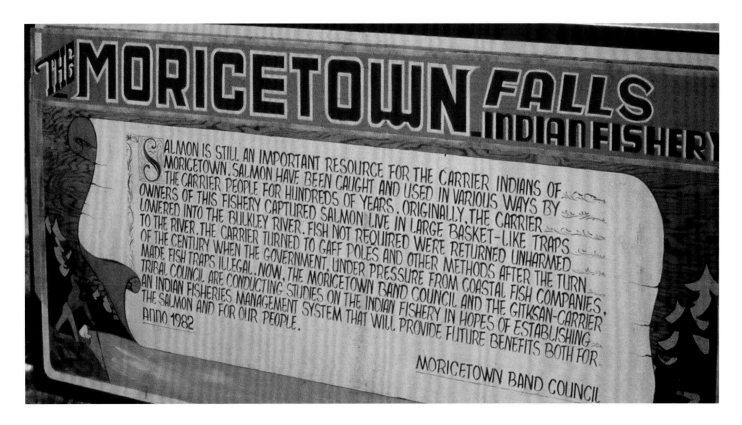

imagined, they accounted for additional exploitation due to mortally injured fish escaping. Fishing activity was restricted to five days per week and later to four and individual fishermen were even restricted to ten fish per day at one point. The residence period of fish in the high harvest rate areas immediately below the falls was strongly positively correlated with the presence of gaffers and with low river flows. The mandated weekly closed periods were remarkably successful in prompting fish to migrate past the falls and therefore escape the gaffs. Excessive harvest rates persisted however, reaching as high as 58% on sockeye one year and averaging 26% for ten years of record. If sockeye and chinook runs in June and July did not satisfy food fish requirements steelhead and coho were targeted in August and September. Both species proved especially vulnerable in low flow years. Two remedial measures were recommended by the scientists - fishways to speed passage and therefore reduce the time of exposure of fish to gaffs and elimination of gaffs in favor of a return to dip nets. The original fishways were partially successful in moving fish through the falls area more quickly. Further fishway measures were studied and justified but never pursued. Other measures resulting from the Moricetown research on migration delays and harvest rates included removal of the fish passage obstruction at Hagwilget and construction of a 12.5 million egg capacity pilot hatchery on the Nanika River to rehabilitate sockeye.[8] Steelhead catch data compiled over the course of their investigations revealed an average annual harvest of 390 in years from 1930 to 1968. The highest catch recorded was 1400 and the lowest 83. If injured fish escaping from gaffs were included the average annual steelhead catch would likely have doubled. Anyone who doubts there were many more fish (other than pink salmon) arriving at Moricetown

in the late 1940s than at any time since need only review Milne's data on the catches of individual gaffers. Catch per minute was the original metric. Years later it became catch per hour.

The fishways constructed by the Department of Fisheries warrant additional comment. The prevailing opinion of the Wet'suwet'en, as expressed by Morrell (1985), is that Fisheries Department officials deliberately blasted away perches utilized by the fishermen and constructed fishways to reduce or even eliminate the Indian fishery. Another quote is evidence enough:

"On the Bulkley all traditional trap sites have been systematically destroyed by blasting carried out by federal agencies in the name of removal of obstacles to fish migration."

Whereas previously noted comments of fisheries officials might be interpreted to lend credence to this theory there is more to consider. The initial attempt to construct a fishway was undertaken in 1929. It involved blasting four equal steps over a total drop of ten feet in the main eastern channel (river right). According to Milne (1948) 140 cubic feet of rock were removed at a cost of $948.65. Limited follow-up investigation revealed almost no evidence of the 1929 undertakings and no amelioration of fish passage difficulties. The next undertakings came in response to recommendations that followed the 1945-1947 investigations of the effect of the falls on the salmon runs. Regardless of who might ultimately benefit from getting a higher proportion of the fish arriving at Moricetown through to their spawning destination, the study results demonstrated beyond doubt that something had to be done to improve escapement. Construction commenced in 1951 and was completed that same year.

The main steelhead fishing areas at Moricetown Falls before and after construction of the fishways. The earlier photo (left) was taken in the mid-1940s, the other one (above) September 10, 2010.

My assumption there would be records of the fishway construction in Fisheries Department archives proved wrong. Pacific Biological Station Library staff and personal contact with retired DFO staff proved only that the engineers of the day were notorious for failing to file reports on their work. The fishways at the base of the falls on both sides of the river have remained unaltered since originally installed despite recommended improvements advanced by the scientists who continued their work at the falls until the late 1960s. Comparisons of photos of the falls and fishery before and after fishway construction do not provide tangible evidence that the number of fishing sites or the effectiveness of fishermen was reduced by any Fisheries Department actions. In fact the fishways provided easier access to most of the best fishing sites and the fishway entrances themselves became highly productive spots during periods of suitable river flow. That begs another question; how it is that harvesting fish at the entrance to a fishway squares with the explicit

forbidding of such practice under decades old fisheries regulations? There is one sobering thought that leaps to mind with respect to fishways and alleged blasting. If the Supreme Court of Canada's settlement of the Hagwilget fishery case is a precedent for Moricetown the future promises to be interesting.

There is more to consider. As indicated previously, one of the major objectives of the FRB staff who were active at Moricetown for more than two decades was to address the depressed Nanika sockeye stock. Now, the FRB researchers were not the same Department of Fisheries folk who were joined at the hip with the commercial fishing industry leaders down in Prince Rupert. They were the professionals at a time when that term carried with it some real credentials. They heralded from an independent arm of the Federal Government based at the Pacific Biological Station in far off Nanaimo. The steps they recommended as a result of their investigations had everything to do with getting more Nanika sockeye through the Bulkley and on to the Morice. Fishways at Moricetown helped.[9] So did the blasting at Hagwilget. In effect all that removal of the Hagwilget rock did was re-establish the historic spatial distribution of fishing effort and harvest on the Bulkley River. If this was such a communal society with strong history of sharing and exchange (as evidenced by the move from Moricetown to Hagwilget when the rock first fell into the canyon) what difference would 20 miles make, especially with all the modern transportation conveniences that existed by the time the rock was removed? The issue of the salmon allocation imbalance that heavily favored the commercial fishery was not the responsibility of scientists. Their work focused on the fish. Had they not been active at Moricetown and had nothing been done to address the problems they so clearly illustrated we can be absolutely certain there would have been even less fish to harvest, no matter where and by whom.

Fast forward to the 1980s and 90s. Fish, once the primary food item of all the Skeena Indians had lost their dominance as successive generations shopped in grocery stores more than in rivers. The number of members of the Moricetown Band was higher than at any time in recorded history and rising steadily. The quality and productive capability of fish habitat in the Bulkley and Morice watersheds was slipping as the cumulative effects of development within the watershed mounted. Fewer fish of all species except pinks arrived at Moricetown with each successive generation. There was no guardian, no permits, no closed periods, no quotas, as many fishermen wielding gaffs and jigs as ever before and fish were sold openly, sometimes even from a well marked roadside stand in the parking lot overlooking the falls not more than 25 meters from the centerline of Highway 16. In hundreds of visits to and through Moricetown over this period I never saw another fisheries agency person on site. The century old power and influence of commercial fishing industry leaders and the Department of Fisheries had obviously been eroded.

Now, how did all this play out for steelhead? More Indian fishermen with only self imposed rules to guide them while harvesting a shrinking fish population did not make for happy times. Fish politics was taking over. Conservation was everyone's mantra as long as it didn't cost them anything. The historically powerful and influential commercial fishing industry refused to accept further restrictions to conserve steelhead subsequently reallocated to upstream Indians to eat or elitist fly fishermen to torture. Indians were increasingly aware of the trump card they held. The bullying was over. Nothing more was going to be given up unless there was an acceptable pay back.

The first step taken to try and move away from the status quo at Moricetown involved MOE paying willing fishermen for each steelhead they dip netted, tagged and released. That opened a door that evolved into hiring Band members to specifically target steelhead with dip nets for tag and release. By the early years of the new millennium that program became ever more sophisticated and expensive. The conservation versus allocation debate was the driving force. Decisions around constraining steelhead catches, whether by commercial, native or sport fishers, could no longer be based on professional judgment. Bullet proof science was the only acceptable route. No one could argue that better information on steelhead stock strength was not a good idea or that tagging and releasing steelhead was a worse alternative than killing them? At the same time no one was going to stop fishing and the burden of proof for any course correction was always on the conservation advocates, never the harvesters. I struggled then and now with how that fit with the precautionary principle regularly trotted out as a central theme of fisheries management.

What began in 1992 with two or three dip netters working a few days during the last week of August and the first two weeks of September to tag 187 steelhead at ten dollars each morphed into a significant economic and employment opportunity for the Band. The 2009 program funneled nearly $170,000.00 just to the hands on fish tagging, let alone the after season cost of organizing and analyzing data. To that can be added the consultant fees and salaries of the growing number of Band officials and DFO and MOE employees that now have to be involved. In recent years the tagging project crews have worked morning and afternoon shifts continuously from July until at least the end of September (to October 20 in 2008) to beach seine and tag fish using custom built jet boats in the tail out of Moricetown Canyon. Three hundred meters upstream at the falls additional crews dip netted relentlessly to catch the largest possible number of fish and tag those not already bearing tags from the beach seine crews. The total number of fish handled between the two sites in climbed past 3,400 in 2009. In 2010 the figure stood at 8,017 by October 1. One consulting firm was responsible for organizing the tagging data and applying mark/recapture methodology to arrive at population estimates. Another was engaged in a sonic tagging program to address problems clearly enunciated a dozen years before, namely that virtually every assumption inherent in the mark/recapture population estimation methodology was being violated and the figures derived would seriously overestimate the population.[10] In the end the attempt to wean fishermen off gaffs to save a couple hundred steelhead became a classic manifestation of the cliché "be careful what you wish for". I'll offer that the present steelhead love in at Moricetown kills more fish than the gaffs and jigs it attempted to replace. (They still fish with gaffs during the chinook migration period and they still harvest some of the steelhead caught while tagging.)

The 2010 situation needs highlighting. It is crystal clear from the many published reports of the FRB scientists of yesteryear just how great an influence the fishery at the falls was on fish accumulated below.

The steelhead capture and tagging process as prosecuted by the Wet'suwet'en First Nation members conducting the mark recapture population estimation exercise at Morricetown Falls in recent years. Photographs were taken on September 10, 2010. The season total number of steelhead similarly captured and processed as of that date was 4,865.

Palmer reported that in 1966 a single dip net used by FRB staff caught 806 sockeye which was 4.5% of the run arriving at Moricetown that year. The business of migration delays and therefore increased vulnerability of tagged and released fish was fully documented as was the consistent pattern of tagged fish dropping back below the falls, some of them never to be seen again. Remember, from a steelhead and coho perspective, the problems were magnified due to lower flows which prevailed during their peak migration timing. In years of low stream discharge and/or when fishing persisted later into the season fishing exploitation rates increased. If sockeye and chinook could be exploited at the rates documented by the FRB staff during much higher flows and when fishing was relatively heavily regulated (e.g. four days per week) it isn't hard to understand that the relentless pressure of today is capable of affecting a high proportion of the fish present. The 2010 numbers are already being touted as conclusive evidence of a Bulkley/Morice steelhead return of unprecedented size. I have yet to see the first glimmer of recognition the record low flows that prevailed in the Bulkley River until the last week of September 2010 combined with the highest ever capture effort had anything to do with the spread between the numbers for that year versus any other. A 250% increase in catch between 2009 and 2010 and a 300% spread between 2008 and 2010 does not reflect the real variation in abundance of Bulkley steelhead. We

know 1998 was the all time high year for the Skeena test fishery steelhead index. If we compare test indices for 1998 and 2010 for the comparable period the latter was roughly 20% lower yet the Moricetown steelhead catch was 325% higher. There is obviously more to the story than simple inter-annual fluctuations in abundance. There's a baker's dozen years of data readily available today. How long will it be before science trumps politics and a thorough analysis of the entire Moricetown business is undertaken? Then there are the fish.

If anyone thinks dip-netting steelhead with knotted nylon nets.......and carrying thrashing fish across rocks and gangplanks to be dumped into another net......and carrying the still thrashing fish across more gangplanks to be dumped into a large black plastic holding tub containing a couple of five gallon pails of stagnant water baking in the summer heat.....and netting that fish again to dump it into a dry trough to be measured and tagged.......and then dropping it into a dry, sun baked aluminum pipe to skid down into a shallow off channel pool immediately adjacent to the rapids it was attempting to ascend is doing that fish any favors they don't have much experience with fish biology or behavior. When upstream migrant Fraser River sockeye are subjected to water temperatures comparable to those not uncommon in the Bulkley River in late August and early September tens of thousands of them never make it to their spawning

Gaffs, nets and tourists aplenty at Moricetown on August 16, 1990. This is typical of how the fishery had developed when the initial pay-to-tag-and-release steelhead project that became the mark-and-recapture population-estimation program of the present was undertaken.

destinations. At Moricetown we have similar conditions plus the added stress imposed by the intensive netting, handling, tagging, etc. On the Fraser alarm bells ring long and loud. On the Bulkley the science goes on. Nowhere in any of the published reports of today is there a single mention of the correlation between capture efficiency and flows or the risks associated with higher water temperature.

For me, the most disturbing aspect of the Moricetown scenario is the fact that none of the information published by the FRB staff has ever been acknowledged by the First Nations at center stage or any of the consultants engaged in re-inventing the wheel for the past two decades. The primary work that was supposed to recount the history of the Gitxsan and Wet'suwet'en fishery in the Skeena watershed (i.e. Morrell's 1985 report) is devoid of any mention. The fact is that report was "supported" (we can assume that term means funded) by DFO and included as one of its explicit objectives "a review of the scientific literature on Skeena salmon management". The silence with respect to the numerous FRB reports is remarkable to say the least. Gottesfeld and Rabnett's 2008 book is similarly deficient in that respect despite the fact Rabnett does mention the gaff introduction business in a separate publication dated three years earlier (Rabnett, 2005). The work that is the substance of all the published FRB reports was conducted well within the life span of people still resident at Moricetown when

Morrell's interviews and studies were undertaken. It seems reasonable to ask why such important and readily accessible elements of a story would be omitted.

It doesn't go unnoticed there is a disconnect between the oral accounts of how carefully the Indians managed their fisheries before contact and what we witness today. I'm of the opinion no one's interest is served by pretending that isn't reality. Quotes from Morrell's 1985 work are revealing:

"Failure to treat fish and other animals with respect was to risk disastrous retribution." (p. 25)

"The paramount rule mentioned by virtually all the advisors was that all fish had to be utilized; waste was forbidden." (p. 26)

"It was forbidden to interfere with fish unless the fish were needed for food." (p. 27)

Twenty-three years later Gottesfeld and Rabnett used this exact material to paint their picture of salmon fishery management by the Skeena First Nations. The impression left is always one where the fishing was prosecuted with live capture techniques, harvest was strictly in accordance with conservation principles, fish were respected and never wasted, etc. Even when notoriously non-selective gill nets arrived on the scene Morrell claimed mesh sizes were adjusted so precisely as to target individual species at specific times and places.

The results of capture and tagging at Moricetown. A Bulkley steelhead caught about half way between Smithers and Moricetown on September 28, 2000. Photograph by Steve Pettit.

Anyone visiting Moricetown Falls or touring fishing sites along the Skeena in the last half of the 20th century saw very different behavior and philosophy in action. At Moricetown countless pink salmon would be flipped or torn off gaffs and jigs and discarded to wash downstream. This was the norm even at times when pinks were so abundant nothing else could reasonably be expected to be caught. (e.g. in the left bank fishway entrance). In a couple of years in the 1990s pinks were dipnetted and hauled away in large quantities for commercial sale but in my extensive experience as a Moricetown observer I never saw a single gaffed or jigged pink salmon retained. The gaffers who targeted the preferred sockeye, chinook, coho and steelhead and, knowingly, fatally injured half of what they hooked didn't exactly paint a picture of respect and utilization either. The fishery took on a carnival atmosphere, far different from anything that existed a decade before. Tourists, sometimes by the busload, seemed either dumbfounded or disgusted. Many of them took advantage to buy fish. Out of sight and out of mind were the gill nets that had become the primary method of harvest everywhere but Moricetown and occasionally in the Moricetown Canyon pool tail out and the reaches below. The discard of pinks from those nets was also 100%. Untended nets containing rotting carcasses of multiple fish species and sometimes things other than fish were also disturbingly frequent. Strangely enough Morrell acknowledged the discarding of pinks from gaffs and jigs, as well as from set nets, deeper into the same report where the quotations above appeared.[11]

I began this chapter saying the Moricetown fishery history was especially important because the Bulkley system supports the largest of the Skeena tributary

Another example of the influence of capture and handling at Moricetown. This tagged fish was also recaptured about half way between Smithers and Moricetown. (September 14, 2005.)

steelhead populations and because what happens at Moricetown sets the tone for First Nations fisheries throughout the Skeena. It is the focal point of the steelhead conservation versus allocation debates, it is the heartland of the steelhead bearing territory involved in treaty negotiations, it is likely to become another Hagwilget court case, and it is the crowning example of how fish become lost in a sea of process and politics. Consider this – after a decade of increasingly costly steelhead mark and recapture investigations the population estimates are beginning to be recognized as upwardly biased. I'll predict that will lead to more exploitation of uncertainty, commonly manifested as recommendations for further study. Millions of dollars and twenty years later we can still find gaffs at Moricetown and there is no better estimate of the steelhead population size than there ever was. If a fraction of the money donated to tagging efforts had been spent, instead, on turning around the DNA analyses of tissue samples readily available from steelhead at the test fishery there would be more reliable information available at no additional cost to the fish and it could be on the table before the fish ever reached Moricetown, not half a year later as is the case with the growth industry tagging program. The influence of every downstream fishery is irreversible history by the time steelhead are tagged at Moricetown. All the players seem anaesthetized to the fact millions more and air tight population estimates will never change that outcome. The agenda would seem to have little to do with fish and a lot to do with using steelhead as a political pawn. If you're a Bulkley or Morice River steelhead angler you need to be nervous about your future opportunities. More of this science at Moricetown means a lot of steelhead are not going to make it to the most popular angling waters in the system or spawn successfully. You can expect to see more fish that are lethargic and/or bearing abrasions and wounds along with their tags and many of the encounters will be downstream from the falls not upstream. Rumblings of discontent that began to surface five and six years ago grew much louder in 2010.

Chapter 7
ELSEWHERE

N ow, back to the rest of the Skeena. The gill nets that replaced former more selective fishing techniques courtesy of the Barricades Agreement at Babine were generally operated from fixed locations along the main stem Skeena for many years following their introduction. Contrary to what some have said, the nets were not forced upon Indians. It was the Hazelton area Indians demanding the same treatment as their Babine neighbors that catalyzed the transformation of the main stem fishery. There is nothing to indicate the pattern of steelhead harvest by those using the gill nets changed until long after they appeared. All available data paints the same picture as emerged at Moricetown. The harvest never amounted to more than about one steelhead per Indian per year. With a relatively small and stable Indian population along the Skeena until well into the last half of the 20th century the actual number of steelhead involved remained at 2-3,000 annually, still not a conservation threat. Through the last 40 or so years of the century, however, things began moving in a different direction.

The appearance of outboard motor equipped boats forever changed the fishery in the Skeena River itself. Hiking to the traditional fishing spots in the semi canyon reaches of the Skeena near Kitseguecla and setting gill nets from gin poles where basket traps and dip nets were once deployed and then having to pack fish out is one thing. Running up and down the river in aluminum boats with outboard motors to drift nets or to retrieve set nets strung from any suitable location and then delivering fish to pick up trucks parked at boat launches is quite another. I found no mention of when the first power driven boats showed up but they were obviously never part of any traditional fishery. By the 1980s and 90s I personally witnessed a much increased prevalence of drift netters in ever more sophisticated boats. The Kitwanga and Glen Vowell reaches of the Skeena were heavily utilized in this respect because the combination of velocity, depth and an obstruction and debris free cobble bottom made for ideal fishing circumstances. These two areas are obviously migration corridors for every anadromous species but also important steelhead staging and overwintering areas for Kitwanga and Kispiox stocks respectively. When commercial fishing license plates show up on boats fishing 150 miles inland one begins to wonder what is really going on. The net being operated by the occupants of the boat in the photograph on page 54 was at least 200 feet long.

Traditionally the primary targets of the in-river net fishery were chinook and sockeye from June through early August but eventually both set and drift nets became increasingly noticeable in late August, September and even October when coho and steelhead were the expected catch. Net fishing didn't end at the

Drift-netting the mainstem Skeena near the Highway 37 bridge crossing at Kitwanga, August 1990. There is an "A" commercial fishing license plate attached to the aft base of the side windshield on the port side of the boat.

Proceeds of a single gill-net drift on the Skeena River adjacent to Glen Vowell on August 18, 1998. Five steelhead were included. Some of the same people involved in this drift were similarly engaged when I was on location on September 14, 2010.

mainstem Skeena either. Some may contend this fishing activity was regulated and that catches were recorded accurately. To them I say that in countless trips I made along the Skeena from Kispiox to Kitwanga between July and October over a 25 year period my Moricetown experience was always duplicated. I never encountered a single person that had anything to do with monitoring or enforcement of the fishery. I never failed to find nets either. If there was any selectivity of gill nets or any respect for fish among gill net operators I certainly never witnessed it. Numerous discussions with netters and boatmen quickly taught me they understood very well there were no consequences to anything they were doing. The days of any heavy handedness by "fisheries", if they ever existed for the main stem Skeena fishery, were a very foggy memory.

Steelhead are harvested in several other locations besides the Skeena and Bulkley rivers. The Bear River, the principle spawning tributary of the magnificent Sustut system has long been a place where steelhead were taken annually. No one except the people involved knows how many but the remoteness of the area and the number of people living there probably kept it to dozens rather than hundreds. The upper Sustut and Johanson rivers are also visited frequently by Indians (not from any Skeena Bands) since mining roads accessed the mile high country first described as Steelhead Paradise by author John Fennelly in 1963. Crews working a steelhead counting weir in that area since the early 1990s have reported frequent occurrences of Indians harvesting fish with everything from gaffs to rifles. No single incident involved more than 10 or 20 fish but it wouldn't take many of those to put a serious hole in a spawning population that has averaged 631 over the past 17 years. Additional harvest likely occurs after the fisheries crews have departed.[12] Snowmobiles are a worrisome tool in some of these times and places. In the Kispiox it is common for local band members to harvest steelhead with angling gear in

the fall season while the rest of the angler population is governed by catch and release regulations. Angling fish in prime overwintering habitats just before the fish move to spawning destinations in spring is also a frequent occurrence.[13] Eye-witness accounts of high grading for large males have been passed to me over the years. The Kispiox Valley residents who make these observations never publicize them, presumably because they fear it would jeopardize relationships in the tight-knit valley community. It isn't hard to find evidence of angling for overwintering steelhead in the main-stem Skeena between Kispiox and Glen Vowell either. These occurrences are strictly a function of ice conditions. Mild winters that are becoming ever more frequent are not steelhead friendly. No one wants to notice that Gitxsans probably harvest more steelhead with fishing tackle now than they ever did with their fishing methods of historic times. Babine is another area where steelhead are now angled by First Nations people. How many and how often is anyone's guess but I have watched Fort Babine Band members anchored over the single best steelhead spawning area in the entire Skeena drainage at the outlet of Nilkitkwa Lake take multiple fish off the beds in a single session.

The First Nations fishery in flowing water was not the only one with a demonstrated pattern of operating without any serious scrutiny or record keeping. There is also an ocean based food fishery that is seldom mentioned. DFO officials remarked in 1987 that a fleet of anywhere from 10-40 commercial fishing vessels fished the best tides and best locations during the weekly closure windows when the rest of the commercial fishing fleet was tied to the wharf (Sprout and Kadowaki, 1987). We're not talking the low end of the spectrum of fishing vessels here. Many of them were large, highly efficient seiners. If you had a blank cheque to go fishing you probably wouldn't be out there in something that wouldn't maximize the opportunity either. Forty of those fishing by their own rules can take a big bite out of the available supply of fish.

The contract seiner (*Ocean Virtue*) flying the obligatory yellow flag engaged in radio tagging steelhead off Smith Island on July 28, 1994. In the background off the starboard stern can be seen the yellow milk carton seiner (*Western Bounty*), government staff and crew members aboard the contract vessel understood should not have been fishing that day.

Not surprisingly the only concern expressed by the managers of the day was the high sockeye catch per effort of these vessels. Steelhead did not warrant mention. The tidal water food fishery continues today under the FSC label. The difference is credible information on steelhead catch is even less likely now than it was in the 1980s. DFO officers have never displayed any interest in addressing that situation. Another of my personal experiences might help make that point.

In late July 1994 a commercially licensed seine vessel was contracted to catch steelhead in the approaches to the Skeena for an important radio telemetry program. That vessel, like any other operating under a government contract, was required to display a standard, industry recognized, yellow flag from its mast whenever engaged in fishing. I was asked to tour a high ranking MOE employee around the Prince Rupert fishing scene while that contract program was underway. We travelled to the area where the contracted seiner was working in a separate unmarked vessel. In the process of locating the contract vessel and while on board I couldn't help but notice a number of

other vessels in the area. Many of them seemed to be fishing. The rules, as explained to us at that particular time, were that no one other than a sanctioned contract vessel was to be fishing and no other contracts were in place. Curiosity got the best of me so I excused myself, untied our own boat from the contract vessel and went to do a little investigation. The nearest vessel was another seiner fully engaged in fishing. At the top of the mast of the vessel was a yellow plastic milk carton that, until observed at very short range (I approached to within 10 m of the stern of the vessel) gave the appearance of the obligatory yellow flag. Many pictures and notes later I returned to the legitimate contract vessel with what I naively assumed was news. On return to Prince Rupert I reported details of the incident to DFO enforcement authorities and noted the one vessel photographed was not the only one fishing in the vicinity. I never heard a word of follow-up. Hours later, the three of us who had been out on the contract seiner that day were enjoying a drink on the balcony of a local hotel bar. From our table we looked straight down on yet another seine vessel that had just tied up.

Setting a gill net from the Suskwa Forestry Road crossing on the Bulkley River. September 26, 1990. The net was eventually set such that it spanned the entire channel.

The catch by a 200-foot length of gill net pulled from the Skeena River near the Bulkley confluence on September 3, 1989. Sport fishermen camped in the area observed the net to have been untended for the three days they were present and retrieved it to prevent any more waste.

Shortly afterward a steady stream of people were coming and going with heavy plastic garbage bags in hand. Sitting inside in the bar were several DFO staff from the Prince Rupert office, among them a couple of high ranking enforcement staff. After watching and photographing the events below us for a half hour or more I approached the senior officer and suggested he might want to come out and have a look. He asked what I thought he should look at and I explained. Without ever rising from his seat he followed with the comment that said it all – "Bob, this is Prince Rupert". Two days later I was returning to Smithers and stopped in Moricetown long enough to photograph steelhead being sold to European tourists. I asked myself why I ever bothered.

Remember this, all the steelhead harvest information from all the accounts of the Indian food fishery from the mid-1930s to at least the late 1960s confirm steelhead never played any significant role in Indian culture nor did they make up more than a tiny fraction of the amount of fish harvested annually by Indians. Sockeye and chinook dominated food demands as well as social and ceremonial needs then and now. At 3000 Indians and one fish each taken as by-catch by traps and dip nets from annual aggregate steelhead populations that could easily sustain such harvest no one would argue there was a problem. Where is the boundary between that and, for example, reefer trucks packing unprecedented quantities of fish out of historic Kisgegas Canyon just so the Gitksan can get their piece of the Babine sockeye pie before they all pass through to Wet'suwet'en territory? What happens when the First Nations population exceeds the steelhead population, as it very likely will in some years two or three steelhead generations hence? Who is paying attention as a steadily expanding, self governing First Nations population applying outdated philosophy to contemporary political opportunity uses unprecedented

Another day, more long untended nets near Kitseguecla—and more steelhead wasted. October 20, 1990.

technology, both offshore and inland, to exercise court sanctioned rights on a steelhead population that can't possibly be exempt from all the same forces conspiring against, for example, Nanika and Kitwanga sockeye or Bear River chinook or Sustut coho or. . .? Somewhere along the way "rights" become meaningless if fish are genuinely of concern.

Chapter 8
ONE FISH, TWO INDIANS

The early commercial fishing industry at the mouth of the Skeena River has been reasonably well described. We know how great a part the Indians along the Skeena and the outer coast played in the formative years. It is equally well known how Indian people were manipulated and discriminated against in later years, especially with respect to the number of commercial fishing licenses made available to them. Whereas Indian participation in the commercial fishing industry was actively discouraged and limited by government supported cannery owners and bankers, it was never eliminated. Over time Indians became firmly established dependents on gillnetting and cannery work. Other employment opportunities such as railway construction, tie cutting, highway construction, logging and saw mills came and went but none of these provided the inherent association with fish and fishing or the seasonal compatibility that the commercial fishing industry did. One hundred years from start up there were many Skeena river mouth gillnetters and cannery workers whose parents and grandparents had been supported by the tidal waters industry. Suffice to say Indians have been and remain a firmly entrenched part of the commercial fishery targeting Skeena stocks.

There is a monumental difference between the past and the present however. Discrimination and oppression with respect to First Nations' participation in commercial fishing is long over. A sharp about face fueled by a relatively rapid succession of events that included public inquiries into the commercial fishery, the Constitution Act of 1982 and the steady stream of court decisions flowing from it, and treaty processes is now much in evidence. One needn't dwell on the details of these events to understand the overall direction. A clear enough picture emerges from an overview of two independent but overlapping processes initiated by government in 2003.

In the first the Federal Minister of Fisheries and two provincial ministers whose responsibilities included licensing the shore based fish processing industry and treaty negotiations respectively appointed two prominent experts in law and fisheries policy to prepare a report defining a vision of the Pacific fisheries (not just salmon) in a post-treaty era. To quote from their terms of reference they were asked: "to make recommendations that would provide certainty for all participants in the fisheries, ensure conservation of the resource, provide for sustainable use and effective management, improve the economic performance of the fisheries and provide equitable arrangements among fishers and fair treatment of those adversely affected by treaty settlements" (McRae and Pearse, 2004). How's that for lofty goals?! The second process involved a steering committee made up of leaders of the

First Nations Summit and the B.C. Aboriginal Fisheries Commission who appointed a panel of their own experts to "articulate a vision for future fisheries management and allocation and to identify what principles would help achieve that vision" (Anon, 2004...Our Place at the Table...) Advocates for the second initiative lobbied successfully for federal government funding on the basis that First Nations were not consulted prior to the appointment of those leading the first. They were subsequently resourced to undertake their own series of public hearings in First Nations communities around the province and prepare a separate report. The recommended policy reforms flowing from the two processes share common themes. Those germane to the salmon fishery along the coast speak volumes about what is and what will be. I'm not naïve enough to believe all the recommendations to government are binding and I appreciated that five years later a lot of what was printed shows little evidence of implementation. But, I also understand how those reports reflect social, political and economic realities. Ignoring those would qualify as negligence.

One report is focused on how to orchestrate management of coastal fisheries given the impending realities of treaties. The governance and administrative recommendations are complex to say the least. The other report leans more toward how the resource itself should (will) be allocated but also speaks to governance. Both address what the fishery of the future might look like but neither goes anywhere near the question of whether or not gill nets should be a significant part of it. In other words its all about tinkering with who gets what and how that will unfold, not in the least with moving away from harvesting technology that has produced so many of the problems of the present. Specific recommendations are foreboding. One states "As a starting point and as an interim measure, Canada take immediate steps to allocate to First Nations a minimum 50% share of all fisheries, with the understanding that this may eventually reach 100% in some fisheries." Another: "Canada must immediately take steps to ensure that First Nations have access to adequate quantities of fisheries resources for food, social and ceremonial purposes." Nervous yet?

Anyone concerned about steelhead should appreciate the word never appeared in one report and only sparingly in the other. Sockeye dominate and so does the Fraser River. The closest reference one can find to river sport fishing was in Our Place at the Table in the context of the perception of the Wet'suwet'en that the Province has denied them the opportunity to prosper economically from guiding wealthy foreigners on prime fishing waters within their territories. There is considerable verbiage about ocean based recreational fisheries and the importance of chinook and coho to those. There is also recognition of the number of sockeye now taken by fresh water recreational anglers but, again, the Fraser is the focus. The pre-occupation with sockeye and the Fraser

is nothing new. It just serves to emphasize one more time that the out of sight, out of mind Skeena country is still an afterthought and steelhead are not part of the equation.

To dwell on steelhead again, there is another feature of both reports that might make steelhead advocates uncomfortable. That involves the ongoing process of expanding First Nations participation in the commercial fishing industry. The process is well advanced under programs already initiated by the DFO. All of those programs fall under the broad category of the Aboriginal Fisheries Strategy, a 1994 undertaking that has as one of its primary objectives "to reach agreement with Aboriginal groups on the management of fisheries, including the food, social and ceremonial fishery and any economic opportunity fisheries." There are millions of dollars involved here every year. Some of that goes to a program (Allocation Transfer Program) to buy up commercial fishing licenses from non-First Nations holders who wish to retire their vessels and licenses. Those are subsequently re-issued to First Nations. Another program labeled the Aboriginal Aquatic Resources and Oceans Management Agreement resources eligible First Nations applicants to acquire administrative, scientific and technical capacity and to participate in advisory processes, etc. Yet another known as the Pacific Integrated Commercial Fisheries Initiative contributes funding to "build capacity, establish commercial fishing enterprises and acquire commercial fisheries access".

Between the transfer of commercial fishing licenses to First Nations and declining abundance of salmon I submit there is little doubt that whatever remains of the commercial fishery in years ahead is going to be dominated by First Nations. In the case of the Skeena and all its First Nations commercial fishing tradition that translates to more gill nets operating in the times and places historically preferred by Indian fishers. Those areas just happen to be the innermost reaches of the Skeena commercial fishing area (i.e. River/Gap/Slough), the ones where steelhead are most heavily impacted. If anyone thinks First Nations gill netters have any interest in conserving steelhead they couldn't ever have witnessed the emotional outbursts I endured from some of their loudest, most aggressive spokespersons. I can't forget the hostility with which they expressed the view steelhead were just one big headache for gill netters and the quicker they could get rid of them the better off they would be.[14] It won't be just the standard commercial fishery that will be a concern either. All those transferred licenses are just as likely to be out there augmenting the fleet fishing under FSC rights when they aren't partaking of a regular commercial fishing opening. A little known fact about the FSC fisheries participants in the immediate Skeena rivermouth fishing areas is that the list is not limited to just the traditional four Skeena First Nations. It also includes bands from Kitwancool (traditionally affiliated with the Nass River) and Takla Lake (traditionally Fraser River territory).

Expanding First Nations fisheries don't stop at the tidal boundary of the Skeena River. The FSC fisheries are non-selective and employ whatever gear is preferred – set nets, drift nets, gaffs or whatever. Anything goes as long as a conservation issue cannot be proven. We don't need more experience than we already have to know steelhead conservation has zero influence on FSC fisheries. All else being equal those will expand purely in proportion to the rapidly growing population. In addition to the FSC harvests there are now two more for steelhead to contend with. One is the "Escapement Surplus to Spawning Requirements" or ESSR fishery. The other is something even more recent, Economic Opportunity fisheries. (How many acronyms can you stand!?) Here again the Federal Government has actively promoted fisheries over and above the FSC fisheries that, on paper, target only surplus fish. The enhanced Babine sockeye stock, the same one that is the sole foundation of the river mouth fishery is the focal point. The ESSR fishery is driven, in part, by weak stock conservation concerns and in part by the progressively greater allocation of allowable harvest of salmon to First Nations. It involves live capture techniques such as beach seines and fish wheels in the main stem Skeena, wheels and traps at Kisgegas on the lower Babine, removal from traps at the Babine weir and sometimes even a small seine fishing vessel in Babine Lake. The closer to their origin the target fish are harvested the less likely the collateral damage to other stocks and species, including steelhead. In other words these inland ESSR fisheries are "selective". That is all good on paper and there is fair evidence of progress in that respect in the early years of this century. If the ESSR fisheries were in replacement of commercial fishing that would be a good thing. They aren't. If any commercial fishing is allowed so too is ESSR fishing thus increasing the influence on, if not the harvest of, steelhead. The Economic Opportunities fishery is in an early stage of development. We're told it involves transfer of commercial fishing licenses from the coastal fishery to inland First Nations fishers. I should add here that none of the discussions around First Nations fisheries ever involve any of the MOE representatives who are supposed to be managing them. I don't think it a stretch to suggest negotiations between a Federal Government with a demonstrated history of steelhead neglect and First Nations fishers who view steelhead as either an impediment to their commercial fishing agendas or a pawn to command more attention in their dealings with the Province is not a happy story for steelhead.

The commercial fishery in the approaches to the Skeena and in the throat of the river is not going to go away any time soon. First Nations will not give it up and governments who just keep acceding to their demands for more investment to strengthen and expand their participation are not going to abandon that approach. The social and political upheaval that would result would be intolerable. For evidence of the passion and conviction of First Nations with respect to continued existence as commercial gill netters I recommend Miriam Wright's thorough documentation of their protests over salmon fishing regulations for the Nass and Skeena through the 1950s and 60s (Wright, 2008). Once again, this isn't Vancouver and the Fraser. This is far away northwestern British Columbia where the First Nations population is highly visible and growing dramatically and where governments are desperate to sustain economic opportunity for those people. Those same governments are anxious to resolve treaty demands as well. When all the trees have been cut and sawmills and pulp mills closed fish is about the only card left to play. The 90% of the population of the province who live in its southwestern corner and have no personal or cultural history of association with fish but who control political outcomes are oblivious to any consequences of handing over what's left.

If there is recognition of the fundamental dilemma faced by First Nations people in their competing interests for, at best, a fixed supply of fish I have yet to find it. The same fish are not going to meet the demands of those who insist on remaining coastal commercial fishermen plus the demands and expectations of the growing number of their brethren everywhere upstream. The First Nations' ability to resolve their internal allocation issues is going to be put to the test, hopefully not at the expense of steelhead.

Chapter 9

ZERO TO SIXTY

The development of the fish-canning industry on the Skeena followed the arrival of transportation options from southern British Columbia and penetration of the interior of the Skeena from the coast by gold seeking miners. When the first assessment of the fish supply and a suitable cannery construction site was made in 1875 there was already regular steamship travel from Vancouver and Victoria to Port Essington just inside the mouth of the Skeena. Paddle wheelers had been transporting miners and supplies from there to the Kitsumkalum (Terrace) area for several years although Indians continued to hire out themselves and their canoes to transport miners and supplies as far as Hazelton throughout the 1870s.

Inverness or, as it was originally known, Skeenamouth was chosen as the site for the first cannery. It was constructed in 1876 and operated briefly that year (Lyons, 1969). Some accounts have it that 1877 was year one but Lyons' thorough review of old cannery records can be taken as the most accurate. At the outset Inverness employed 225 people, mostly Indians, supported by a fleet of 40 boats. The Aberdeen Cannery on the Skeena at the mouth of the Khyex River commenced operation in 1878. In 1883 three more canneries began operating on the opposite side of the Skeena at Port Essington, right at the confluence of the Ecstall River. At the turn of the century there were 11 canneries working the estuary of the Skeena and, at the peak of it all from 1913 to 1927, there were between 13 and 15 competing for the annual supply of fish (Fig. 11). The number of boats fishing grew commensurate with cannery capacity and peaked at more than 1300. How many people were employed at the height of this flourishing new labor intensive industry is unclear but its dependence on Indians from all the upriver communities on the Skeena system is undisputed. From the verifiable records of the Indian population of the time it is clear a high proportion of it occupied the cannery villages for the summer fishing season.

The accounts of the rise and fall of individual canneries, all the corporate and political maneuvering that concentrated control of the salmon industry in the hands of a few wealthy and powerful men, the early technological innovations, the ethic partitioning and discrimination and the labor disputes are fascinating to say the least. Those subjects as well as the on again off again attempts by government to restrict the number of cannery licenses and individual boat licenses dominate the early years of the north coast canneries. Thorough descriptions are available in a number of books (e.g Lyons, 1969; Newell, 1989; Meggs, 1991; Blyth, 1991; Meggs and Stacey, 1992). What is generally absent from those and so many other records of the day, however, is the impact of the burgeoning industry on the fish themselves, especially steelhead. As was the case with early accounts of the Indian fisheries, the exercise of patching together the steelhead component is complicated by the lack of documentation of anything to do with that species. Thousands of pages of material from museum archives and numerous library collections are consistent in that respect.

An appreciation of what the arrival of a gill-net fleet at the mouth of the Skeena meant for fish is probably best derived from some geographical perspective. The area over which all the early canneries and boats operated was not extensive. The fishing vessels themselves were small, open boats with a single sail and a set of oars. Aboard were two men, one to work the oars and the other to pull the net. They were towed to and from fishing locations daily in long lines behind company owned steam powered vessels. The entire fishery was conducted within the tidal reaches of the lower Skeena River, an area subject to tidal fluctuations of up to 23 feet. Tides were the major controller of the location and duration of gill net deployment. The beginning of the flood tide was always the most productive. In the very early years of the fishery there was no upstream boundary. In 1910 there was one established about 8 miles upstream from the mouth of the Khyex River or about 12 miles upstream from today's test fishery location. At that boundary the width of the river channel at low tide was 0.4 miles or about 2,100 feet. By the time an upriver boundary was in place the length of the gill nets employed by the cannery owned fishing vessels was 1,200 feet. At Inverness, the site of the first cannery at the mouth of what was commonly referred to as "the slough" and one of the two main entrances to the Skeena, the channel width was about 3000 feet Slightly further along the migration route adjacent to the cluster

Fig. 11: The names and locations of all the canneries that operated on the north coast of British Columbia at one time or another from the earliest days of the commercial-fishing industry in the late 1870s until the late stages of the 20th century. (Figure adapted from Gladys Young Blyth's 1991 book *Salmon Canneries: British Columbia North Coast*.)

of canneries around Port Essington the channel widened to about 1.7 miles. That gives the illusion of a relatively broad expanse of river for fish to pass through. In reality that was never the case. Anyone familiar with salmon and steelhead in rivers appreciates they move through relatively defined corridors in highly predictable patterns. Whereas the channel width was significant the migration corridor was not and is not. Some spots are consistently productive, others a waste of time. None of this was lost on those who controlled the fishing. A transcription of an interview with one of the early Skeena gill-netters about his experiences as a boy of 13 fishing in the first decade of the 20th century appeared in the Provincial Archives of British Columbia (Anon., 1976). It creates a remarkably clear picture of the concentration of fishing in the migration pathways and reveals much about how fishing was prosecuted.

"In the central mouth of the Skeena River – the passage between two Islands, Kennedy and De Horsey – this passage was called The Gap. There was a neck of land that stuck out just below the passage, stuck out well into the river on this low stage of the tide. When the salmon came in with the incoming tide from the ocean they would come in behind this point. The tide striking that point would swirl around in a semi-circle and the momentum of the tidal current made a complete vortex, and in this vortex, the fish would become bewildered and they would circle around there. Well, it was a great place for the fishermen to get in. Thirty and 40 fishermen would get into this hole – we called it the Glory Hole. They would throw their nets in every and all directions, criss-crossing one another, cursing one another, fighting one another, to get this salmon as much as they could, but as the tide came up and found its higher level then the tide would slow up in its movement and the fish would continue on around the point and up the river to the spawning –ground. But there were some terrible fights in that Glory Hole. Indians trying to keep the Japs out, they would jump on their boats, cut their anchor lines, throw their anchors overboard, rip their sails to get them out of there. They never bothered the white much. They hated the Jap because they felt he was a despoiler, for the reason that, they would fish night and day legally or illegally and the Indian felt that the Jap was taking more than his share. That was the reason. There was always an enmity between the Indian and the Japanese fishermen."

The total length of river environment over which the early row boats were deployed, from Inverness at the north tip of Smith Island and along the inside route through the slough or along the outside of Smith Island to the southern entrance through the Glory Hole, to the first ever upstream fishing boundary above Khyex was about 32 miles. A liberal estimate of the average width of the channel used by a large majority of the fish migrating through the fishing area would be half a mile. Here is what upriver bound salmon and steelhead faced as progressively more canneries and boats came on line. Five hundred boats with 500-foot nets amounted to more than 47 miles of net between ocean and river. One thousand boats with

1,000 foot nets was 190 miles of net. When the gill-netting effort peaked at 1300 boats (mid 1920s) each with 1200-foot nets there was the equivalent of 295 miles of net being strung across a half mile migration corridor 24 hours per day six days per week.[15] If uniformly deployed that would be enough to seal off the pathway almost 600 times. The irony was that one of the few regulations governing fishing at the time stated that at least one third of any channel or river must remain unobstructed for the passage of fish. Evil lurked at Babine and Kitwanga where weirs were employed for periods long enough for local Indians to feed themselves but a thousand gill nets constituting a maze no less effective for straining every fish possible from the river was something to be applauded.

The upstream boundary had already been moved downstream for "conservation" when the peak in fishing effort occurred so the length of river being fished at that time was reduced to about 24 miles. Lyons' (1969) account of the 1909 fishing included complaints from the canners that the boundary that had been established by the Department of Fisheries prior to that season served only to concentrate 800 boats in four square miles of rock and debris infested river. The boundary was subsequently rescinded. The first boundary that stuck came into effect for the 1910 season. It was many miles upstream and had no impact on the distribution of fishing boats. There was no escape for fish underneath the nets either. They were generally deep enough to seal off the entire water column. And, one more thing – the Department of Fisheries or its predecessor took on as a high-priority task the removal of sunken logs and debris from the fishing area so that entanglement with gill nets would be minimized. A specially equipped barge was brought all the way from Vancouver for this purpose (Sprout and Kadowaki, 1987). The remarkable outcome of all of this is the fish still weren't eliminated. We can thank big tides, frequent winds, fog, occasional unfavorable river flow conditions and the odd labor dispute for that.

I should also mention here that the Ecstall River was open to gill netting for its lower eight miles until after 1925. In fact the first three miles remained open until 1948. The average wetted width of the Ecstall, even at high tide, did not exceed a half mile. With six canneries operating in the immediate vicinity of its confluence with the Skeena around the turn of the 20th century one can only shudder at the impact on fish destined for that river. Whatever survived that gauntlet and may still be represented today couldn't possibly be anything other than a pale shadow of what once existed.

Concentration of the commercial fishery in the throat of the Skeena persisted until the arrival of gasoline engines. They were introduced on the Fraser in 1900 and were in general use by 1906 but were banned on the entire north coast until 1924. Lyons (1969) reported that was intended to protect Indian fishermen who would be unable to afford gasoline engines and fuel and would therefore be eliminated from the fishery. This would be a

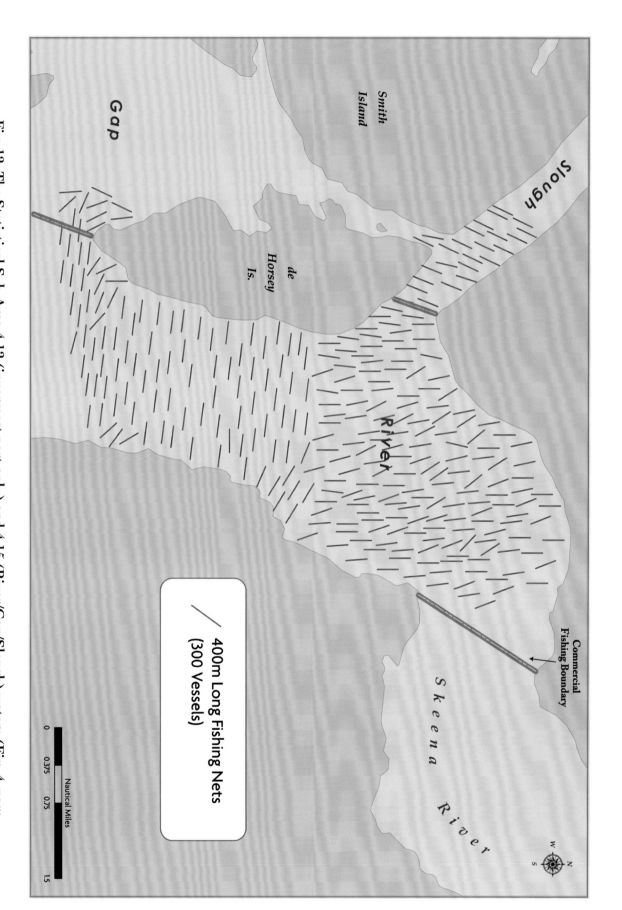

Fig. 12: The Statistical Sub-Area 4-12 (innermost part only) and 4-15 (River/Gap/Slough) waters (Fig. 4, page 21) where all of the traditional gill-net fishing was concentrated and where a disproportionate amount of the annual steelhead harvest has always occurred. Each red line represents a scale version of one 1200-foot-long gill net. There are 300 shown. That is a conservative average number of vessels that fished in those sub areas during a typical mid-July to mid-August commercial-fishing opening in most years in the past many decades.

major problem for cannery owners who were well aware of the risk of losing the cheap cannery labor provided by Indian women and children if they alienated their fishermen husbands and fathers. By 1924 the cannery owners still employed significant numbers of Indians but there were other ethnic groups, notably the Chinese, who were performing jobs formerly the exclusive preserve of Indians. Eventually the Skeena cannery owners, the same ones that owned the Fraser canneries, concluded they needed to do something to reduce pressure on Fraser sockeye (Blyth, 1991). New opportunity in the north was promoted as a way of encouraging southern fishers to move to greener pastures. Not only was that perceived as a partial solution to overexploitation of Fraser sockeye, it was also seen as a method of improving the efficiency of the northern industry. Regardless of the rationale, the introduction of power boats revolutionized the fishery. The new gas-powered vessels were no longer dependent on company tow boats to deploy them nor were they confined to the river. Now they could move to areas outside the river and estuary and intercept the fish before they got there. I'll speak to the progression of other technological changes later.

Conveying an image of what several hundred vessels, each equipped with 1200 feet of gill net looked like in the early days of the Skeena fishery or any time since is not something that could be done with conventional photography. No single frame or even a panorama of the rivermouth fishery could begin to capture what fish were faced with. An alternative is to utilize GIS technology to paint the picture. Figure 12 does that nicely. It demonstrates clearly the capacity of fleet of 300 gillnetters to repeatedly block the passage of any fish intent on moving through the commercial-fishing areas. Imagine the same figure when more than four times that number of nets were deployed. Then and now the areas where steelhead were most frequently encountered are those over which the nets are distributed in the figure.

Some other features of the early, river-focused fishery should also be considered in order to appreciate more fully what fish were subjected to. The sockeye fishing season commenced in mid to late June and continued until about the third week in August. Before that, from sometime in April until late July, it was chinook fishing season. Different gill-net mesh size was the only distinction between these seasons. As near as I can determine the mesh size was the choice of the fisherman rather than prescribed by regulation, at least for many years following fishery start up. Thus the overlapping seasons. The coho season began as soon as the sockeye season was concluded and extended into late September. Other than the preferences of cannery owners for a given species at a particular time there was no reason for distinguishing between seasons. Steelhead that would have been present as emigrating kelts anywhere from late April to late June and as newly arrived immigrants from mid-June through September were obviously subjected to gill nets at both ends of their adult freshwater life history.

Initially there was no such thing as a closed period. That didn't come until there were already five canneries in operation, at which point the fishery was closed from 6:00 PM Saturday until 6:00 PM Sunday. Six-day-per-week fishing persisted until the late 1930s. Twenty-four hour-per-day fishing was the norm anywhere tides permitted, even if it took two crews per boat to achieve that. Cannery location together with the limited range of fishing boats and no ability to preserve undressed fish kept fishing concentrated in the mouth of the river and its lower reaches until gas-powered vessels became commonplace. By then the fishery had been underway for fifty years. There was no such thing as in-season management because there was no method of communicating with fishing vessels out on the grounds and no enforcement presence. The single purpose of the fishery was to provide a steady supply of fish to the canneries for as long a period as possible and it was the cannery owners who determined how that would unfold.

In referring to the early catch records compiled by the canneries the first thing that leaps from the tables is the dearth of information on species other than sockeye and chinook. That was the result of canning being focused entirely on those two species for several years after canneries commenced operation. Any fish other than red fleshed was not marketable as a canned product at the time and was therefore discarded without ever being delivered to a cannery. Pinks, chums, white springs and, of course, steelhead were on that list. The accounts of the waste are legion but impossible to quantify conclusively. Coho fared somewhat better in that the records show they were utilized several years before these other species. Cannery owners dictated what they would pay for from their own catcher boats and those boats had finite capacity to hold fish. Earnings depended on the number rather than the pounds of saleable fish delivered and sockeye fetched, by far, the highest price. If a 15-pound steelhead or a 50-pound chinook was worth less than 6-pound sockeye that were in such abundance they could quickly fill a boat what choice did a lowly fisherman have? The waste of pink salmon was appalling. Even when canneries finally began accepting them (effectively not until after 1900) they had a limit of 100 fish per boat at 1 cent per fish. The archival material referenced earlier included an account of a single boat crew having to pick as many as 5000 pinks from their net to get their 50 cents each for the day's catch. Another particularly revealing account of waste came from the pages of the Vancouver Sun newspaper in a January 23, 1962 article by Barry Broadfoot recounting an interview with life long fisherman Marco Vidulich who spoke of the early days on the Fraser (the late 1890s). Granted, this was the Fraser and not the Skeena, but the same companies owned and operated the canneries in both locations.

"We'd leave at four in the morning, my partner and me. In our big, 25-foot rowing skiff. Four hours hard work out to the net. Pull it, take

out the sockeye. Throw away all the cohoe, chum, pinks and big, big springs. Canneries wouldn't take those fish. No good: but we'd have about 500 sockeye. There would be just room for us to row."

Another account from the Provincial Archives of British Columbia referenced the 1891 season at Aberdeen, the furthest upstream cannery on the Skeena (Anon. 1970). That year the fishermen were paid 6 cents per sockeye and 25 cents per red spring salmon, regardless of size. The cannery would not accept any other species, including the relatively common white springs. When the boats could be filled readily with sockeye the fishermen could only lose by keeping a large spring salmon that took space otherwise available to pile sockeye. An interesting sidebar to that same archival account was the first reference to steelhead. It stated they were a fine-looking fish but of no use for canning owing to their light flesh color but the Indians smoked them for winter use.

Discarding of fish was not restricted to the fishing-

boats crews. In the canneries there was also an abundance of waste. When fishing was better than anticipated the capacity of cannery crews and equipment to process fish was quickly exceeded. Uncleaned fish piled high in scows or on the floor of canneries passed the point of salvage and were dumped or shoveled back into the river. There was no such thing as waste management. The river tides took care of that. At times only select parts of the best fish would be retained for canning. All the offal, trimmings and carcasses that couldn't or wouldn't be processed went down the chutes or through holes in the floor into the river. That situation persisted for at least thirty years after the first case of canned salmon was produced.

The early catch records consisted of the canned pack of fish, by species. That reflected only the number of 48-pound cases of final product. How many tons of fish may have been picked from nets and thrown away and how many tons of what was delivered to the canneries but never made it into the canned pack will never be known.

Chapter 10
THE STEELHEAD ABUNDANCE BENCHMARK

I stated previously the question of how many summer steelhead entered the Skeena in an average year before the first gill net arrived could never be answered definitively. I said also that Indians could not have influenced that number any time before. That leaves me to work with the period from cannery start up until the recorded catches of all species peaked and declined to try and piece together what the steelhead run might have looked like before that influence was felt. The period from 1876 to not later than 1930 is central to this discussion.

The domestic fisheries for Skeena stocks occurred exclusively in the tidal reaches of the Skeena River for most of this period. More distant fisheries that developed in Canadian waters with the introduction of gasoline engines were just beginning and not yet confusing interpretations of where fish landed may have originated. We can be reasonably confident the Skeena landings represented nothing other than Skeena fish and all Skeena fish landed were being accounted for *if* they were delivered to canneries or other fish processing facilities and *if* they became a sold product.

The fishery within the Skeena River was not the only one influencing Skeena steelhead when the first records of catch began to appear. Fisheries in Southeast Alaska escalated sharply between 1900 and 1925. In fact the SEA catches of sockeye, pink and chum salmon all vastly exceeded the Skeena catches of those same species in those years. Knowing what we do today of the origin of fish taken in SEA we can be sure there were Skeena-bound steelhead falling victim to Alaskan fishermen. I'll deal with some specifics of that later. The other thing to recognize was that the productive capacity of the Skeena's tributaries over this span was still as good as it ever was. No one could yet blame habitat degradation for any trend toward smaller annual returns of salmon and steelhead to the Skeena.

The exercise of patching together the steelhead landings in the early days of the Skeena commercial fishery relies heavily on a report prepared by DFO staff in 1986. That report (Argue et al, 1986) examined all the historic records of the amount of canned, salted, fresh/frozen, smoked, mild cured and other salmon products compiled by all known processors in various geographic locations along the coast. Product statistics were adjusted for the amount of waste associated with producing them and average weights per species applied to arrive at estimates of how many pieces of individual species were involved.[16] For example, the estimate of the round weight or green landed weight (not yet cleaned) of a steelhead that ended up as smoked was 1.7 times greater than the smoked product weight. For fresh or frozen the conversion was 1:1. For canned it was 1.75:1. Those figures were used to convert the final product weight to the gross round weight of steelhead landed. The long term average round weight of Skeena steelhead that arrived in the fish plants was about 10-pounds and showed little variation over time or between years. Dividing the total pounds landed by the average weight per fish provided the estimate of how many pieces of steelhead were represented in the product statistics.

A second set of numbers of steelhead landed in the early commercial fishing days on the Skeena surfaced in 2008. It was discovered by a long time commercial fishing industry representative in old files in one of his company's offices. There was no information other than the numbers themselves so, unlike Argue et al, the methodology employed in compiling them is unknown. The reason they are acknowledged here is that they have been circulated broadly in recent months and would almost certainly be brought forward by others if not considered in the context of this discussion. This second set of numbers shows similarities with Argue et al's originals in terms of the steelhead catch trends and peak catch periods but they are consistently higher. Both sets of numbers are part of the interpretations that follow.

The Skeena commercial fishery was a decade old before there was any record of a steelhead being processed. For the next 28 years (until 1914) the estimated number of steelhead processed remained relatively low. Up until that point the records refer only to products other than canned. According to the earliest accounts from the industry steelhead was never a species valued for canning so it is no surprise they would not figure prominently in the canned pack statistics. That said there was a sharp rise in the number of steelhead being processed beginning in 1915. In that year the steelhead number rose to 27,000 in Argue et al's data set and 37,000 in the other. Those higher numbers were consistent in both data sets until after 1930. The rise in 1915 appears to have been linked to the emergence of fresh fish plants but that was also the year when some steelhead were first reported as canned. The fresh fish plants developed commensurate with cold storage capability and would seem to have provided an outlet for selling fish not valued for canning. The separation between steelhead sold for purposes other than canning and those canned was abandoned after 1929 so the statistics after that point give no indication of what trends, if any, may have existed with respect to steelhead processing. Between 1915 and 1929 as much as 77% or as little as 5% of the steelhead sold was reported as canned. There was no obvious pattern or explanation for the differences between years but the increasing trend in steelhead numbers paralleled the increase in the number of fresh fish plants. I would add here that the fact steelhead were not valued as a canned product would only be part of the reason they were seldom canned. A more logical explanation and one never alluded to in any of the material I uncovered describing the early history of the BC canneries is that steelhead would never have been abundant enough to support a canning run devoted exclusively to them. The early canneries were set up specifically to handle the dominant species of the season. With every other salmon species outnumbering steelhead many fold it would probably be a rare event for enough steelhead to accumulate at any point in time to justify canning them.

The increased number of steelhead pieces appearing in the product statistics through the early 1900s was likely also the result of expanding interest in canning species other than just the traditional sockeye and red chinook. Chum and, especially, pink salmon were considered a nuisance until market conditions were such that they too could be processed and sold. Coho appeared to be slightly ahead of pinks and chum in marketability. All three of these species exhibited run timing that overlapped steelhead more than did the timing of chinook and sockeye. It would follow then that expanding effort on the species with the greatest overlap in run timing would result in higher steelhead catches as well. The statistics compiled by Argue et al indicated a sharp and sustained increase in the number of both pink and chum salmon canned in the five years between 1911 and 1915. The ten year periods over which the highest average numbers of pink, chum and coho made it to the product statistics were 1917-26, 1917-26 and 1921-30 respectively. These years overlap the decade during which the highest ten year average number of steelhead appeared in the processing records (1926-35 in Argue's report and 1920-29 in the other data set). The trend in steelhead presence in the commercial fishery processing statistics from fishery start up until the fishery began to move outside the confines of the Skeena River and its estuary is revealed in Table 1. The data after 1935 are not included because they are influenced heavily by the seaward movement of fishing vessels, competing fisheries elsewhere, new technology and movement of fishing boundaries.

According to Argue et al the peak number of steelhead pieces processed in a single year was 63,504 in 1927. The second data set had the highest catch occurring in 1918 (68,824) but a similar catch (68,634) occurred in 1928. Those numbers coincide with peak numbers of gillnetters, peak canning capacity (although not the peak number of canneries) and the highest number of fresh fish processing plants yet seen in the area. The period from fishery start up until the peak in numbers processed represented between eight and ten steelhead generations. The period from start up until major declines in catch and, presumably, abundance occurred (early 1950s) would cover an additional four or five.

Translating the early catch records and fishery characteristics into an estimate of steelhead abundance is the next step in creating the historical Skeena summer steelhead mosaic. This requires interpretations that are constructed around sockeye because those data constitute the best and only evidence of stock sizes and harvest rates that prevailed in the period of concern. If anyone has a plausible case why harvest rates applicable

Period	Average Number Canneries	Average Number Fresh Fish Plants	Average Number Boat Licenses	Average Steelhead Pieces Processed (Argue et al)	Other
1876-80	2	0	60	0	0
1881-85	3	0	160	0	0
1886-90	5	0	269	1,400	1,562
1891-95	7	0	385	1,800	2,436
1896-00	8	0	448	1,000	1,607
1901-05	11	0	781	1,600	4,188
1906-10	13	0	811	4,100	7,995
1911-15	13	1	872	9,600	15,092
1916-20	15	2	930	36,600	46,335
1921-25	13	3	1,022	17,800	52,745
1926-30	12	7	1,175	42,800	54,455*
1931-35	9	7	1,126	32,600	unk

Table 1. The five-year average numbers of canneries, fresh fish plants and gill-net vessels accounting for the five-year average estimated number of steelhead processed in and around the Skeena River between 1876 and 1935.

* No figure available for 1930; figure is a four-year average.

to sockeye should not be applied to co-migrating species I'm happy to listen. In the meantime let the numbers speak for themselves.

When the FRB scientists arrived in the Skeena fisheries management world in the mid-1940s and began their work assessing sockeye production they were quick to point out that the period of chronic overfishing of sockeye began around 1925. Years later that was determined to be a period when about 50% of the annual run was being harvested. Given the uniformity of fishing effort over the course of a season and the fact the season bracketed the entire steelhead run timing we can reasonably assume that if half the sockeye run was being harvested half the steelhead run was also being harvested. Add to that the known tendencies of both fishermen and processors to discard at least some of the steelhead caught plus the fact that Alaskan nets and traps were taking Skeena-origin fish, doubling the annual figures for the numbers of steelhead processed to arrive at the number of fish that started the journey to the Skeena from the central North Pacific in that same year would significantly underestimate the true population size.

The two questions that surface immediately are what is the validity of the 50% harvest rate estimate and why 1925? The canned pack records reveal the peak catch of sockeye occurred in the 1906-15 decade when the average annual number of sockeye canned fell just short of 1.5 million with a peak of almost 2.5 million in 1910. The 1925-34 figures show an annual average of only 0.94 million and a peak of 1.7 million. The numbers declined steadily after the mid-1930s. On the basis of all those figures I would argue the chronic overfishing was already evident by 1925 and the period for assessing its impact should have been at least a decade earlier. If the 50% harvest rate was applicable to the 1906-15 figure the average annual sockeye run would have been at least

3 million. If it is applied to the 1925-34 average it was well below 2 million. If we applied the 50% rate to the decade when the highest number of steelhead pieces appeared in the processing records the average run size that reached the Skeena would have been at least 75,000 fish according to one set of processing records and well over 100,00 according to the other. The various scenarios that can be assumed to bracket the range in the size of the pre-harvest summer steelhead population entering the Skeena in the first third of the 20th century are outlined in Table 2.

We need to examine some of these figures and assumptions a little more carefully to appreciate what the range in steelhead abundance may have been before there were nets. The canned pack records for sockeye from which the number of fish represented were back calculated are believable right from the beginning because that was the species everything was focused on. But, we need to remember those data do not account for the waste associated with dumping of excess fish or high grading or spoilage, nor do they address Alaskan interception. All those same factors apply to steelhead and all of them contribute to underestimating Skeena River stock sizes if only the local processing records are considered. Also, the period most appropriate for estimating the unexploited population size for sockeye should have been well before 1925. That may not be the case for steelhead because their large number of life history combinations serve to compensate for any single year or even two or three successive years of high exploitation. All else being equal it would take longer for the effects of chronic overfishing and reduced recruitment to show up among steelhead than it would among sockeye which exhibit a much simpler life history pattern. Given the absence of any believable data on the steelhead catches during the period of maximum sockeye catch it is impossible to know if there was already an overfishing effect occurring among steelhead when the peak numbers for steelhead pieces show up in the early processing records. In that context, once again, any estimates of steelhead abundance based on the available records can only be considered conservative.

Keeping firmly in mind all the issues that could be at play in using the fish processing records to estimate steelhead abundance the range of possibilities looks as follows. The smallest steelhead run size estimate results from using the lowest estimate of the decade average number of fish processed in combination with the highest harvest rate. In Table 2 that would be 37,700 and 60 % for a population of 62,833. At the high end, using the peak number of steelhead processed in combination with the lowest harvest rate the population would have been 172,000. I am satisfied the low figure is highly conservative. The high figure can't be considered as a typical summer steelhead run size because it represents the peak number of steelhead processed and peak numbers of any species always exceed longer term averages. One cannot deny, however, there really was that many summer steelhead entering the Skeena in the highest year in the early part of the 20th century. In terms of an average annual run size a conservative approach would be to use the median between the two ten year average figures in Table 2 (i.e. median of 37,700 and 52,100 is 44,900) and apply the 50% harvest rate estimate of the sockeye researchers. That gives a figure of 89,800. To that we can add what the Alaskans had already removed and whatever estimate we like of the waste and discards that never figured in any of the figures derived from fish processing records. Those additions would easily take the figure to 100,000.

The Alaska scenario is not speculation. It is well illustrated by reference to data compiled in the late stages of the 20th century. Those are the only steelhead-specific data ever compiled on the Southeast Alaska fishery impacts. Whereas they cannot necessarily be translated straight across to circumstances that prevailed in the early part of the 20th century they clearly indicate the migration pathways of Skeena summer steelhead and the fact that any net fisheries operating along that route exacted a toll. The one thing constant over time is the location of the major Southeast Alaskan fisheries.

The case for Alaskan interception of Skeena steelhead is built on recoveries of tagged fish in the two main Southeast Alaskan net fisheries, Cape Fox and Noyes Island. Their location was noted in Fig. 2. page 20. In 1980s MOE staff embarked on an experiment involving the release of adipose-clipped, coded wire-tagged summer steelhead fry in several different Skeena tributaries. The objective was to try and refine stock specific run timing and, if possible, harvest rates. Brood fish were removed from their Skeena tributary, spawned locally and their fertilized eggs shipped to a southern BC hatchery where suitable water temperatures prevailed. Fish were reared to a stage large enough to be fin clipped and tagged (coded wire tags or CWTs) and then transported back to their river or origin for release at a size of 3 or 4 grams in late September or October. Sampling programs to recover CWTs from salmon harvested in both northern BC and Southeast Alaska had been in place for several years under objectives and provisions of the Pacific Salmon Treaty. Steelhead were added to the contractor's agenda for the years when the tagged Skeena steelhead were expected to be present. The contractor's sampling target was 20% of the commercial landings of salmon for any given fishing opening (typically three or four days per week).

The Skeena-origin tagged steelhead began to appear in the Southeast Alaska and northern BC fisheries in 1989. Recoveries continued through 1993 when the last

		Estimated Population Based On Harvest Rate		
Highest 10-year average catch		0.4	0.5	0.6
Sockeye	1,484,000	3,710,000	2,968,000	2,473,000
Steelhead 1	37,700	94,250	75,400	62,833
Steelhead 2	52,100	130,250	104,200	86,833
Highest single-year catch				
Sockeye	2,450,000	6,125,000	4,900,000	4,083,333
Steelhead 1	63,000	157,500	126,000	105,000
Steelhead 2	68,800	172,000	137,600	114,667

Table 2. Estimated abundance of Skeena summer steelhead and sockeye based on different combinations of the average and peak numbers of those species processed and the proportion of their runs harvested during the first one-third of the 20th century.

Highest 10-year averages: Steelhead 1, 1926-35; Steelhead 2, 1920-29; Sockeye, 1906-15
Highest single-year catch: Steelhead 1, 1927; Steelhead 2, 1918 & 1928; Sockeye, 1910

return expected from the release groups was seen. The results from the port sampling of catches on both sides of the border were revealing. For all years combined the Alaska recoveries totaled 87, of which 36 originated with the Cape Fox fishery, 41 at Noyes Island and 10 from unspecified Southeast Alaska locations. The BC recoveries totaled 118. The majority of these (76) were from Area 4 while 16 others were taken in Area 3, sandwiched between Area 4 and Southeast Alaska. Twenty-six more CWT bearing steelhead were recovered from packing vessels whose catches were collected in both Area 3 and 4. That makes 42% of all tag recoveries from Southeast Alaska. Occasional known origin hatchery steelhead from other distant locations such as the Columbia basin showed up as well. What never showed up was any fish, other than a half dozen winter steelhead kelts, that could reasonably be expected to have originated from Southeast Alaska.

When the total number of steelhead fry released across all rivers and all years is summed and viewed in the context of the likely range of fry to adult survival the catch figures are brought sharply into focus. Even at the highest survival there couldn't have been more than 3500 tagged steelhead present and, more likely, about half that many. That would place the Southeast Alaska harvest rate between 12% and 25% of the Skeena summer steelhead before they ever entered Canadian waters. Now, if anyone thinks these numbers are trivial or lacking in statistical significance, perhaps a bit of sockeye data thrown in will help adjust that perception. Wood (2001) reported that even with the Canada-U.S. treaty in place, Alaskan exploitation rates on Skeena sockeye exceeded 20% in 1994 and 1997 and reached a maximum of 25% in 1998. The report of the Independent Science Review Panel in 2008 (discussed in greater detail later) took that a step further. It stated that over a longer term Alaska accounted for 23% of the total number of Skeena sockeye harvested by the combined commercial fisheries on both sides of the international border. Still not convinced? Then consider the sensitivity that emerged as soon as the steelhead CWT recovery data were presented to a group of Canadian and American participants in the Pacific Salmon Commission processes (pursuant to the Canada-U.S. Pacific Salmon Treaty) in Bellevue, Washington in 1993. In a classic move to kill any prospect of those troublesome Canadian steelhead causing any discomfort the Alaska managers responded shortly afterward by forbidding the sale of steelhead caught in their net fisheries. Fishermen could still keep them but there was no reporting requirement. BC took a slightly different approach in that non-retention and non-possession of commercially caught steelhead became a condition of commercial fishing licenses at about the same time Alaska terminated selling them. In BC the condition of license approach was replaced by a formal regulation forbidding the retention and possession of commercially caught steelhead anywhere on the coast in 2003.

There was always a catch reporting requirement for BC-caught steelhead but we know how much attention was paid to that. Commercial-fishery steelhead interception of steelhead evolved similarly on both sides of the border. No data = no problem. The entire business of Skeena steelhead interception in Southeast Alaska has been as dead as the steelhead themselves ever since their sale was banned.

Another incriminating sidebar to the Southeast story is the number of southern BC-origin marked hatchery steelhead that showed up in the port sampling of their catches through the last few years when the CWT programs for BC steelhead were still in place. Between 1982 and 1992 there were 150 Vancouver Island origin summer steelhead recovered in Southeast Alaska ports. In some years the number of BC-origin CWT's recovered in Alaska exceeded the cumulative total number recovered in all the BC ports sampled.

How closely did the Southeast Alaska interception of Skeena-bound steelhead in the latter stages of the 20th century resemble what may have occurred at its other end? No one will ever know with certainty. What we do know is the SEA fishery was well advanced before the Skeena fishery was realizing its highest catches. The SEA fishery was dominated by enormously efficient floating and anchored traps of which there were about 20 operating in 1906 (Cole, 2000). Almost 7 million fish were harvested by those traps that year. Catch data indicate an equal split between sockeye and pinks, the principle commercial targets and the only two species for which accurate records were kept. By 1920 there was an order of magnitude more traps feeding more than 100 canneries in SEA. Milne (1948) reported there were 284 traps and 37 canneries operating in Southeast Alaska at that time and that 65% of the salmon catch was by traps and 30% by seines. Gas-powered seine vessels had entered the scene in about 1910. The fish traps were so efficient and such a socio-political lightning rod they became a central issue in the drive toward Alaska statehood. Other than a few situations with a long history of Indian use (e.g. three traps were still in operation at Annette Island in 1991), fish traps were banned when Alaska became a state in 1959. That was the good news. The flip side is that paved the way for proliferation of seine and gill net fleets that may have redistributed the social and economic benefits derived from fish but certainly never saved any. I'd say it is safe to assume the migration pathway of Skeena steelhead and sockeye is the same now as it was when the fish traps and canneries in SEA were at their zenith. Given that, the magnitude of the early 20th century SEA catches and the data now in hand on the proportion of Skeena steelhead (and sockeye) harvested in those distant waters, even the most conservative estimate of the steelhead removed, when added to the number reaching the Skeena itself, would take the estimate of the average annual pre-fishery stock size for Skeena summer steelhead well over the 100,000 mark.

Chapter 11
TECHNOLOGY AND INNOVATION

It's clear by now I like to illustrate messages with clips and quotes from bygone days. There is often great instruction in the words of those who took time to record them. Here are two more cogent pieces to introduce another chapter. The first is from 1919 personal papers of Henry Doyle one of the principle figures in the evolution of the Skeena salmon canning industry and architect of the original amalgamations leading to the formation of the dominant player in that industry. The second from the 1948 publications of D.J. Milne, the Fisheries Research Board scientist who led the Skeena River Salmon Investigation.

"It appears that despite warnings given them fishermen and cannery workers the world over work on complacently at exterminating the industry that supports them and give no thought to the future until the disasters that have befallen others are experienced by themselves. Then they will howl for relief and call upon government to take action to save them from themselves. To-day, those interested in the salmon fisheries in northern BC are quietly working under the new regulations the government has put into effect. Tomorrow, the inadequacy of these regulations to maintain the fisheries will be apparent, and then the unrest and dissatisfaction will be as great or greater than it was prior to 1918. As they are administered to-day, the regulations governing fishing in District No. 2 are not satisfactory; they do not protect the supply of raw material, nor can they conserve the fish." (In Newell, 1989)

"A competitive industrial system has made it virtually impossible for a brake to be applied on exploitation except by government control. Thus the function of conservation is to offset the dangers to supply inherent in technological advance. Social control of fish resources is now an accepted philosophy; it is within the province of the government to protect and supervise yields and it is its duty to do so. Fishing should be allowed only to the escapement limit. Paradoxical though it may appear, it is nevertheless true that none are more anxious to save and perpetuate the salmon than the canners themselves and yet their methods are such as, if continued, will very soon destroy them."

Together these pieces speak volumes about the quest for profit that drove an accelerating war on fish for more than half a century before the first scientist arrived on the scene and before there was any meaningful or rational attempt to apply some brakes.

The government response to the demands of canning industry leaders to address steadily accumulating evidence of overfishing through the early 20th century consisted of moving fishing boundaries and increasing the weekly closed periods. One wonders what utility there was in the sequential movement of the upstream fishing boundary from where it was first established in 1910 to the various downstream locations in 1925, 1935 and, in 1948, to where it is located today. Apart from the 1948 measure which may have saved some of what little remained of the Ecstall River populations after 75 years of sealing off the migration corridor, the only thing accomplished by any of the moves was concentration of the fleet. Limiting the number of canneries and boats would have made sense and the early accounts indicate much discussion of these options occurred. In essence, however, it was the cannery owners who determined how many canneries would operate, how big they would be, how many boats would fish, who would own and operate them, how long seasons would last, what the closed periods would be and even where the fishing boundaries would be located. Small wonder the comments of a visionary like Henry Doyle who, by the time of his quote above, was a spectator rather than a player in the commercial fishing game.

There were several milestone events that created the situation first addressed by Milne and his cohorts. The proliferation of canneries was obvious but the investment in labor-saving equipment such as the "iron chink", can making and sealing machinery, fish-offloading systems, automatic retort loading and casing machines, etc. added to individual plant capacity substantially. Gluts of fish that swamped canneries and led to much waste in former years could now be handled easily. The collective processing capacity that just kept on increasing created an almost insatiable demand for fish. The ability of sail- and oar-powered catcher boats to supply enough fish to achieve expected economic efficiency was slipping steadily. That heralded the authorization of gasoline engines which had been in broad use in southern BC for two decades. The gas motor restriction for District 2 was lifted in 1924. Accounts of how long it took for complete conversion of the fleet from oars and sails to internal combustion engines conflict. Some say it was only three or four years until virtually all the useful vessels were fishing with power while others say there were still several hundred non-powered boats fishing until well into the 1930s. Apart from facilitating boats moving seaward, power also substantially increased the ability to deal with the river's tidal influence that previously limited movement and net deployment. Innovations in net composition and construction added to efficiencies.

Seine nets were also part of the push to supply more fish. Drag seines made their first appearance in northern BC in 1890. They were made from cotton and measured up to 200 m long and deep enough to reach the bottom, where employed. According to Harris (2008), by 1916 there were twelve drag-seine licenses allocated for specific sites along the shorelines of Dundas, Stephens and Porcher Islands and three more for sites on the mainland coast immediately north of the Skeena estuary. Gill netting was forbidden in these areas. The licenses were usually held by canning companies and focused on the bays and estuaries of smaller creeks with nearby Indian villages that supplied cheap labor. "Creek sockeye" were the original target but, as the supply of those relatively unproductive stocks dried up, markets for other, more abundant species such as pinks and chums developed, and drag seining lived on. Drag seines were highly effective in removing a large proportion of the potential spawning fish that typically milled about in large schools prior to entering their creek of origin. They were ineffective for harvesting significant numbers of Skeena-bound fish and highly unlikely to have ever been a factor in that river's steelhead population status.

Steadily improving technology around vessel configuration and mobility adopted by the gill-net fleet was equally applicable to seining. Ultimately the precursor of the modern drum seiner replaced the drag seines but not as quickly as elsewhere on the coast. The drum seine was introduced in the 1950s. That allowed nets to be wound on and off the vessel more easily. Power blocks that facilitated even faster net retrieval showed up in 1953. Those innovations occurred at the same time federal authorities unleashed seiners along the outer migration corridors used by Skeena fish, extending the gauntlet created by the gill-net fleet in the throat of the river behind them. In 1960 metal and fiberglass hulls began to replace older wooden vessels. Concerns about overcapacity of the fleet finally registered with government and limitations on the number of seine vessels licensed and the size of any new vessels that replace ones retired. Industry countered with new vessel designs that dramatically increased carrying capacity while staying within length limitations.

The commercial fishing industry's quest for labor-saving opportunities and efficiency improvements to reduce dependency on people and for means to transport fish long distances so that processing facilities could be concentrated and utilized for the longest possible season was relentless. Among gill-netters, technological innovations that followed gasoline engines included the first echo sounders and radios in the late 1930s, mechanical drums in 1942 and nylon nets that replaced high-maintenance linen nets in the mid-1950s. All of these were additions to increasingly larger, faster boats with greater fish-packing capacity and catch preservation systems that maximized time spent on the fishing grounds. Newer gill-netters were operated by a single fisherman rather than the historic twosome of oarsman and net puller. Seiners carried crews of five or six and commonly handled as many fish in a single trip as several dozen oar-powered gill-netters did in an entire season short years before. No one but the fisheries scientists (and Henry Doyle before them) chose to acknowledge or speak to the cumulative effects the latest, greatest equipment had on the resource. Call it willful blindness or the tragedy of the commons or elements of both. As long as individual vessels could employ new technology to prop up their efficiency and maintain their catch at some reasonable level escalating harvest rates were masked or, when not, ignored.

I mentioned previously that fixed-location traps that were the primary harvesting method in the coastal waters of Southeast Alaska from the late 1800s through 1959 when Alaska became a state. Traps located in the Fraser River approaches in southern BC and adjacent Washington (120 of them in 1899 according to Meggs, 1995) were also a prominent feature of fisheries focused on Fraser-bound sockeye and chinook until deep into the 20th century. They never became a factor in the northern BC waters for reasons not entirely clear from historical documents I have been able to retrieve. The personal diaries of Henry Doyle referenced previously (Newell, 1989) indicated he and his BC Packers Association had carefully examined the entire area in and around the lower Skeena River immediately following their arrival and staked, for land purchase and foreshore rights, 36 sites. Doyle confessed that even if their applications were approved and permission given to operate traps he would not recommend their introduction in the neighborhood of Smith, De Horsey, or Kennedy islands. Another of Doyle's comments says all.

"To my mind there is no question but that, properly construed, these islands are within three miles of the mouth of the river, and were traps put in there so as to withstand the currents and tides, they could completely shut off from the Skeena River every salmon working toward that river. That such a result would be harmful to our interests, as well as others', goes without saying, and the attention attracted to the dangers that could be expected from injudicious trap fishing might result in an order from the government prohibiting their use in any part of the province."
(Newell, 1989)

So, it seems reasonable to assume that between geography, tides and the vision of Henry Doyle Skeena salmon and steelhead were spared death by trap.

The other feature of ocean harvest of Skeena steelhead that occasionally gives rise to finger pointing is the high-seas fishing fleets of foreign nations. This is an issue shrouded in secrecy and deception. On paper the international agreements would imply this never was a problem. Considerable investigation by credible authorities, both inside and outside Canadian and American governments, produced information otherwise, at least for some years. Evidence of significant interception of North American-origin salmon and steelhead by western Pacific-based drift-net fleets operating in defiance of the rules in the late 1980s and early 90s sounded alarm bells. That prompted increased intensity of surveillance and enforcement that would seem to have curtailed most of the problem of foreign nets operating in times and places frequented by North American steelhead. How much of a factor this may ever have been for Skeena-origin steelhead is highly speculative. Given the latitude of the Skeena relative to the countries of origin of the offending vessels and their areas of operation Skeena fish were likely well north of any detectable impact. Also, the ratio of steelhead to salmon is so low as to obviate any purpose in targeting steelhead even if foreign nets were operating so blatantly as to be targeting Skeena sockeye in utter contempt of all the international agreements. Between the sheer economics and the threat of detection and reprisal the likelihood of such a worst-case scenario is remote. There interception of Skeena steelhead by net fleets originating on our side of the Pacific was and is a far more significant issue.

Part 4: Management Arrives

Chapter 12

EARLY MANAGEMENT

A brief overview of governance was given in Chapter 3. Recall that the distinction between the terms management and governance is frequently less than clear. I favor describing management as the application of policies and regulations to the variables affecting fish and fishing. I'll try and describe the major management events in that context. Some repetition may show up here but only as much as needed to emphasize management milestones as I perceive them.

Federal Government fisheries folk have broken the history of management of the Skeena sockeye fishery into three stanzas. The first was termed the pre-research period (1876-1942), the second the research period (1943-1971) and the third the mixed-stock management period (1972 onward) (Sprout and Kadowaki, 1987; Wood, 2001). The stanzas are reasonable but I'd offer less flattering labels – no management, some management and institutional inertia. Sockeye were clearly the only species of concern for a century or more. The word steelhead is conspicuously absent from almost every formal record of that period. How much more evidence does one need to appreciate there was no such thing as steelhead management for a very long time? Everything that can be pieced together stems from interpretations built around sockeye and that information base was effectively non-existent until the so-called research period arrived. I hesitate to brand good people of yesteryear naïve or negligent but the fact remains steelhead never entered the collective consciousness of management authorities for most of the history of the Skeena fisheries. When they did they weren't exactly a welcome addition.

The pre-research or no-management stanza is well enough understood by the labels given it. From the steelhead perspective there is nothing that can be said about this period that hasn't already been covered. As it drew to a close steelhead were still well represented in the Skeena watershed in spite of two thirds of a century of neglect and indifference. The next stanza didn't see any meaningful change in terms of the attention accorded steelhead. The forces conspiring against them were ever increasing however. Habitat degradation was on the rise, access was improving, river sport fisheries were emerging and growing and the commercial fishery exploitation wasn't diminishing. By the end of the stanza a worst-case scenario was about to unfold.

The Skeena River Salmon Investigation (SRSI) was highlighted earlier. To refresh, this was the first-ever entry of government representatives trained specifically in fish biology and fisheries management. In essence it was the federal government's response to the economic chaos descending on a once lucrative Skeena salmon fishery. The cannery men were increasingly desperate for solutions to the problems they were singularly responsible for. The response – invite the scientists to define the fix. The Investigation started in 1944, 68 years after the first cannery went into operation at the mouth of the river. It continued until 1948. The fishery the investigators were greeted with was already markedly different from that which preceded it. The gill-net fleet had shrunk from a peak of more than 1300 boats to about 800. Seven canneries remained in operation, half the number present 20 years before.[17] Fishing effort had not been altered much though. Gill nets were still soaking five days per week, down only one day per week from the standard that prevailed from the late 1880s until the mid-1930s. The season was similarly unaltered, still extending from the first of July to the end of September. Sockeye and coho were the preferred species for those three months. There was still substantial net-fishing effort from April to early July but that entailed larger-mesh nets targeting chinook. The upstream fishing boundary had been moved downstream three times already when the scientists arrived but it remained upstream from the Ecstall River confluence. The lower Ecstall itself remained open. The entire period prior to the arrival of the first scientists was devoid of any technical expertise in terms of understanding the fundamental elements of the fishery, namely, how many fish were present, how many of them were needed to sustain the returns and how can the fishery be regulated to let the right number of spawners through. In the absence of escapement targets there was no such thing as manipulation of the fishery to ensure they were met. Not until the early 1950s was there any effort to monitor commercial-fishery catches other than from season-end submissions from fish processors. It took several years longer to establish a rudimentary catch reporting system that provided in-season estimates of catch by species by area. By the time a functional catch estimation process was in place the dispersal of fleets to areas progressively further away from the river of origin of the fish they caught did little to enhance understanding of what catch should be ascribed to what stock. Seven decades is a long time to be lost in fog. Who knows how a mid 20th century assessment of Skeena fisheries should be interpreted? All we can say with certainty is the catch of every species had diminished markedly from levels evident from canned pack statistics of years before and technology had exceeded the capacity of the stocks to withstand it.

Most of the early work of the SRSI was centered on Moricetown and Babine. Moricetown has been dealt with previously. Babine was obviously important because it supported the largest and most commercially valuable sockeye stock in the Skeena. At the time Babine sockeye production was estimated to represent 70% of the Skeena total. This origin of this figure is a bit mysterious. Whereas a counting fence was installed on the Babine in 1946 I have yet to discover the methodology underlying the pronouncement that the Babine counts taken there represented seven-tenths of the Skeena total. With so many years of intensive commercial fishing already done, estimates of historic sockeye abundance and proportional distribution within the Skeena can't be considered any more accurate than those I can offer for steelhead. "As much as 70%" becomes a story unto itself in later years when Babine sockeye came to represent more than 90% of the Skeena's sockeye production. I'll come back to that.

The next pivotal event in the evolution of Skeena fisheries management was the aforementioned rock slide that occurred on the lower Babine River in 1951. As was the case with the Hagwilget slide on the Bulkley, this was a natural event. The difference was the Babine slide occurred in a very remote section of the Babine River canyon approximately 20 miles upstream from the Babine/Skeena confluence and 60 roadless miles beyond the village of Hazelton. It is not known precisely when the slide occurred but it was sometime in the late spring or early summer of 1951. Alarm bells didn't ring until August of that year when dead and dying sockeye began showing up at Hazelton on the Skeena and few fish were arriving at the Babine fence. Those that did were in very poor condition. On August 17 government officials located the blockage via aircraft. Eleven days later a fisheries team reached the site by pack train and confirmed its seriousness.

A sidebar to the Babine slide event is the latter-day claim of the significance of the Babine fishery to Indians, particularly at Kisgegas but also elsewhere between there and Kispiox. If Kisgegas, ten miles downstream from the slide, was such an important fishing site how is it that massive numbers of dead and injured salmon discovered by the fisheries people were not reported by the Indians alleged to have relied so heavily on the fishery at Kisgegas? The written records indicate the only reports of dead or damaged fish came from Indian gill-netters in the Hazelton area 60 miles downstream. I submit this is more evidence of the fallout from the Barricades Agreement. By the time of the Babine slide that agreement had long since seen the replacement of site- and time-specific, labor-intensive tributary fisheries such as once existed at Kisgegas, by the white man's passive gill nets targeting multiple stocks and species in the mainstem Skeena.

The Babine slide, the engineering work required to access and overcome it, and the intensive sockeye-focused studies it initiated were thoroughly documented by the fisheries scientists of the day (see, for example, Godfrey et al, 1954). The impetus was obvious. The commercial fishery in far off Prince Rupert was seriously at risk if 70% of the Skeena's sockeye were denied access to their spawning areas in the Babine Lake system.

Once again the science community was called into service. Enter the Skeena Salmon Management Committee (SSMC) described previously. Its mandate is worth repeating in the present context - *"to investigate thoroughly the condition of the Skeena River salmon stocks to improve the management of the runs and increase the yields"* (Withler, 1960). The Babine Lake sockeye run which had been seriously depressed in 1951 and 1952 as a consequence of the 1951 rock slide was the priority. The fishing seasons of greatest concern were 1955 and 1956 when the majority of the recruits from the slide-impacted spawners would return. Looking back from this point in history it is instructive to read through the annual reports of the SSMC and understand that, irrespective of the composition of the committee, it was the science community that ruled the day. The majority of the board members may have been commercial-fishing industry leaders but their demands were clearly subservient to the recommendations of the scientists involved. The transfer of responsibility from something less than professionally trained staff to scientists had begun with the SRSI in the mid-1940s. With the establishment of the SSMC the transfer of management authority to scientists was complete. For the first time ever scientists began estimating run sizes and harvest rates and implementing regulatory measures to ensure adequate escapements.

It is a sad commentary that it took a catastrophic natural event to catalyze the eleventh-hour oversight of the Skeena fishery by qualified professionals. That aside and, irrespective of the relatively short life of the SSMC in the grand scheme of things, that group did leave its mark. Foremost in its legacy were the test fishery initiated in 1956, extensive surveys of all the largest sockeye-producing lakes in the Skeena drainage, and thorough analysis of the historic commercial-fishery catch and effort data. The test fishery remains to this day as the primary in-season fishery management tool. Limnological surveys of the major sockeye lakes illustrated the differences in productivity between different stocks and thus the outcome of targeting the mix of stocks dominated by Babine fish in the rivermouth fishery. The consequences of mixed-stock fisheries were described at least, even if they weren't addressed.

The limnology investigations on the sockeye lakes were the precursor of the sockeye spawning channels on Fulton River and Pinkut Creek, two major sockeye spawning tributaries of Babine Lake. Construction of the channels and attendant flow and temperature control works began in 1965. Those facilities were designed to better utilize the juvenile sockeye rearing capacity of Babine Lake, much of which was untapped as a result of chronic overfishing by the commercial fleets of years gone by. Recalling that the mandate of the SSMC was, in part, to increase yields, the spawning channels made perfect sense. Years later it became abundantly clear just how damaging the enhanced sockeye production was in terms of aggravating the mixed-stock fishery already taking its toll on steelhead and every other species as well. The first returns of adults to the spawning channels occurred in 1970. By 1972 the science community was relieved of responsibility for managing the Skeena fishery. That heralded a return to days of yore where the fishery was controlled by Federal staff in Prince Rupert, the community dominated by the commercial-fishing industry.

One other often neglected output of the SSMC was the programs they initiated in 1957 and 1958 to tag sockeye and pink salmon in the vicinity of Noyes Island in Southeast Alaska. The data on recovery of those fish was clear evidence of American interception of Canadian sockeye (Nass and Skeena origin). The major concern expressed by the Canadian researchers was that the Noyes Island commercial fishery was much less regulated than any of those on the Canadian side of the border and threatened Canada's efforts to rehabilitate Skeena sockeye and pink runs. Steelhead, of course, were never mentioned in any of the tagging study results in spite of the fact they couldn't possibly have been absent from the catches of the seine vessels involved.

Chapter 13

THE SKEENA TEST FISHERY

No single aspect of management of Skeena steelhead is more influential nor more misunderstood and abused than is the test fishery data. For that reason the origin and application of the data commands special attention. Recall that test fishery was one of the principle products of the SSMC undertakings that commenced in 1955. Its outputs represented the first-ever data to estimate how many fish were traveling upriver each day over the course of the season. The data set stemming from the test fishery has been continuous since 1956, the year following all the preliminary work conducted by the SSMC scientists brought in to address the sockeye crisis created by the Babine slide. Once again, the site of the test fishery has been unaltered from the outset as has its location in the first area of significant channel constriction as one progresses upstream on the Skeena about 6 miles upstream from the commercial-fishing boundary established in 1948. The test-fishing process involves setting a 200-fathom-long by 3.3-fathom deep (1200' x 20') gill net comprised of ten equal length panels of mesh sizes varying from 3.5 to 8 inches. Sets are made for exactly one hour at the same location on every slack tide during daylight hours from early June until at least August 25 and, in most recent years, deep into September. Depending on the time of the high and low tides the number of test-fishing sets per day could be as high as three or as low as two. The methodology has remained unaltered since 1956 although the net construction material has been adjusted and calibrated against the original. For each species catches are translated to daily test indices by averaging the catch per set and standardizing the figures to catch per hour.[18]

For most of its history the test fishery has been all about sockeye and management of the downstream fisheries targeting them. Standard procedure was to count the escapement at the Babine fence, use 70% as the Babine proportion of the total Skeena sockeye return and then reconstruct what had happened in the commercial fishery by comparing the reported commercial catch to the total upriver escapement. When Babine represented 70% of the Skeena sockeye production the margin for error was perhaps larger than it became after full production from the Babine spawning channels was realized. At that point Babine-origin fish represented 90% or more of the total Skeena return and nothing else mattered. Two critical issues surrounding the test-fishery data from day one were, first, that they came after the most recent commercial opening had exacted its toll and, second, the Babine fence counts that verified or refuted the in-season estimates of sockeye run strength at Tyee were never available until well after the commercial-fishing season was over. The test fishery was therefore more a tool to

The test-fishing vessel at work on the lower Skeena during prime time in August.

measure the harm done by the downstream commercial fisheries rather than a mechanism for assessing whether or not the nets should have been unleashed in the first place. Ultimately the only real measure of what should or shouldn't have happened in-season was determined by the actual count of fish passing the Babine fence weeks after the last sockeye was canned in Prince Rupert.

Test-fishery catches of steelhead were recorded right along with catch data for all the other species. Nothing was ever done with the data, however, until 20 years later when provincial government staff undertook the inaugural SEP financed investigations of Skeena steelhead. That was a century after launch of the commercial fishery. Some of the initial investigations involved translating hourly and daily test-fishery catches for steelhead into estimates of abundance. Until the steelhead run strength could be estimated and the commercial-fishery harvest rates documented there was no clear understanding of what management measures should be implemented and no hope of ever changing the status quo with respect to the commercial net fishery. This was probably the first good illustration of the theme that pervaded all things steelhead forever after, namely, change required conclusive evidence of need.

The steelhead scenario contrasted sharply with sockeye that could easily be counted as they passed through the Babine fence under low-flow conditions in late summer. Steelhead spread out over an entire watershed and spawned on the opposite side of the annual hydrograph. Spring flow conditions precluded counts even in the few situations where aggregations of steelhead did occur. Painting the steelhead abundance picture commenced in about 1975 and gained momentum through the decade that followed. Intensive surveys of the commercial-fishery catch of steelhead were undertaken. Those data were coupled with tributary-specific catch and escapement estimates derived by radio tagging, creel surveys and Indian fishery surveys. Collectively the data indicated the daily test-fishery indices compiled at Tyee should be multiplied by 223.7 to arrive at daily

estimates of steelhead passing that point. The figure was later adjusted to 245, the one still applicable today. Not available from the early estimates of abundance was the breakdown of what proportion may have been bound for individual tributaries such as Bulkley, Kispiox or Babine to name a few. Those estimates followed as the result of combinations of a plethora of tagging projects, juvenile population surveys, scale interpretations, some fence counts, electronic counters in select locations, creel surveys, mailed questionnaire surveys and monitoring of Indian fisheries. More recently DNA analyses have served to confirm and refine the previous knowledge base on stock specific abundance and time of return.

The accuracy of the 245 expansion factor remains a subject for debate. Unless and until virtually every steelhead in the Skeena can be counted the number lends itself to use or abuse by anyone with an agenda. Those who dislike steelhead and the influence they bring to bear on the commercial fishery continue to demand proof positive of the relationship between daily test-fishery indices and abundance. Never has there been any recognition of obvious relationships between commercial fishing and steelhead escapement in spite of continual lip service from DFO about the evils of mixed stock fisheries, the need for precautionary management, the importance of bio-diversity and sustainability. Needless to say the burden of proof for all things steelhead was never on the commercial fishing industry or DFO. To critics of the veracity of the steelhead expansion factor the question to be answered is why isn't the same microscope perennially focused on steelhead applied to the other five species? Why the institutional resistance to accepting and applying the test-fishery data for steelhead when the impoverished upper Skeena coho are supposedly managed with surgical precision solely on the strength of the test-fishery data?

What needs to be understood is the Tyee indices for all species represent in-season estimates of the number of fish passing that point. Estimates are simply that. They are figures that can vary in and between years. Factors commonly believed to be of influence to test fishery results include river volume, tidal amplitude, debris, saturation of nets by sockeye and/or pink salmon and a growing seal population that has learned the easiest way to make a living is to pick fish out of a gill net. The commercial fishing industry to this day consistently claims the Tyee index for steelhead underestimates abundance. The vitriolic speeches about all the steelhead passing right on by because the test net was full of pinks, or sockeye, or debris, or the tides were too big, or too small, or the water was too high, or too low, or too clear, or too warm, or the fish were swimming underneath, or... The rhetoric was relentless during my years as a steelhead management biologist. Not once did I hear an acknowledgement that test net sets on ideal conditions (2010 was replete with them) could possibly overestimate abundance. And not once did I hear DFO officials commonly present when the diatribes were delivered address the biases and misconceptions of their friends and neighbors. One doesn't have to dig deep into the correspondence files for any year in the past 20 to find examples of federal people using a high steelhead index to cast doubt about any notion of a conservation issue or need for management action. But, try and find any evidence of the same people doing anything other than remain silent or discredit the validity of the steelhead index when it was low.

The original published material that rationalized the establishment of the test fishery and its methodology confirmed all suspicions about the efficiency of the commercial net fleet operating in the Skeena approaches. Withler (1956) reviewed all the commercial-fishery catch records for the years 1944-1950 and concluded the average rate of harvest of sockeye was 50%. In those years the fishery operated five days per week over the entire time that steelhead would have been present. By 1955 when all the preliminary work leading to the establishment of the test fishery was unfolding the weekly closed period for net fishing had increased to three days but the sockeye harvest rate had risen to 65%. This was ascribed to the increased efficiency and mobility of the fleet. Any case for steelhead not being subjected to similar harvest rates would make for interesting reading. Incidentally, Withler and his colleagues also reported investigating the hypothesized influence of all the environmental factors on test-fishery catches ("wind, clouds, time of day, debris, seals, tide levels, etc."). Their analysis: "Only the stage of the tide had a consistent effect, catches being higher when low tides confine the run to a narrower channel." (Anon, 1962). Apparently none of the latter-day DFO folk and their commercial-fishing confreres ever read Withler.

There were highly significant but rarely acknowledged lessons from Withler's original work with the test fishery. During the weekly closed periods the sockeye population in the commercial-fishing areas downstream built up steadily. When the four-day-per-week fishing periods commenced on Sunday evening the highest commercial catches for that week always occurred in the first 24 hours and declined steadily for each 24-hour period until the fishery closed on Thursday evening. The supply of sockeye entering the fishing area replenished itself over the following 72-hour closed period whereupon the fishery re-opened and the cycle repeated. I couldn't help but notice the pattern of fishery openings followed by rapid and dramatic reduction in catch and escapements measured immediately upstream was a carbon copy of the situation well documented at Moricetown by Withler's colleagues from the Fisheries Research Board ten years before the Skeena test fishery began.

It is not clear from Withler's original test-fishery work if the number of vessels fishing during a four-day opening remained constant but it is clear there was a point of diminishing returns in terms of the overall catch. In other words it didn't take a large fleet or consistently high effort to virtually eliminate the available supply of fish

shortly after any opening commenced. His observations of sockeye in 1955 were mirrored by steelhead year after year from when the data were first plotted in my own shop for every year from the mid-1980s onward. Examples of the relationship between the number of gill-net vessels operating and the test-fishery steelhead indices in four different years in the decade of the 1990s appear on page 83. Pardon another cliché but you don't have to be a rocket scientist to figure out what happens to steelhead and everything else when the gill-net fleet is operating. The pattern of depletion immediately following virtually every gill-net opening has been staring everyone in the face for decades. Equally obvious is the huge disadvantage facing any steelhead entering the commercial-fishing area in July or early August. A century after the nets were first deployed there aren't many of those early run fish to begin with. Those that remain are still the most vulnerable. What does it take to have industry and DFO recognize the obvious? It is their data is it not? How can the case for added protection for the early run steelhead stocks be stonewalled for so long? Remember, this is just the scenario in the commercial-fishery management area closest to the Skeena (Area 4). Before any steelhead even entered that area it had to run the gauntlet of the fleets operating on the highway to the Skeena immediately north (Area 3), as well as the Cape Fox and Noyes Island fisheries in Alaska.

I hesitate to dedicate so much space to the test fishery but there are more features around its history and application that scream for recognition. Arguably some of this is tangential to the test fishery itself but the data are highly instructive in terms of the overall business of gill nets and all the angst that accompanies any measures to constrain their impact. I'll get to that. In the meantime the figures presented below illustrate chronically neglected patterns with respect to gill-net openings. Two things show up. First, the number of vessels participating on any given opening is consistently highest during the sockeye season in July. In earlier years when there was no such thing as area licensing this was partially explained by the argument boats could move freely anywhere they chose up and down the coast. It made sense southern boats would arrive to fish the earlier, high-value northern BC sockeye runs and then head south to fish the central coast and Fraser River sockeye runs that always arrived later. However, the pattern didn't change when boats were no longer afforded that flexibility. The actual fleet size present in the north did diminish but not enough to make any difference in the total catch or the pattern of removal of almost everything with fins on any given opening. Second, on multiple day openings the fleet sizes were commonly largest in the first 24 hours following the start (6:00 PM Sunday) than for any 24-hour period that followed.[19] Presumably the early departure of vessels from fishing areas was related to depletion of the fish supply and lowered catch and earning expectations. Later in the season when low-value pinks dominated

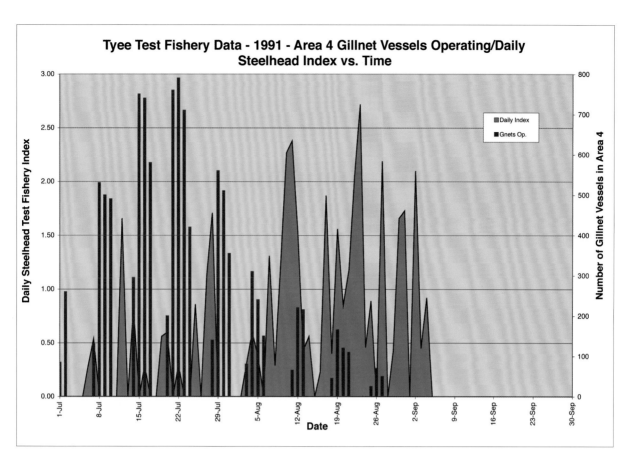

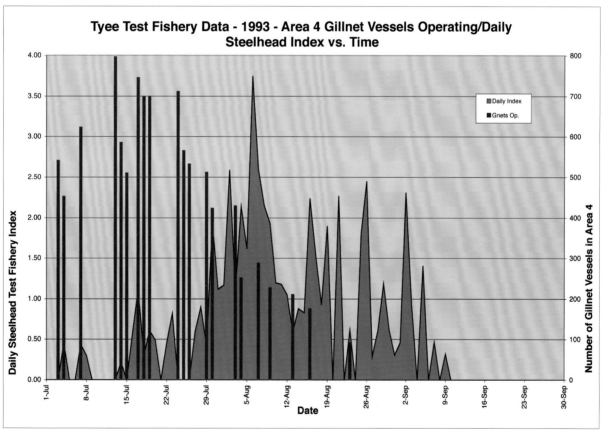

the catch the same day-to-day pattern prevailed but the number of vessels partaking at the start of any opening was always vastly reduced from the number present in July. The question to keep in mind when presented the steelhead conservation scenarios that follow is how do claims that hundreds of diligent, hard-working fishermen and shoreworkers were denied their "right" to make a living because steelhead needed to be protected square with the fact half of the fishermen didn't even bother to go fishing when they had the opportunity?

The next point to be made about the test fishery is the mortality rate of steelhead caught in that net.

This is important because it clearly refutes the mythology so prevalent among commercial fishermen and the industry in general. Over all years and all circumstances endured at the test fishery, half the steelhead caught by the vessel(s) involved were dead when landed.

We're not talking about small sample sizes here. For example, the test-fishery log books for years 1988 through 2001 inclusive revealed that 6,528 steelhead had been caught and 50.4% of them were dead when landed. This is a best-case scenario for steelhead survival in a gill-net fishery.

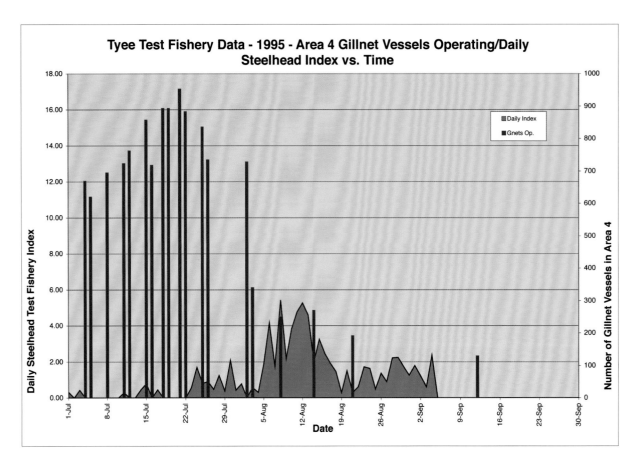

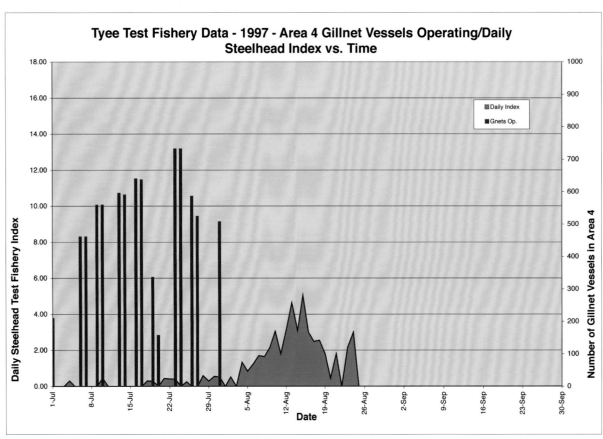

The test fishermen are extremely skilled, experienced and committed to what they do and they never make sets that last for more than one hour. That is hardly the norm for the fleet in general. Consider also that steelhead arriving in the test-fishing area are home free if they survive that one last net. Contrast that with a steelhead navigating through a maze of several hundred nets when a commercial-fishing opening is underway. So, when the fleet and its masters extol the virtues of short nets, short sets, recovery boxes, etc. and claim their fishery is harmless keep that 50% DOA test-fishery experience and the gill-net fleet distribution firmly in mind.

Continuing in the vein of lessons from the test fishery, it is well worth mentioning the long-term results on recoveries of tagged fish that originated from that other half of the test-fishery steelhead catch that wasn't DOA. Over the years a lot of steelhead were tagged with anchor tags supplied by MOE. I'm not about to argue the data are of great value in any statistically significant sense but there are important revelations nonetheless. Foremost is the paucity of recoveries made in the original year of tagging and the almost complete absence of any in later years (i.e. as emigrating kelts in the spring following tagging or as repeat spawners returning the year after that). The same applies to any tagged fish that were released in the commercial-fishing areas and subsequently available for recapture in the commercial fishery and at the test fishery. Those patterns were completely consistent over time. That alone is clear evidence of poor survival among net-caught and released steelhead. Then there are the data on recoveries of test-fishery tagged steelhead by commercial fishermen back in the fishing areas downstream. As small as they were, the numbers reported were roughly equal to those reported from the combined Indian and recreational fishery catches upstream. Put all that together and think about the likelihood of survival of a steelhead caught and released in a normal commercial fishery where dozens more nets would be encountered on any line drawn between the point of release and the upper limit of the commercial-fishing area (assuming the fish went upstream and not down).

The observations of MOE staff who conducted a radio telemetry investigation in 1989 using test-fishery caught and released steelhead shed more light (Beere, 1991). In that study 49 outwardly healthy steelhead were high graded from the sample of those alive when landed by the test boat (49% were DOA) and tagged by the most radio telemetry conversant and caring fish handler I have ever known or worked with. The results were devastating but enormously instructive. Only eight (16%) of the radioed fish made it as far as the Lakelse confluence near Terrace. The other 84% were never detected on receivers, other than three that were found dead and covered in fungus within days of being tagged. The results demonstrated beyond any doubt that handling and stress in combination with the delicate physiological state of fish transitioning from salt water to fresh was lethal. It was impossible to determine how much of what factor was to blame but there should have been major caution flags raised about the assumptions typically applied to survival among net caught and released steelhead in the inter-tidal areas where most of the net-fishery interception of steelhead occurs. Supporting data comes from the neighboring Nass watershed where hundreds of steelhead have been tagged and released following capture in fish wheels operated in the mainstem river upstream of tidal influence. Recapture rates in Nass River tributaries have been consistently high.[20]

One might assume the accumulated evidence of the devastating effects of gill nets on steelhead in the intertidal Skeena was conclusive enough to eliminate the need to reinvent that wheel. Not so. Another sophisticated telemetry investigation was undertaken in 2008 (Welch et al. 2009). That study resulted from recommendations included in a report (the Independent Science Review Panel report) whose origin and purpose will be discussed in greater detail later. The point here is that all prior information on steelhead mortality in gill nets was ignored by those in control. Instead they orchestrated the expenditure of tens of thousands more dollars to place sonic tags on high graded test net caught steelhead to track their post-release movement.[21] They called it a pilot program, thus implying the first of its kind and more to come. Thirty-four steelhead were outfitted with tags. Only 19 (56%) made it as far as the Lakelse River confluence vicinity downstream of Terrace and only four (12%) to the Bulkley River, by far the largest steelhead-producing system in the Skeena and the expected destination of three or four times that number and proportion of the original tag sample.

Anyone who took time to familiarize themselves with the history of test-fishery steelhead mortality rates and the well-documented experience with radio telemetry at that site would immediately conclude the results of this latest pure science endeavor simply confirmed decades-old facts. Unfortunately there was nary a hint of any such recognition by the latter-day scientists. The result is we have a nice color glossy report that dances around the edges of the blatantly obvious mortality problem but only enough to build a case for recommending more studies. Those would involve receivers deployed downstream of the test fishery as well as in some of the tributaries between the test fishery and the Lakelse River. How the pilot study was sold and conducted in the absence of receivers downstream from the test fishery is, to me, incomprehensible. Equally distressing is the fact this government-sponsored report recommended monitoring Skeena tributaries downstream from the Lakelse because some of them may have been the destination of the missing 44% of the sonic-tagged sample. How does that make it to print when those tributaries have long been known to support only small populations of winter steelhead?

One final anecdote on the test fishery will close out the subject. I bring this forward mostly because

The frozen leviathans held by MOE staff members Dana Atagi (left) and Ron Tetreau (RIP) as they arrived in Smithers in December, 1998 after purchase arrangements were completed and shortly before shipment to the taxidermist. The final product, the diorama now at the Smithers Airport lobby, was shown on page 15.

The two leviathans captured at the Skeena test fishery on August 1, 1998. The photos were taken at the Tyee test-fishery dock shortly after the fish were caught. Each is being held by one of the test-fishery vessel operators active at the time. The test fishermen reported they weighed the fish at 38 and 42 pounds at the dock. The estimated weights based on length and girth measurements (44.5"x 26.0" and 43.5"x 26.5") and commonly used formula suggested the lowest weight would have been 40.1 pounds and the highest 44.2 pounds. The photographs were e-mailed to the author in Smithers. The photographer was not named.

the airport lobby in Smithers, the hub for a great many visiting steelhead anglers, is now graced with an impressive diorama containing two very large steelhead captured at the test fishery (see page 15). There is a much deeper story behind that display than anyone reading the accompanying plaque would ever know. Those fish were caught on August 1, 1998. They were recognized instantly as something special and hustled away to a freezer in the DFO's equipment storage compound in Prince Rupert. A phone call from DFO alerted me to the fact shortly afterward. MOE, through myself, was offered first right of refusal on purchasing the two fish. Otherwise they would be sold to the highest bidder by the test fishermen. The test-fishery contract specified any steelhead caught were the property of the fishermen and they could do whatever they pleased with them.

I had known for some years that the test fishermen could sell (dead when landed) steelhead. In fact I had commented frequently on how inappropriate and distasteful it was for steelhead caught under a federal contract to be sold when the license conditions for commercial fishermen (however unenforced) specified non-possession, non-retention and when the entire upriver sport fishery was regulated on a catch and release basis. I had also proposed taking all the dead steelhead from the test fishery, adding them to those that obviously showed up in the Prince Rupert fish plants and giving them to the Wet'suwet'en at Moricetown to relieve demand for steelhead there.[22] What I didn't know until after the two leviathans showed up on August 1, 1998 was it had become common practice for the test fishermen to sell the big steelhead to at least one of the owners of the high-profile sportfishing lodges on the Skeena River near Terrace. Those highly prized fish were far more valuable if marketed to wealthy Europeans than if sold through a local fishmonger. I submit that if DFO was the least bit interested in demonstrating a measure of good faith toward

the other users of steelhead they would have eliminated the sale of test-fish-caught steelhead years before. I can't get a response to my question of what happened to all the dead-when-landed steelhead on the test boat in 2010 (likely about 800 "pieces"). All I can tease out of anyone is they probably didn't throw them overboard!

To continue the 1998 story – the price commanded to prevent the two prize steelhead falling into other hands was $1000.00 each. Orchestrating payment was a delicate administrative process but key contacts in the Province came through. The fish were picked up and deposited in a provincial freezer in Smithers and delivered to taxidermist Jack Gibson's Richmond BC studio in December, 1998. Some will remember his diorama was the focal point of the entrance to the Smithers MOE office for several years before being transferred to its present home. The above photo shows the fish as they appeared at capture and when delivered frozen to Smithers four-plus months later. Close examination of the photograph does not reveal any of the marks typically present on fish that had succumbed to the effects of a gill net.

Chapter 14

THE MIXED-STOCK MANAGEMENT STANZA: THE TREADMILL OF CONFIRMING THE OBVIOUS

When the so-called mixed-stock management stanza began in the early 1970s, Skeena steelhead could be considered to be facing their worst ever circumstances. The chronic overfishing that had plagued sockeye, as well as every other species, for a half century but that had eased pursuant to the Babine slide was now back with a vengeance courtesy of the Babine spawning channel production. If the consequences of targeting a single stock of sockeye weren't apparent before they certainly became so afterward. The river-mouth net fishery was increasingly concentrated on the enhanced sockeye production. With that came all the predictable effects on every other stock and species that swam with them. Skeena steelhead run timing always overlapped with that of the aggregate Skeena sockeye population and obviously subjected them to harvest. The concentration of net fishing during the return period of the Babine spawning channel sockeye made an already bad situation for steelhead worse. The mid-July through early August steelhead comingled with enhanced sockeye were disproportionately valuable to the upriver sportfishing community because they arrived in the preferred tributary fishing locations first and were available longer than any that followed. The fishing in the upper Morice and Sustut river systems described by John Fennelly in his 1963 classic *Steelhead Paradise* is evidence enough of the time of arrival and abundance of steelhead in those waters in the late 1950s and early 1960s. Seventy-five years of intensive commercial fishing had already altered the circumstances found by Fennelly and his cohorts but the more serious impacts came after the Babine sockeye channels reached their productive potential a dozen years after *Steelhead Paradise* was published. The figures illustrating the relationship between gill netting effort and test-fishery indices are ample evidence of the problem.

That other management agency, the provincial one that had been delegated responsibility for steelhead by the big brother federal agency years earlier was gaining a toe hold as the mixed-stock era unfolded. The hold strengthened following initiation of the SEP initiatives mentioned in the chapter on governance. Now there were two agencies on the Skeena steelhead map, one with deep roots in the commercial-fishing industry, the other with strong ties to the recreational fishery and fully committed to representing those interests. Narrowing the gap created by the 100-year head start of the commercial industry was challenging to say the least.

Steelhead management circa SEP, and for the decade or so the substantial funding accompanying it persisted, was all about defining and illustrating the damage done by the net fisheries operating in and near the Skeena estuary. The term mixed-stock fishery was at the forefront. All the other non-target stocks of sockeye, chinook and coho were equally vulnerable but it was steelhead and the momentum steadily building behind them that became the center of attention. Chum salmon were probably even worse off but no one cared enough about them then (or now) to be their advocate. Pink salmon were treated similarly. A sport fishery had arrived, a guiding industry with it and DFO itself was beginning to understand its stakeholder community extended beyond Prince Rupert. The MOE and its pesky steelhead were seldom accorded anything other than lip service in meeting rooms dominated by DFO and its commercial brethren. But, when DFO's own consultative processes gave the sportfishing fraternity seats at its table MOE had proxy voices that became louder with each passing year.

Getting a wedge in the door leading to management decision-making processes was slow and painful. First came the compelling evidence of the number of steelhead being harvested by both gill nets and seines in the Skeena approaches. Most of that was compiled in a series of three reports stemming from some of the earliest investigations funded under the new SEP in 1975, 76 and 77 (see Andrews and McShefrey, 1976; Oguss and Andrews, 1977; Oguss and Evans, 1978). Publication of those figures confirmed what MOE and knowledgeable sport fishers had said for years. A disturbing proportion of the steelhead entering the Skeena approaches were being removed by the net fishery and many of those harvested were never accounted for in the statistics kept by DFO. Coincidentally the test-fishery calibration process illustrated the harvest rates that were being exerted on steelhead. Nowhere in British Columbia was there a more prominent example of the fisheries-management issue of the day—mixed-stock fisheries. Skeena was it. All of this came together in the mid 1980s when there was an abundance of steelhead entering the Skeena. At the time it wasn't appreciated just how unusual the return years of 1984, 85 and 86 were. Whereas the catches and harvest rates of Skeena-bound steelhead were obviously high there were still relatively large numbers of steelhead escaping the nets. Fishing was considered to be good but no one could put that into any longer-term context because there was no good baseline to work from. The only defensible debate at the time was who should get those steelhead—hard-working multiple-generation families of commercial fisherfolk in Prince Rupert or upstart elitist sport fishermen upriver. Throw in the Indian fishers who were either commercial or upriver gill-netters themselves, and strictly opposed to anglers playing with their livelihood and/or food, and the meeting halls became theatres. Years later it became well understood that the mid-80s abundance of Skeena steelhead was a coast-wide phenomenon resulting from unprecedented high ocean survival of steelhead smolts. One steelhead generation later the opposite end of the abundance spectrum descended and steelhead conservation preempted steelhead allocation. Traditional ways of managing the Skeena fishery were getting tougher to sell in DFO's new, self-imposed world of consultation and consensus.

When steelhead and steelhead advocates emerged from the primordial management soup in the late 1970s and into the 80s the Skeena commercial fishery was disturbingly similar to its distant past in terms of the impact on fish. We know the capacity of the fleet was still well in excess of the ability of the stocks to withstand it. Sequential fishing restrictions were always retrospective and did little more than delay the inevitable decline of weak stock after weak stock. A good deal of willful blindness must have been at play not to address the demise of everything but enhanced Babine sockeye. The commercial fishermen and industry leaders themselves may have been oblivious but, if the professional managers were, they could only be considered negligent, incompetent, impotent or all three.

I mentioned earlier the proportion of the Skeena sockeye return made up of just the Babine stock. When data were examined by the first scientists arriving on the scene in the mid-1940s the estimate was 70%. Fifty years later that figure had become 90-95%. In other words a long succession of federal managers had knowingly allowed numerous other smaller stocks of sockeye to be depleted to the brink of commercial if not biological extinction just so the net fishery sustained by enhanced Babine sockeye could remain. Chinook were salvaged by agreements pursuant to the Pacific Salmon Treaty in 1985, although they continue to remain far below historic abundance. Besides, by that time, the chinook scenario was all about the outside troll fisheries, not the river mouth nets. Pink and chum salmon commanded as much attention as steelhead. Coho dwindled to a small fraction of what once returned to Skeena and most of them were late-returning stocks that did not have to run a gauntlet of nets targeting sockeye and pinks. Some DFO people today would have it the summer-run coho that entered the Skeena coincident with sockeye have been "rebuilt" through commercial-fishery restrictions of latter years. Arguably that is true by 1990 standards but it is a Grand Canyon separated from what existed when the canned pack statistics of the early 1900s are examined carefully. Alternately they might want to review their own Babine fence counts of coho in the first couple of decades following installation. . . and those were more than a half century after the nets.

A Federal Minister of Fisheries took center stage in 1998 as soon as he familiarized himself with the status of coho in British Columbia. David Anderson (a west coaster and a steelhead angler to boot) quickly recognized the crisis at hand. His response was to close fishery after fishery up and down the coast before any more damage was done. The measures he imposed in advance of the 1998 fisheries were not exactly warmly embraced by the commercial and recreational fishing industries or, for that matter, by staff of his own organization but, finally, a politician with brains, integrity and guts did the right thing. Anderson's 1998 line in the sand represented the most significant action ever taken to address the mixed-stock fishery and inherent conservation problems infinitely well known and thoroughly described by DFO staff years and even decades earlier. Commercial fishermen wanted to burn him at the stake. I say his bronzed likeness should be the centerpiece of a Pacific fisheries management hall of fame. The linkage between the 1998 coho measures and steelhead will be more evident later.

From a steelhead perspective the years of greatest momentum and those responsible for everything that followed were the early 1990s. By then all the information necessary to demonstrate that a northern British Columbia commercial-fishing fleet of as many as 200 seine nets followed by 800 gill-nets was bad news for Skeena-bound steelhead. The eyes of the steelhead advocates were squarely focused on the basic fisheries management questions: how many fish are there in advance of the fishery, how many are being removed by it and is the number escaping the nets sufficient to meet modest upstream use and sustain stocks? MOE was reasonably comfortable with the estimates of steelhead escapement and both governments had agreed on what the escapement requirements were. The lingering uncertainty was how many steelhead were being caught. The initial investigations funded by SEP in the mid-1970s (cited previously) were the beginning of the story. That was the wake-up call for seiners and gillnetters, as well as the shore based processors to avoid divulging how many dead steelhead they were accounting for. By the 1990s steelhead catch reporting was a complete sham. Some examples to illustrate that fact and the difficulty in addressing it follow.

The best example I can use to expose the problem is the test fishery itself. When one examines the test-fishery catch data the first thing that jumps out is the actual number of steelhead caught by that single net. For example, for the ten years from 1998 to 2007 the number of steelhead caught at the test fishery ranged from a low of 284 in 2007 to a high of 1539 in 1998. The annual average was 740. If we go with a 100-day season from mid-July to mid-September that translates to 7.4 fish per day or at least 2.5 fish per set. Remember, the set time for the test net is one hour and no more than three sets are ever made on a single day. In contrast the commercial vessels generally make much longer sets and many more of them on every day fished. Straight across comparisons between averages at the test fishery over the course of an entire season are open to denial. The appropriate comparison is the test-fishery catch on the days when the commercial fishery is open to the commercial catch by vessels closest to the test-fishery location on those same

days. Not unexpectedly the reported steelhead catch for the fleet is small in comparison. What is remarkably similar between the two sets of catch data, however, is the ratios of other species. The ratio of sockeye to chinook or sockeye to coho for the commercial vessels when compared the same ratios in the test-vessel catch are consistently similar. But, if one compares the sockeye to steelhead ratio for the test-fishing vessel to the same ratio for the fleet, the test-fishery ratio is always far lower. The only plausible explanation is the steelhead caught by fleet vessels were grossly underreported. The analyses were performed on data that pre-dated any of the so-called conservation measures adopted by the commercial industry so we can dismiss that as a credible explanation for observed discrepancies.

Another example comes from the report of the contractor in charge of the federally sponsored head recovery program for the entire BC coast. His job was to sample the north coast net-fishery catches for steelhead and to recover marked fish present as a result of a stock-specific migration timing study initiated years earlier. The marked fish recoveries were discussed previously in relation to Alaskan fishery interception of Skeena-bound fish. I made special note of a conversation I had with the contractor at the height of the 1993 sampling. He told me his staff commonly sampled more steelhead while achieving their target sampling level of 20% of the landed catch than was reported by the entire industry. Even more incriminating was one particular quote from his final report (Thomas, 1993).

Contact with processors encountered a variety of problems, foremost involving an intransigent attitude to handling and reporting steelhead. Although catch reporting problems were established, attempts to further mask landed steelhead or impair sampler contact with steelhead were confronted. Sampler interference during this difficult time originated from tally staff. Commonly steelhead were intercepted during unloading and hidden from samplers or tally staff altered weighing procedures in an effort to restrict fish access. Importantly, tally staff also exhorted fishers to take fish home and as a result not have them recorded on fish slips. The actions of tally personnel were remarkable when considering the dimension of their intrusions with both samplers and fishers.

My personal experiences anonymously touring the Prince Rupert waterfront at the peak of the fishing season, camera in hand, added to the opportunity to expose the ubiquitous cover-up of the steelhead landings. As confirmed in the 1993 Thomas report and all the way back to the original reports of the mid-1970s, many more steelhead were always caught but never reached any of the commercial packing vessels or shore-based processors where there was at least some chance of being counted. I'll note here as well that of the dozens of packing vessel and seine vessel deliveries I observed on the Prince Rupert waterfront in the late 1980s and 1990s

Quick, find the steelhead and get them safely into a holding tank so they can be tagged.

The ladies wearing blue hats were employees of the contractor whose job it was to sample landings for adipose-fin-clipped steelhead.

there wasn't a single one that failed to reveal at least one steelhead. This was the case even in years following the regulation forbidding the retention or possession of steelhead by any commercial vessel. I never encountered a DFO employee whilst skulking about the waterfront fish plants either. Then there was the well-known situation of one prominent processing plant operating a two for one deal with all of its fishermen. For every two steelhead turned in the fisherman got one back smoked. No data ever reached paper.

Other examples of disguising the steelhead catch are readily available from commercial-fishery records circulated by DFO after the conclusion of any season up until at least the mid-1990s. Without more than minutes spent looking back on some reports retrieved from my personal files from those years I found all sorts of DFO figures further illustrating catch-reporting issues. In 1994, for example, the published figures on steelhead catches in the north coast fisheries indicated

Shift change at the BC Packers cannery on the Prince Rupert waterfront, July 27, 1995. Each of the plastic bags contained steelhead that were being removed from the facility without ever being recorded as fish landed.

Area 3 seines caught 57 steelhead for 698 boat days fished. That equates to one fish for every twelve seiners on any given day. Remember, most of the Area 3 seine fishery occurs on the steelhead migration corridor to the Skeena. There was no seine fishery in Area 4 that year but the gill-net fleet reported 1383 steelhead for 8130 boat days. That's one steelhead for every six gillnetters. The Area 5 seine fleet which operates at the southern entrance to the Skeena reported nary a steelhead for 74 boat days and the gill-net fleet 24 steelhead for 504 boat days. All of these figures are gross underestimates but they made it to press nonetheless.

The real issue with steelhead-catch reporting is not so much that individual fishermen deliberately contravene regulations and that DFO deliberately ignores that reality. Rather it's the fact information known to be false is published without qualification. Years later such drivel has a nasty habit of being accepted as accurate. Small wonder I came to refer to steelhead-catch reporting as a conspiracy of silence. Ask if it is any different today.

I'll add one last personal experience with catches of steelhead by commercial nets. If not revealing it is at least entertaining. In 1988, when interest in the unfolding Skeena steelhead scenario was assuming new heights, MOE took the lead in a radio telemetry program that involved a seine vessel contracted by DFO to catch steelhead to be tagged and released in the commercial-fishing approaches to the Skeena. The primary objective was to learn more about time of passage of individual stocks of steelhead through the fishery. The skipper of the vessel was a seasoned and highly successful fisherman. I'm reminded of the legendary Bill Schadt in Russel Chatham's *The Angler's Coast* and Tom Skerritt's documentary video "Rivers of a Lost Coast". I spent two days aboard the vessel trying to drink up as much as I possibly could about the operation of a seiner and the skills and perceptions of the captain and crew. The dates were August 4th and 5th, very near the estimated longer-term peak of the summer steelhead returns to the Skeena.

A bag full of fish coming aboard on August 4, 1988.

Going in I was very familiar with all the commercial-fishery steelhead catch data or lack of it. I also knew the full story underlying the reports written by former colleagues Andrews, Ogus and Evans. Throw in the numerous interactions I had over the years with the mark recovery program guru and I was satisfied there weren't going to be any surprises. Wrong! On the first day out the crew made five sets. They caught 51 steelhead, including 42 in one set. Another five sets on the second day produced 31 steelhead. Contrast that 41-per-day average with any of the federally published figures on seine catches of steelhead in any of the north coast statistical areas in any year you like (1994 data referenced above was anything but unique). My surprise at the number of steelhead caught didn't go unnoticed by the skipper. He went to great lengths to explain away the numbers. Never before in his long history of fishing the north coast had he or any of his crew seen 42 steelhead in a day, let alone one haul. What was I to believe? What were the odds that I would just happen to witness what I'd been led to believe was more than a season's take of steelhead in a single set? This off-the-chart catch was reserved for the day when the pesky steelhead biologist from MOE first sets foot on a seiner? Back at the wharf on the evening of August 5 a talkative crew member on another seiner that had been on the grounds that day was busily filling a plastic bag with steelhead as I walked by. He told me their vessel had caught 30 that afternoon. I struggled with accepting my experience over the two days was as rare as the skipper would have me believe.

Another important dimension to my experience on the seiner was the number of sets made to catch the fish we tagged. Five sets was about one quarter of the number that would have been made on a regular fishing day. Finding the steelhead and removing them alive from sets that commonly contain at least 50-fold more salmon takes time. In the commercial-fishing business time is money. Those who believe the seine fleet is reducing its total number of sets to the point where the care and attention steelhead received when I was out there in 1988 ever became standard practice are deluding themselves. Why would it if there were never any consequences for those who failed to comply with the conditions of their license and/or the catch-reporting regulations? Those who deny that should be compelled to produce the list of the convictions for non-compliance with the standard posting for every north coast seine fishery in the past decade: "Fishers are required to release all coho, steelhead, and chinook to the water with the least possible harm. Brailing and sorting your catch prior to placing fish in the hold is mandatory. Operating revival boxes are also mandatory, and may be used to revive fish prior to release." Even the officers from the Federal shop who occasionally visited the fishing grounds to observe the seiners (and gill-netters) operating under those license conditions openly admitted the compliance was abysmal. This will come up again later on. MOE staff once shot some remarkable video footage to illustrate the disdain with which some commercial seine crews treated non-target fish they were compelled to release. DFO officers who were present during at least some of that filming remained idle while crews on one vessel punted coho and caber tossed steelhead off the deck.

Chapter 15
THE ROOTS OF INSTITUTIONAL INERTIA

An appreciation of the climate steelhead advocates were faced with in the late 1980s and into the 1990s is fundamental to understanding the difficulty in altering the commercial-fishery status quo. I've said numerous times already that steelhead never warranted any attention and rarely even any mention for a century of commercial-fishery exploitation of Skeena salmon stocks. Generations of attitude and behavior, fully supported by a long-standing management regime weren't about to change just because some neophyte steelhead managers and their sportfishing friends arrived on the scene. There is a plethora of examples to illustrate how difficult and incestuous the contemporary circumstances facing steelhead and steelhead managers were. I've short listed three personal experiences to help paint the picture.

Example one. In the late 1980s MOE staff in Smithers were frustrated over their inability to elevate the profile of the Skeena steelhead commercial-fishery interception issue to a point where higher authorities might begin to address it meaningfully. Contemporary thinking was that managers in offices surrounded by commercial-fishing interests and those closeted away in Vancouver, Victoria and Ottawa were too insulated from the world where steelhead were perceived differently. An idea advanced by one of my colleagues was to produce a weekly one-page update on steelhead as the commercial-fishing season progressed and send it to a representative audience. It was a work saver as well in that it eliminated the need to respond to endless phone calls and letters inquiring about the status of the steelhead run. The weekly updates became known as the Skeena River Steelhead Run Status Report. They included nothing but basic numbers most of which were obtained directly from DFO in Prince Rupert - weekly totals for the number of steelhead estimated to be passing the test fishery, the number of days the commercial fishery was open, the reported catch of steelhead (as negatively biased as it was), the harvest rate (the reported catch divided by the total run size for that week) and the spawning escapement target for Skeena summer steelhead. The reports were surface mailed to approximately 400 destinations including every sportfishing advocacy organization in the province, conservation groups, all angling guides licensed for the Skeena and its tributaries, dozens of media outlets, chambers of commerce, sports shops, DFO offices in Prince Rupert and Vancouver, MOE offices in Victoria and dozens of others who later requested they be included. This was still the pre-digital world. The test-fishery data were accessible to only a miniscule fraction of those who are a mouse click away today and e-mail didn't exist. Even MOE regularly waited two or three days for updated test-fishery figures. Prior to the newsletters the vast majority of the target audience knew nothing of the test index, the commercial fishery or how those were, or in the case of steelhead, weren't linked.

The reports received rave reviews initially. This was not unexpected because they all came from those with connection to the sport fishery. Over time, however, cries of foul began to surface. Most were traceable to the commercial-fishing sector and DFO although one prominent and vocal steelhead guide best described as a compulsive liar and con artist did his best to build opposition within the sport-fishing sector. His position was self defense because numerous disgruntled customers were seeking retribution for alleged fraud. They had bought trips predicated on guide-supplied information that promised fishing success far beyond anything that could reasonably be expected according to the actual run-size estimates. The solution among all those opposed to distributing factual information about the influence of the net fishery on steelhead was to kill the messenger. Senior DFO staff in Vancouver led the charge. They demanded Victoria instruct its underlings in the hinterlands of the Skeena to cease and desist. I heard some amazing accounts from Victoria staff who were party to comments from senior DFO staff in Vancouver who would never dare commit such remarks to paper. The reports lasted four years before the political heat was enough to bury them. In retrospect, as unpalatable as it was to have such innocuous material suppressed, it didn't really matter at that point. The reports had elevated awareness as much as was ever hoped they would. Figures 13 and 14 show examples of the reports and perhaps a bit of evidence of their context and the climate in which they were distributed.

Example two. In December, 1991 I was an invited speaker at an annual convention of the Northwest Guides and Outfitters. This was a long-established group representing virtually every hunting guide in the northwestern quarter of British Columbia. Collectively they had an impressive client list with connections that could make noise in high places. Traditionally the hunting guides were not particularly interested in happenings around steelhead but some of them did own territories through which the Skeena and its tributaries flowed. Their hunting clients frequently availed themselves of fishing opportunities when their primary objective of hunting was not on the day's agenda. The hunting guides were also recipients of the weekly steelhead run status reports and had become familiar with many of the issues of the day. They made their living out there in the wild and they were every bit as concerned about livelihoods and lifestyles dependent on fishing and hunting opportunities as were those who depended on gill-netting.

At their convention the guides organized a panel discussion on the Skeena steelhead situation. Participants included one representative from each of the two fisheries-management agencies, a tourism-sector representative and two commercial-fishing industry representatives (one a gill-netter, the other a processor). This was the time when high-seas drift nets were very much in the news. The federal government had just endorsed a United Nations resolution calling for an end to drift netting on the high seas by June 30, 1992. The top Canadian fisheries participant had referred to the nets as a crime against nature. At the same time an Alaska-based organization, Seacops, had been making great progress in alerting the world to the same problem. Seacops was concerned specifically about steelhead. In the course of my presentation I made reference to the UN resolution and noted that world opinion was strongly in favor of selective, non-destructive fish-harvesting techniques replacing those that weren't. I asked those present what the difference was between 170 miles of gill-net that amounted from 750 gill netters, each with one 1200 foot net and the equivalent amount of gill nets strung by a high-seas fleet in the mid-Pacific? I suggested that, whereas high-seas drift nets may have caught a few Skeena steelhead every year, the real problem was the near-shore drift nets that killed thousands. Well, the commercial-industry representatives were apoplectic over any hint of a parallel between them and those evil drift-netters. By the Monday morning following my Friday comments a letter demanding a public apology and retraction was on the desk of the Minister of Environment in Victoria. That was the nice part. The letter was another classic demonstration of the utter intransigence of the Rupert based fishery. It should have been dismissed immediately but the politics of the day turned another mole hill into Everest. In the end it took an overwhelming outpouring of support from recreational-fishing representatives for the weak-kneed politicians in Victoria to politely reject the commercial-industry recommendations. The DFO representative who participated on the same panel when my drift-net analogy was made was never heard from.

Example three. By the time the mid-1990s arrived there had been numerous studies aimed at demonstrating gill nets either did little harm to steelhead or that any potential harm could be minimized by applying measures such as weed lines (sinking the top of the net about 4 feet below the surface), manipulating hang ratio (the ratio of the length of stretched out net to the cork line to which it is attached), varying the net construction material, shortening the soak time of the net, retrieving gill-netted fish and live transporting them to a central holding barge to be emptied after the commercial-fishing opening, and so on and so on. A decade worth of studies and huge sums of money had been spent. The wheel was reinvented repeatedly. In the end any steps with any realistic potential to measurably reduce the impact on steelhead were dismissed as unacceptable to commercial fishermen and their masters. Sometime in June of 1996, well before the commercial fishery had begun, I received a phone call from a newspaper reporter from Prince Rupert. He asked for my thoughts on the latest proposal that had been advanced by the commercial netters and their federal supporters. It was yet another study aimed at demonstrating that gill nets could distinguish between

Province of
British Columbia

BC
Environment
Lands and Parks

Bag 5000
Smithers, B.C.
VOJ 2N0
Telephone (604) 847-7303

SKEENA RIVER STEELHEAD RUN STATUS REPORT

July 28, 1992

This is the third in a series of weekly reports outlining the status of 1992 summer run steelhead returns to the Skeena River system. To date, approximately 3320 steelhead are estimated to have entered the Skeena River past the test fishing site at Tyee. The current number of steelhead ascending the Skeena is more than double the 1991 return to the same date. However, the present total represents 65% of the long term (1956 - 1991) average and 50% of the most recent 10 year average to this point in the season.

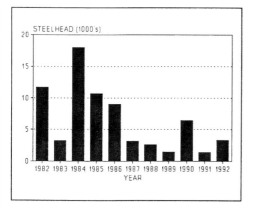

Numbers of steelhead entering the Skeena River up to and including July 25, 1982-1992.

The commercial gillnet fishery near the mouth of the Skeena operated slightly more than 4 days over the past week. Vessel numbers peaked at 700 and averaged approximately 600 during this opening.

Efforts to release steelhead caught in this fishery continue. Reports from fishermen suggest they have released nearly 50% of the current total reported catch of 1309. Of the 614 steelhead released to date, approximately 130 have been transported to a centrally located facility for holding, tagging and subsequent release at the end of the opening. Although initial survivals of fish from this facility appear good, the longer term health of these steelhead and others released immediately by fishermen are unknown at this time.

As part of the current catch and release initiative, observers are being placed on gillnetters to provide data on steelhead condition at the time of capture. The success of this program will hinge on the willingness of fishermen to allow observers on their boats during the fishery. The cooperation of vessel operators contributing in this way is greatly appreciated by those involved in organizing the program.

Week ending	Days fished	Number of gillnetters	Steelhead Catches		
			Harvest	Release	Total
July 4	3.0	273	39	14	53
July 11	2.0	458	78	35	113
July 18	3.0	548	187	98	285
July 25	4.3	605	391	467	858
Total	12.3		695	614	1309

Fig. 13. Two examples of the Steelhead Run Status Reports that were broadly circulated each week during the commercial fishing season. Note how truncated the reports had become by the 1993 fishing season. This was entirely the result of pressure brought to bear on the report producers. Even the 1992 report had to be carefully worded so as not to overly offend the commercial-fishing sector or its managers.

a target salmon and a non-target steelhead. The reporter referred to it as the selective gill net study.

Call it a weak moment but I thought it worth the time to try and give this fellow some perspective. In doing so I went through the recent history of studies and results to try and acquaint him with some basic facts and I suggested to him the term 'selective gill net' was a classic oxymoron. Weeks later, in the thick of the commercial-fishing season, my classic oxymoron remark was quoted in an article in the Prince Rupert daily. The reporter had been astute enough to recognize an opportunity to fan the flames of controversy and had gone to one of the local DFO people well known for his ties to the industry and asked for his opinion on my remarks. Our man didn't disappoint and confirmed in spades the tight relationship between his agency and the industry.

The newspaper story catalyzed a flurry of high-level discussions I was oblivious to until I answered my Smithers office phone well before our normal opening hour about

ten days after the newspaper hit the streets. The opening remark of the caller is forever burned in my brain. "Bob, you're in big trouble". No good morning, no hello, just those icy words from the easily recognized voice of the province's Assistant Deputy Minister of Environment at the time. The one-way conversation was well advanced before I connected enough dots to understand its origin. He was compelled (probably ordered) to reprimand me following a formal complaint from the top gun in the United Fishermen and Allied Workers Union direct to the Premier of British Columbia's office. My head on a plate was the objective. Well, it didn't happen that time either, but not because the ADM was the least bit supportive, cared about the issues or was prepared to speak to the futility of more useless studies. His only concern was keeping the heat in the fisheries political kitchen at tolerable levels. Making issues disappear was paramount. Before this one did there had to be another show of support from an irate sportfishing community

Province of
British Columbia

BC☙
Environment
Lands and Parks

Bag 5000
Smithers, B.C.
V0J 2N0
Telephone (604) 847-7303

SKEENA RIVER STEELHEAD RUN STATUS REPORT

August 20, 1993

The status of the Skeena River steelhead run for 1993 is best illustrated by reference to present and past indices of the number of steelhead escaping commercial fisheries and entering the lower Skeena River (i.e. the Tyee test fishery index).

Index to August 19, 1993..................................42.12

Index to same date 1992....................................30.86

Average index to same date 1982 - 1992................78.06

Target season ending index..............................180.00

An approximation of the actual number of steelhead represented by the index can be developed by multiplying the index by 245. The target season ending (early September) index of 180 reflects the number of steelhead which must pass Tyee to ensure the identified summer steelhead habitat is utilized by the prescribed number of spawners, that provision is made for upriver Native and sport fisheries, and that losses to disease and predators are compensated.

The Skeena steelhead run normally peaks at the index site on approximately Aug 7. Early season results do not always mirror season end totals but the figures to August 7 can be expected to provide a strong indication of what to expect through the remainder of the season.

Fig. 14

---

disgusted that a public servant might be disciplined for stating the obvious. Victoria was beginning to understand the fisheries union wasn't the only voice in town.

Such was the climate of the day. The only difference between 1890 and 1990 was the entrenchment of the beliefs and positions of both the commercial-fishing industry and DFO and the steps they were prepared to take to defend themselves against upstart sport fishermen and their MOE friends. The litany of correspondence I saved in personal files in almost 14 years in office in the Skeena country bears testament to that. When the Mayor and Council of Prince Rupert, the fisheries union heads, the Prince Rupert-based Save our Communities Committee, the entire commercial-fishing industry caucus and senior staff of DFO in both Prince Rupert and Vancouver are lining up for the funeral of someone who dared orchestrate a steelhead run status newsletter or claim minor tweaking of gill nets would never achieve significant reductions in harm done to steelhead you know they're getting nervous. A measure of the astuteness of the authors of so much of the hate mail generated over those years was most of them never spelled my name correctly.

If the preceding examples don't sell the story on how unyielding the commercial-fishing industry had become

as the 1990s unfolded we can look to some less personal evidence. Consider statements contained in a 1992 letter written by the Chair of the North Coast Advisory Board to the publisher of this book. These followed an article that appeared in a popular sportfishing magazine owned and edited by the publisher. The caucus chair:

Unlike you, however, we attempt to represent our interests by employing scientifically valid data, proper research, fairness and a social and regional consciousness.

The four most recent fisheries which have started up and had the most recent impact on steelhead are the high seas driftnet fleet, the United States seine fisheries at Noyes Island, the US gillnet fishery at Tree Point and the commercial sports fisheries on the Skeena and its tributaries.

The Skeena steelhead is not endangered. Steelhead return to the Skeena from early July through to April when they spawn. Only a small segment of the run returning in mid-July to early August is impacted by international, US, Canadian and Aboriginal fisheries.

So, there we had the senior commercial-industry spokesperson chastising others for being unscientific, data deficient, socially irresponsible and unfair in the same breath he clearly demonstrated a remarkable lack of familiarity with the most basic life-history features of Skeena summer steelhead and made completely unsubstantiated claims about everyone but the net fleets that sustained him. Hypocrisy was never a word that entered the lexicon of the steelhead critics.

How about a 1993 letter from the same individual shotgunned to all the industry heavyweights, chambers of commerce, city councils, numerous elected representatives, all the First Nations in the watershed and beyond, media outlets, etc? Quotable quotes:

The fundamental principles of natural resource management as defined by the Province are to provide fish for recreational anglers to play with while destroying the livelihood of thousands of people employed in the commercial salmon fishery.

Any damage to the economic and social fabric of the region is being created by the Province of BC. Their ill considered demands are bankrupting individuals, destroying small businesses, and producing economic and social strife in both aboriginal and non-aboriginal communities.

Furthermore, all selective harvest technologies that have been tried on the Skeena to date have been total failures. . . . If they want more steelhead for their sportfishing clients the Province should pay for it through enhancement. They shouldn't force another sector to pay for it through lost jobs, social upheaval, and poorer communities.

This last piece about selective harvest technologies is particularly noteworthy. This from the man in the forefront of all the initiatives touted by industry as the solution to "the steelhead problem". Apparently we agreed on something. I should add he was also one of the participants on the Northwest Guides and Outfitters AGM panel and author of the letter demanding my retraction and apology for the drift-net analogy.

The other thing to understand about how DFO prosecuted fisheries management by the time the Skeena steelhead issues were heating up was the commitment to consultation with stakeholders. The days of a few commercial-fishing industry representatives and DFO operating in isolation of others with an interest in fish and fishing were over. Some of this was already covered in the governance chapter. What may not have been clear and is worth emphasizing here is the influence the sportfishing stakeholders were beginning to exert as the 1990s unfolded. Industry continued to be represented by the North Coast Advisory Board (NCAB) much as it always had been. In contrast sportfishery representation took on a much more structured and visible role. The Sport Fishing Advisory Board (SFAB) was re-constituted to include north coast and south coast sub-committees. This second tier of the SFAB was known as the North Coast Co-Management Sub-Committee (NCSCC). A third tier of the SFAB followed with the establishment of local sub-committees in the various larger communities in the Skeena watershed. The First Nations of the Skeena also started to become major players as a result of their constitutionally guaranteed rights, a number of precedent setting court decisions and policy direction from DFO headquarters in Ottawa. Each of the three sectors dealt separately with the Federal conveners of the various consultative processes. MOE participated directly at all NCSCC meetings, some SFAB meetings, most local NCSCC sub-committee meetings, some NCAB meetings but was never invited to attend any of the meetings or discussions between DFO and the First Nations community. I liked to refer to the times as the golden age of consultation. The leader of the Skeena sportfishing community in those days, John Brockley, frequently reminded me that consultation was the blood sport of the 90s. Everything considered, the complexities of the individual consultative processes, the difficulty of linking the outputs and translating any of that into management actions that complied with a never-ending stream of policies generated by people distantly removed from the influence of their product became the recipe for all ahead stop.

Chapter 16
THE SWC AND THE WSC

I f the Skeena River Salmon Investigation of the mid-1940s and the Skeena River Salmon Management Committee of the 1950s are taken as management milestones the Skeena Watershed Committee (SWC) of the 1990s qualifies as well. That initiative was born of the climate that developed by the time that decade began. A growing and enlightened public was beginning to create an intolerable situation for federal managers still perceived to be preoccupied with sockeye and unjustifiably in support of net fisheries. To that point in time no fisheries management issue in British Columbia ever generated the amount of correspondence and public debate as did the Skeena net-fishery influence on steelhead. Media of every description from throughout Europe and across the United States and Canada were relentless in their following of the Skeena steelhead dilemma, much to the chagrin of commercial-fishery advocates inside and outside government. Letters complaining of abrogation of responsibility and worse were pouring into DFO offices from sources unprepared to accept glib responses or denial. The volume of internal government briefing notes, decision notes, cabinet submissions, media positioning statements, multi-draft communiqués, etc., etc. was staggering by any previous standard.

As the 1991 season unfolded the steelhead estimate at the test fishery was alarmingly poor and no significant reduction in the net-fishing effort was about to occur. The weekly steelhead newsletter parroted the figures which, in turn, generated the federal authorities' most amusing ever condemnation of the accuracy of their own test-fishery results for steelhead. They even went as far as suggesting the test fishery wasn't that good for sockeye either but, predictably, that never had any bearing on the number of days of conventional gill-netting. In the midst of it a group known as the Skeena Watershed Sport Fishermen's Coalition emerged. That local group partnered with another long established and respected provincial organization, the Steelhead Society of BC, to orchestrate a fall public forum in Smithers. It was officially titled "Bio-Diversity and the Integrity of the Skeena Watershed – A Consensus Approach" but was popularly referred to as the steelhead symposium. The intensive day-long session consisted of three moderated panels, each populated by well-known figures in their respective disciplines. Panel subjects included perspectives on the salmonid resource, habitat issues and views from the management community. The latter panel was the one of greatest interest to the gathering because it included the Director of the Fisheries Branch of MOE and the Director of DFO's Pacific Region, as well as the head of the Skeena First Nations fisheries management authority.

A symposium such as this was not just another typical stakeholder sessions of the day. It involved numerous organizational meetings of local Steelhead Society members who dedicated hundreds of hours to arranging for the facilities, the panel moderators, the participants, the travel and accommodation, a meet and greet session the evening before and for the emcee and guest speaker at an impressive banquet and auction fundraiser at the conclusion. Any doubt about the symposium's profile was put to rest when the Mayor of Smithers stepped to the podium to welcome a packed house in an opening address. Cameras and microphones were there to record every detail.

The most significant commitment ever regarding Skeena steelhead and the commercial net fishery was made during that November 9, 1991 symposium. Straight from the mouth of DFO's Pacific Region Fisheries Director came the promise to reduce the interception of Skeena steelhead in commercial nets by 50% within the next three years. This was the fisheries equivalent of nine on the Richter scale. The federal managers who had steadfastly opposed any notion of a steelhead conservation problem for as long as anyone could remember suddenly admitted there was one and committed to doing something substantial to address it. The mechanism for delivery was the Skeena Watershed Committee (SWC). With that the management stanza I labeled earlier "institutional inertia" entered virgin territory. The SWC was as much about governance as management but it seems best dealt with here. Some extensive discussion of the SWC is appropriate. Just as the Moricetown fishery history is central to the entire First Nations fisheries scenario of the Skeena today, so too is the SWC an important lesson on what can reasonably be expected in terms of managing Skeena fisheries to deliver better outcomes for steelhead.

The people involved in orchestrating the November 1991 symposium were also the principle organizers of a parallel effort to bring the plight of Skeena steelhead into the public eye. That effort became known as the Wild Steelhead Campaign (WSC). The Steelhead Society of BC led that charge. It began with an April, 1991 meeting between three key Terrace based Society members of the day and two MOE staffers. That inaugural meeting evolved into a dedicated group of well-informed anglers and guides supported by substantial financial contributions from the international sportfishing and conservation communities working tirelessly to put the Skeena steelhead commercial-fishery interception problem on the world stage. Not the least of the contributors was Patagonia founder Yvon Chouinard, *Fortune* magazine's choice as the most successful outdoor industry businessman of our time. Chouinard's reputation as a world leader in environmental conservation and ethics needs no further explanation. What may not be so public is his love of Skeena steelhead. I'll put him high on my list of those who appreciate what treasures are.

The WSC intended to pursue a two-pronged education effort. The first output was a video which was to be followed closely by a comprehensive report that detailed the management circumstances surrounding Skeena steelhead and salmon. Momentum was firmly behind the video and it was first out of the gate. Well known and respected Smithers based photographer, filmmaker, angling guide and friend of the environment Myron Kozak spearheaded production of a 27-minute video titled "Steelhead, Symbol of Survival". Myron worked closely with another highly regarded film media professional, Rick Rosenthal from Washington State. The video contained powerful messages from one of the most distinguished and respected fisheries scientists of the past half century, Dr. Peter Larkin, about the consequences of mixed stock fisheries and the problems with artificial enhancement. The WSC video was distributed in August, 1993 which, at the time, was understood to be year two of the three year period over which Skeena steelhead interception was promised to be reduced by 50%. Tragically, Myron died in a plane crash on Vancouver Island in August, 1995, before the results of his efforts could be appreciated fully.

The companion effort of the Steelhead Society, the written report, progressed through a number of iterations and editorial inputs from the likes of Dr. Larkin, Lee Straight, Rob Brown and several others experienced in professional and technical writing. Suffice to say it slipped from view over the succeeding months and years as the Skeena Watershed Committee process seized the spotlight. Coincidentally the Steelhead Society, provincially, fell into disarray over events that unfolded elsewhere in the province. The obligation of the Society to produce a report remained, however, and did result in a document that was released in October 2000 (Lewis, 2000). Had the report been completed eight years earlier, as anticipated when the idea was conceived, it may have had some influence. In 2000 the obligation to complete it was fulfilled but the Steelhead Society was a shadow of its former self, the WSC had faded with it and the SWC that had been inspired by the 1991 symposium had come and gone.

The video experience was quite different. A measure of its impact was the response from the anti-steelhead lobbyists in Prince Rupert. Before the end of the month in which the WSC video was released the Save Our Communities Committee (recall it was comprised of the Mayor of Prince Rupert, the Tsimshian Tribal Council President, and the fisheries union head, among others) hired a Vancouver-based film maker to produce its own seven-minute-long counter video. The Prince Rupert City Council which included several members who also sat on the SOCC, donated $15,000.00 toward its production. One of the most vociferous commercial-fisheries activists and a spokesperson for the SOCC revealed more about how uninformed and unyielding the anti-steelhead fraternity was. In a newspaper headliner dated September 15, 1993 he claimed the sportfishermen's point of view was biased and inaccurate and added "we" were going to try and win the minds and hearts of the coastal communities and let those upcountry people know there was another side to the story. He went on to say he had never even watched the WSC video. The WSC video aired in forums from British Columbia to Ottawa and in numerous international venues. The SOCC video languished in obscurity. Look up the WSC video and see how little has changed since it was first aired. It's 27 minutes well spent. While you're at it ask yourself who is more credible, Dr. Larkin or the commercial-fishery spokespersons?

Returning to the SWC, the first order of business for the newly formed group was to clarify its founding principles and its roles and responsibilities. Typical of any government-led multi-stakeholder process of the time a memorandum of understanding (MOU) signed off by all the participants was mandatory. The initial founding principles document listed 20. Imagine the difficulty of getting consensus on 20 principles among 15 people representing interests as diverse as commercial and recreational fishermen, conservationists and unionists or upriver and downriver communities. Who could define or agree on ethics, biodiversity, conservation, proper management, accountability, mutual respect, honesty, aboriginal rights, etc, etc? By April of 1992, almost a year and a half after the genesis of the SWC an MOU was finally signed off. It took just over two more years (May 1994) to sign off a consensus document and another six months for the signatories to agree on what was termed a framework for the management of the fishery. By then the man who made the 50% promise was a fading memory, having been replaced at the start of 1993 by an Ottawa plant with zero fisheries management experience. The word on the street was the dethroned Director was perceived as treading too heavily on hallowed industry ground. Internal correspondence pointed to the outgoing Director being sidelined for expressing dissatisfaction with the intransigence of his superiors. In the meantime the more fundamental question of what the 50% promise actually meant was being punted back and forth between DFO and MOE shops.

Surprise, surprise, the status quo prevailed with respect to the commercial fishery while all the behind the scenes negotiations and deliberations were transpiring. Out there in the real world things were getting interesting though. In early August of 1993 federal authorities announced plans to reduce gill netting by one day per week when the steelhead test index failed to meet the 1992 level at the half-way point of the steelhead return. The immediate response of the industry was to mount a protest fishery involving more than 100 gill-netters. They pretended they were all First Nations vessels legally fishing for food. Coincidentally, other commercial fishers descended upon the federal fisheries office in Prince Rupert, wrapped it in gill nets and blockaded it around the clock. Still others dumped 18 tons of ice on the only access road to DFO's Prince Rupert waterfront dock.

There were no consequences for any of these actions except that security at the fisheries office was upgraded.

On the surface the notion that the test-fishery index for steelhead had finally become a management tool was immensely significant. On analysis, however, the veneer was a bit thin. Choosing 1992 as the benchmark was the perfect out. It was one of the lowest years on record, only marginally better than 1991, the second lowest year ever. Magically, the highest daily index of the season occurred immediately following all the insurrection of the commercial fishermen (3.75 on August 6). That figure was just enough to bring the cumulative total index for the season up to the heretofore undeclared 1992 standard. The threatened steelhead conservation oriented gill-net restrictions disappeared immediately. Pure coincidence I'm sure. The steelhead index bump lasted just long enough to justify the gill-net openings expected by industry weeks before. By the end of August the test-index figure for the pathetic 1993 return was disturbingly similar to that for 1992. Both were little more than one third of the escapement goal.

The agonizing process of clarifying what the 50% promise meant produced three outcomes all too reflective of past history. First, it was not to be at the expense of the harvest of the target stocks of sockeye (i.e. the enhanced Babine stock) and pink salmon. The same agency that committed to halve the steelhead harvest rate dropped the other shoe and declared it was equally committed to maintaining and even increasing the Canadian commercial catch of those target stocks. The concept of mutual exclusivity was obviously not on the radar. Oh, and by the way, it took forever to get on the table the fact that all those steelhead traditionally caught around Dundas Island in Statistical Area 3 were part of the Skeena equation and therefore needed to be incorporated in the steelhead harvest rate reduction plans. That didn't happen until 1997.

Second, the promised reduction was partitioned into early and late seasons. Early meant sockeye run timing or up to about August 7, the estimated longer term mid point of the steelhead run timing. Late was everything after August 7. That would be the period when pink salmon were becoming so low in value the commercial fishermen struggled to recover fuel costs even if they did leave the wharf. In the final analysis the 50% became 42%. Half of that was 21% but 33% was set as the harvest rate ceiling for steelhead for that first half of the run, the half chronically overharvested by the net fleets and the half of greatest value to the upriver sport fishery. So, the November 1991 promise and the expectation that only half as many steelhead were going to be removed by commercial nets as of the 1994 fishing season ultimately translated to something far less significant.

Looking back I still marvel at how DFO managed to convince a lot of pretty intelligent people they could manage an indiscriminate net fishery so precisely that the difference between 42% and 33% could ever be delivered. I'm thinking consensus by exhaustion.

The steelhead ambulance. This was the vessel contracted for the commercial-fishing seasons of 1992 and 1993 to race from a central holding barge to any gill-net vessel whose operator radioed to it that a live steelhead had been retrieved from his net and placed into an onboard live tank ("blue box"). The ambulance picked up the steelhead and brought it back to the holding barge where it was confined until the gill-net opening had concluded. At that point all steelhead that had been delivered to the barge and were still alive were dip-netted out and released, oftentimes downstream from where they were caught originally.

Third, there were no consequences if the steelhead harvest rate ceilings were exceeded. In fact those rates were never on the table until long after the commercial-fishing season was over. There was no in-season accommodation of steelhead unless one counts the silliness and king's ransom that went with a succession of useless industry-biased studies of tweaked gill nets, observer programs that relied on unemployed commercial-fishery advocates to play the "what steelhead, I don't see a steelhead" game aboard vessels of their choice, and hyping a steelhead ambulance running through a maze of gill nets to collect a few dozen still alive steelhead and deposit them in an aquatic prison to be paroled after the latest fishery was finished with its sockeye (and just in time for the next one). No one can show that even one day's commercial fishing was ever eliminated on the strength of steelhead abundance or harvest rate. The failed attempt in 1993 was as close as it ever came. The truth was the fishing time supposedly sacrificed by the gill-net fleet to conserve steelhead and coho in August of that year was more than compensated for by increased fishing in July. Furthermore, the pattern of the number of gill-netters typically fishing in August when low value pinks dominated the catch mirrored that established repeatedly in all the years back to the early test-fishing era. All of this was just more evidence that the number of people affected and the value of the catch foregone was nowhere near what the industry, First Nations and union spokespersons continually trumpeted from their podiums.

I've expressed disgust several times already about the purported efficacy of various modifications of a typical gill net to achieve measurable reductions in steelhead harvest and harvest rate. I should explain some of this a bit more thoroughly. Tweaking was my choice of a term that best describes the spectrum of modifications that were advanced in the 1990s as potential solutions to the chronic problem of gill nets killing too many steelhead. The measures employed in the Skeena fishery included alteration of the basic net composition material, weed lines, daylight-only fisheries, half-length nets, short sets and hang ratio adjustments. Notice that closing areas where steelhead encounter rates are always much higher than elsewhere (i.e. statistical sub-area 4-12 and, especially, 4-15) is not on the list. Think about the deception that is involved here.

Changing the net composition material is all about catching more fish of every species. It has absolutely nothing to do with selecting one over another. Hang ratio is another illusion. Messing with it over the range prescribed in regulation or condition of licenses accomplishes absolutely nothing in terms of steelhead conservation. Weed lines have been shown to be effective in clear water situations (i.e. not the tide-influenced turbid waters of the highest steelhead encounter areas) and in low commercial-fishing traffic situations. Under those circumstances steelhead sometimes travel in surface areas and might be less prone to gill net capture if the top of the net was roughly one meter below the surface. (The weedline option eventually became 1.2-1.5 m.) Several things here. First, and again, the highest steelhead encounter area is not clear water and it is always relatively heavily fished

Releasing steelhead from the steelhead barge, August 1992. The program was discontinued after 1993 when it could no longer be ignored that potential benefit to steelhead escapement was negligible.

whenever a commercial opening occurs. Even if steelhead were prone to travel near the surface the disturbance from vessel traffic would push them deeper. Gill-netters never cease to complain about the noise driving the fish underneath their nets whenever seine vessels are fishing coincidentally. Second, the evidence from the test fishery is black and white. The vertical distribution of steelhead in that net is random. A weedline would have no benefit. Third, the deal on weedlines is that any fisherman who opts for one is allowed to add 50% more depth to his net. A standard sockeye net is 60 meshes deep (roughly 24 feet). A weedline net is 90 meshes or about 36 feet deep. In return for sacrificing 4 feet of fishing space on top of a net a commercial fisherman is rewarded with 12 feet more at the bottom. If steelhead are known to be randomly distributed vertically how can this possibly reduce encounter and harvest rates? Another side to the weedline charade is the fact the highest steelhead encounter areas are commonly too shallow to fish the deeper net.

Daylight-only fisheries are focused strictly on coho, not steelhead. In the highest coho encounter areas there is some utility in avoiding the daylight and dusk peak catch hours typical for that species. Those high coho encounter areas are seaward from the high steelhead encounter areas. The primary coho conservation measures combine daylight-only fisheries with moving the gill-net fleet inshore in August. That concentrates gill-netting in the highest steelhead encounter areas just as the long-term peak of the steelhead run is arriving. Daylight-only fishing has been the norm in that area for decades simply because the tidal influence is so great no one could fish effectively at night anyway. Besides, it was just plain dangerous.

Fishing with gill nets shortened to 100 fathoms (600 feet) from their normal 200 fathoms and requiring them to reduce the time the net is soaking amounts to more

fiddling while Rome burns. With hundreds of vessels overlapping nets that repeatedly choke-off the migration corridor and water column the prospects for a steelhead avoiding a net are slim to begin with. Releasing a fish that may still be alive (remember the long-term test fishery results of 50% DOA) to face more of the same is futile. Even in a dream world where there was sufficient enforcement presence to police the short net, short set, recovery tank, mandatory release conditions of gill-net licenses there is no realistic prospect more steelhead could ever escape alive or healthy enough to contribute to a spawning population.

How much investment and study of gill nets should ever have been necessary to put the realities on the table? In the past two decades millions of dollars have been spent proliferating illusions. Tens of thousand of steelhead were wasted while those in command ignored history, science and their own policies and regulations in a game played to convince each other they were doing something progressive. The only credible studies of gill-net mortality were already on the shelf before the political window dressing gill-net selectivity nonsense started.

Seines shouldn't escape discussion in the context of the alleged steelhead conservation measures that emerged from the SWC years. The boardroom talk frequently centered on alternatives to gill-netting. It was always understood gill nets were anything but selective but they obviously lived on in spite of the overwhelming evidence of the ineffectiveness of any of the measures implemented to teach them to avoid non-target species. Seines were a readily available alternative to gill nets but tradition demanded they each have their place in the fishery. Gill netters and seiners didn't like each other and neither was prepared to forego fishing opportunity perceived to benefit the competition. The DFO approach to demonstrating the effectiveness of seines as a selective harvest tool was to authorize special fisheries for seines in those same inside, high steelhead encounter areas traditionally the exclusive preserve of gill netters. The special seine fisheries always occurred during the weekly closed periods when the gill nets were tied to the wharf. In other words, the special seine fisheries were never in replacement of the gill nets but in addition to them. For steelhead that meant more fishing, not less, and that fishing was never without cost to the stocks. The sales pitch of industry and DFO was the mandatory treatment and safe release of steelhead was delivered and no damage was done to steelhead while surplus sockeye and pinks were mopped up to prevent them from overpopulating spawning grounds.

In the chapter on governance I made brief mention of the group within the Provincial Government that was responsible for licensing the shore-based fish processors. Prince Rupert and the Skeena fishery was important territory for them. Enter more conflict. The license administrators were never visible on the steelhead management front until the Pacific salmon fisheries were in a tailspin in the mid-1990s and the Province seized the political moment to remind the world of its interest in the commercial-fishing industry. It was campaigning for a more prominent role in management. DFO wasn't doing so well and fed bashing was fertile ground for enhancing profile in public opinion polls. A new provincial Ministry was created. That gave the process-plant licensers a much higher profile and they began to assert themselves in forums where they had never been before. The SWC was one of them. With that came the debate about who should speak for the Province and what the message would be. The internal provincial government correspondence dealing with the division of responsibilities between the two Ministries was extensive. Stated simply they didn't like each other. Naturally, as with all things government, process took over and led to another Memorandum of Understanding between Federal and Provincial governments, including terms of reference for a review of Pacific salmon fishery management. The verbiage in a joint news release was all too familiar.

"The guiding principles of the review are far-ranging, and include maintaining and enhancing the conservation and long-term sustainability of the resource while providing for the long-term viability of the industry. The objectives are to bring decision-making closer to clients and stakeholders, and to create effective partnerships to better manage the fishery. The review will also recognize the constitutional protection provided to aboriginal people and treaty rights."

Those were testy times and they certainly didn't benefit steelhead. Industry was quick to embrace its new friends in the Province and exploit the provincial divisiveness at every opportunity. I won't say that DFO was openly supportive of the new kids on the block but they never demonstrated the slightest support for the traditional steelhead management voice, MOE, or any hint of reluctance to include more friends of industry at the SWC table. In weaker moments I sometimes lapsed into thinking it was all a master plan. Then I'd remember the comment of one of my closest colleagues in the Victoria headquarters office. "You give them too much credit if you think there's anyone home capable of making a plan".

The federal/provincial Pacific fisheries management responsibilities issues continued for the remainder of the decade of the 1990s and into the next millennium. From the provincial steelhead management perspective the only thing worth remembering is the emasculation of all such capability through progressive downsizing and reorganizations of the Ministry at its center. That turned the Skeena steelhead clock back at least 30 years. The Premier in charge of the Province made great fanfare in extolling the virtues of living in British Columbia in a widely publicized address in the lead up to the 2010 Winter Olympics. He claimed it was the best place on earth to live and, among other things, promised the

electorate "the best fisheries management, bar none". Days before he resigned in November, 2010 he re-organized his government agencies yet again. If there wasn't enough evidence of the dismembering of any fisheries management capability on the table already that was it. Search out any veteran of the business, if you can even find one, and ask how much influence they think they can possibly bring to bear on the status of fish and fishing now.

Next on the list of discussion points central to the SWC era is the modeling work undertaken by federal and provincial technical experts to estimate the steelhead harvest rates. That was deemed necessary because there were no reliable data on commercial catches of steelhead. In the absence of harvest rate estimates any achievement of the promised reductions could never be detected. The estimates were developed on the basis of real migration and harvest data for sockeye for the years 1985-1991, assumptions around steelhead migration timing and rates and relationships between sockeye and steelhead harvest rates. Later, as various attempts to reduce steelhead harvest were applied (e.g. weedlines, hang ratios, short nets, short sets, recovery boxes, steelhead ambulance/barge, seines, daylight-only fishing, etc.) credits were assigned according to the expected reductions. Theoretically the model(s) were sensitive enough to assess impacts on individual steelhead stocks. On paper and in the meeting halls that all sounded wonderful. A SWC-endorsed tool to predict with promised statistical reliability what the consequences of any particular combination of fish abundance, fishing effort, the distribution of that effort and the new harvest rate reduction methods advanced by industry would be was just what the steelhead doctor ordered. Unfortunately there was never any such thing as in-season application of model outputs. The only tangible product of the model was the early and late steelhead run harvest rates prepared for the fall retrospectives on the season past.

The essence of the modeling exercises and how they were applied to calculate the post-season harvest rate figures is captured in the following quote from material tabled by the DFO at the 1996 post-season review. Notice the assumptions and data manipulations required to come up with the final figures and forgive the technospeak. I include it, not to try and impress anyone with the complexities of the issues involved but merely to demonstrate the distance between the boardrooms and the killing fields.

"The methods used for the post-season review were the same as those for 1995 and 1994. Total sockeye escapement was first applied to the Tyee test index to generate daily sockeye escapement. Daily escapement was then moved back through the four sub-areas of Area 4 to generate daily stock and daily harvest rates by sub-area. The daily sockeye harvest rates were then used to generate reconstructed run-timing curves for steelhead and coho. The 50% dates from the steelhead and coho reconstructions (non-smoothed)

were then used in the Skeena model to generate new normal run timing curves (12.5 day standard deviations). The reconstructed daily sockeye harvest rates were applied to these curves to generate the post-season steelhead and coho Area 4 harvest rates. In an attempt to address catch and release benefits for steelhead and coho, the daily harvest rates for special seine days were set at 0% of the reconstructed daily seine sockeye harvest rate, while those for the regular seine days were set at 50% of the reconstructed daily seine sockeye harvest rate. Daily reconstructed harvest rates for regular gillnets were reduced by 5% to account for catch and release via the blue box program. Daily harvest rates for special test gillnets were set at 60% of the reconstructed daily sockeye harvest rate to account for potential weedline benefits, etc."

If that doesn't make your brain sore you're a special person. Ask yourself what value such a contorted, assumption-riddled, after-the-fact process and outputs had when all anyone ever had to do to see the real-life black-and-white story on the results of any commercial fishing opening was to look at the test fishery numbers before, during and immediately following. Let's not forget 1996 was five full commercial-fishing seasons after the promised steelhead harvest rate reductions. One is left to marvel at how that many seasons could pass with so many people buying the notion the ever more sophisticated modeling exercises would pave the way to delivery of the November, 1991 promise. Let's not forget either that benchmarking all the harvest rate modeling exercises against the aggregate steelhead run-timing curves of the 1985–91 stanza did nothing to recognize or attempt to reverse any of the damage done to the front half of the curve by a century of commercial fishing.

The legacy of the steelhead harvest rate deliberations should resonate with everyone interested in the future of Skeena steelhead. Originally those rates were defined as ceilings, not targets. How target became the surrogate for ceiling remains a mystery, to me at least. I was in the forefront of the steelhead conservation discussions at the time and would have red flagged that one immediately if I ever sensed it was in the works. By the time I did hear about it, the transformation of harvest ceiling to harvest target was a *fait accompli*. The steelhead advocate's expectation that the worst-case scenario of the upper limit on steelhead harvest rate being reached would be a rare event was replaced by the sockeye seekers' determination to fish to that worst case scenario harvest rate every year. A quote from a press release issued by the facilitator of the SWC process dated May 10, 1994 sums up just how toothless the original 50% promise had become.

Consensus was reached through the Skeena Watershed Committee process on Area 4 target harvest rates for steelhead (21%) and early timing steelhead (33%) and coho (19%). These rates will apply for the next three years.

The annual fishing plan which is developed in close coordination between the North Coast Advisory Board and the Department of Fisheries and Oceans will be developed within

these target harvest rates. If these target harvest rates are not achieved in any particular year, the Commercial Sector will be accountable to review within the Skeena Watershed Committee process the changes that might be necessary to restore the level of confidence that these target harvest rates will be achieved in subsequent years."

The seriously depressed steelhead returns of 1992 and '93 came on the heels of the second worst return on record in 1991. Those two return years bracketed two thirds of the time available to deliver the promised 50% harvest rate reduction. In the final analysis they were allowed to slip from view while the SWC process was being defined and organized. For the next four seasons (1994-97 inclusive) the early steelhead harvest rate ranged from 33%-49% and averaged 39%. For the late half of the steelhead run the harvest rate ranged from 29%-39% and averaged 31%. I don't believe those figures included the harvest of Skeena steelhead in Area 3. There definitely wasn't ever any attempt to quantify the harvest in Southeast Alaska. Obviously no one could do anything about that anyway. In later years the Area 3 steelhead harvest was definitely included but I'm holding to the assumption that wasn't the case in those pivotal years following the promised harvest rate reduction and the birth of the SWC. Regardless of what was or wasn't included in the calculations in any given year none of them were made available until at least mid-October. The last gill-netter left the fishing grounds two months earlier. The fact that the 50% harvest rate reduction promised by 1994 wasn't delivered then or in any subsequent season during the life of the widely heralded multi-sectoral consensus-based SWC was accorded as much significance as steelhead catch reporting.

The final fishing season in the life of the SWC (1996) was classic proof of how ineffective the entire investment was. The Skeena sockeye return was large and a large fleet of gill-netters arrived to mop up the surplus. Long after the season ended DFO tabled the outputs of its steelhead harvest rate modeling exercise. The early steelhead harvest rate was 49% and the aggregate steelhead harvest rate was 39%. There wasn't even an "oops" from either the industry or DFO. Ultimately the entire harvest rate scenario was a lose-lose proposition for steelhead. There was never any payback if the targets were exceeded due to excessive fishing and never any relief from demand for more fishing time if they weren't. Five years after the promise and millions of dollars spent and that was the result.

The most troubling aspect of harvest rates then and now is their lack of connection to abundance, at least for steelhead. The problem is anything but difficult to see or understand if one looks at some of the real numbers that prevailed in the critical years of the early 1990s. To make it as simple as possible I'll round numbers off slightly and start with an escapement target of one million Babine sockeye. No other sockeye stock was on the federal agenda at the time so any criticism about oversimplifying the

management scenario by restricting discussion to a single stock is baseless. When the test-fishery index indicates the returns are tracking well below the day-by-day, week-by-week numbers that would see the one million target realized the commercial fishery is stopped. In some years there is no fishery at all. We've seen several examples of that in the last decade. There wasn't and still isn't any such thing as a harvest rate ceiling for sockeye when the escapement estimate is below the minimum escapement requirement. Contrast that with steelhead. For that lowly species it doesn't matter how poor the in-season returns are as long as the harvest rate target is not exceeded. Even then, as noted previously, it doesn't make any difference if it is. So, for example, if 10,000 steelhead managed to run the gauntlet of nets and make it to the river beyond the fact that less than one third of the escapement goal has been met means nothing to DFO or industry. (That was very close to the situation that prevailed in 1991, '92 and '93). If the steelhead return was six or eight times as large the same harvest rate figures would be used. Either way both the commercial sector and the DFO were in lock step in contending they had met the terms of an agreement carved in stone through the SWC process. Under the latter circumstances the upriver sport fishery and tourism economy would be alive and well. Under the former it would be a repeat of the early 1990s when the sportfishery was sinking into oblivion. Is the term institutional inertia starting to make sense?

The run size and harvest rate combinations were easily detectable from the test-fishery data. How those data were or, more accurately, weren't applied appropriately in any of those contentious years in the early 1990s is more evidence of what a misnomer "management" really was. The industry and DFO interpretation of low test-fishery indices and/or little evidence of steelhead presence in the fishing areas was no fish = no problem. Therefore unleash the fleet. That was the doctrine of July and early August. In fact few steelhead at the test fishery should have sounded the conservation alarm. If there really were no steelhead out there on the fishing grounds (as opposed to flagrant mis-reporting of catches) that should have been taken as confirmation of the conservation problem, not a green light for more fishing. Harvest rate analyses and arguments were hardly appropriate when the river was empty. The precautionary principle had no application to steelhead.

There is one last product of the SWC era that deserves to be woven into the steelhead mosaic. That was the business of the regulations governing their harvest by sport fishermen. Relative to most of the rest of British Columbia the Skeena steelhead sport fishery had been managed conservatively since well before the arrival of the SWC. A more comprehensive account will be given later. The point here is that the disaster steelhead return of 1991, the one that finally aroused the world to the plight of those fish and catalyzed so much of what followed, was the first time an emergency order was issued to regulate the sport fishery on a catch and release

only basis. It took effect August 1, 1991. In subsequent years the MOE strategy was to maintain a highly conservative harvest regulation (one summer steelhead per year from the Skeena) as the underlying regulation but issue in-season variation orders annually to reduce the quota to zero before the season started. If the test-fishery results warranted a return to the formal one-fish-per-year quota it could be done immediately. Keeping the sportfishery harvest door open that way was a statement from MOE that it had gone far enough in the direction of conservation and it wasn't prepared to take the final step in amending the underlying regulation framework on any longer-term basis. It was time for anglers' concessions to be matched by the other sectors. That position held until 1997 but by then the expectation of all the commercial-fishery advocates, the commercial-fishery managers and the First Nations representatives was the steelhead sport fishery would remain on a catch and release only basis forever and ever. Anything less would have been interpreted as a transgression of perceived conservation agreements struck while the SWC was in place. Peace in the valley was paramount. Thus MOE abandoned the in-season variation orders and amended the underlying formal regulation from one steelhead per year to zero. What followed became a story unto itself.

The zero quota measure for Skeena steelhead was opposed by the BC Wildlife Federation, the largest hunting advocacy organization in the province. Fish and fishing were always a distant second on the Federation's priority list but that organization never avoided an opportunity to speak to fish issues if it could enhance their profile with a province-wide fishing community that vastly outnumbered hunters. The northwestern BC representative of the BCWF was the ultimate critic of virtually everything MOE's fish (and wildlife) managers ever did in the Skeena Region. Somehow he managed to convince the Federation's executive that evil lurked within the walls of the Smithers MOE offices. No one from the executive ever questioned or investigated the perceptions of their local man, even as his personal vendetta entered the realm of the absurd. A measure of his salesmanship is evidenced by a remark by the BCWF President in an article he wrote for *The Outdoor Edge* (touted as Western Canada's most widely circulated hunting and fishing magazine) for its September/October 2000 edition. Speaking in reference to the Skeena steelhead non-retention regulation he said:

"That opportunity cannot be used as an excuse for mismanagement of habitat or the resource nor can it be used as a testosterone substitute for those anglers that need that kind of nobility. Learn to share, not to think of one's self as any better or more ethical than your fellow users of the resource."

The Province had grown weary of vitriolic attacks by the local BCWF representative and no longer paid any attention. Apparently that only inspired the man to take his personal campaign to a soap opera level. In February, 2001 a plain envelope with no return address arrived on my office desk. Inside were copies of two documents best described as blockbusters. One was a letter dated December 30, 2000 from the BCWF's man in Smithers (then a Director), the other a formal sworn information (i.e. a legal document) indicating the Board of Directors of the BC Wildlife Federation had commenced proceedings to charge five provincial employees, myself included, with contravening two sections of the criminal code. We were being charged with criminal fraud and breach of trust in the implementation of the 1997 regulation. The letter accompanying the sworn information was on BC Wildlife Federation letterhead and had been copied to the Federation's Board of Directors and its legal counsel. It was an extremely malicious and bizarre interpretation of facts woven together as the justification for the actions of the BCWF executive. How these documents found their way to my desk remains a mystery but they must have been leaked by someone close to the top of the BCWF. I forwarded copies to the other four individuals named in the information. All material was subsequently turned over to Ministry of the Attorney General officials of the Provincial Government. The lawyers took over from there.

The promise of a defamation suit it was certain to lose prompted the BCWF to distance itself from any association with its Smithers Director. A settlement was reached whereby the Director was compelled to issue a written retraction of the comments made in his letter and apologize for any distress or damage the letter caused. The Director was also required to resign his position with the BCWF. The President of the Federation signed another letter to the five plaintiffs stating the correspondence that initiated the government response was not authorized by the Federation and did not represent its views. The President also apologized for any distress and damages that distribution of the material had caused. Months later a former member of the Federation executive told me the out-of-court settlement was desperately sought because the Federation would have faced financial and political ruin if it had been forced into the courtroom to defend itself for the actions of its Director. All the retractions and apologies were essentially confidential, unlike the material the BCWF had in its possession and obviously distributed for more than a month before it hit my desk. That damage could never be undone. The settlement was legal but hardly just. A measure of the BCWF's sincerity in all of it came with the discovery the banished member's wife had replaced him as its northwestern BC spokesperson.

The preceding account was no sooner written than another interesting letter hit the airwaves. It was penned by the spokesperson of a new Skeena-area group whose genesis and modus operandi ties directly to the former member of the BCWF. The letter was addressed to the province's Minister of Environment and copied to enough other federal and provincial politicians and bureaucrats to ensure the world saw it. The song was familiar. Restore the steelhead harvest opportunity unjustifiably removed years before. And, while you're at it, turn over responsibility for managing steelhead to DFO because they know how to do it better. Then there was the predictable rhetoric about fanatical non-residents being favored over salt-of-the-earth locals. Completely escaping this man and his organization is the fact an overwhelming majority of anglers has long favored catch and release as the management centerpiece for Skeena summer steelhead. In fact, careful analysis of the MOE steelhead angler data base for the years when harvest of those fish was permitted revealed the number of Skeena-resident anglers who claimed to have harvested any never amounted to more than 100 in any of those years. That's less than one percent of the BC-resident steelhead anglers. A dozen years later the self-proclaimed champions of the other 1% still don't get it.

Let me put a wrap on the SWC years. In spite of all the pomp and ceremony, the enormous travel and accommodation costs, the high-priced facilitation, the pots of gold doled out for numerous projects sold on the basis of everything but good science and in spite of all the accolades from process evangelists from Victoria to Ottawa the SWC had no discernable impact on the status of Skeena steelhead. To those who spent days on rivers instead of the meeting circuit it was as clear then as now. Then again, the agenda ultimately had little to do with fish. I often said the times demanded a t-shirt and bumper sticker campaign, the slogan being "Process is the product, don't ask how the fish are doing".

Some were disturbed by the fact the SWC was disbanded in the months leading to the 1997 fishing season when the commercial sector withdrew because it felt the upriver steelhead folk were gaining too much influence over the tidal net fishery. That outcome was inevitable given the commercial sector's (or any of the others') power to bring down the process by simply notifying the other participants they no longer wanted to play in the sandbox. The only real debate was how long that might take. To those who felt steelhead returns were influenced one way or another with or without the SWC I would assign the task of producing real evidence. All that ever mattered was the annual abundance of sockeye and, for a couple of years when David Anderson was the Federal Minister, coho. From the perspective of intergovernmental relations, development of mutual respect, building relationships between divergent sectors and all those warm fuzzy things that too many upwardly mobile government staff seemed to want to build careers around, there was a cost associated with the collapse of the SWC. The connection between that cost and the benefits to fish is an entirely different discussion. Anyone who desires the more politically correct overview of the SWC years might like to look up a report prepared following a reunion of the players ten years later (Sigurdson et al. 2008).

Chapter 17
CLOSING OUT THE CENTURY

"There is no record of a major fisheries management scheme that was not introduced in an atmosphere of desperation after the evidence of severe depletion had become too obvious for any explanation other than over-fishing." [23]

I think it worthwhile at this stage to try and summarize the major features of the commercial-fishery/steelhead interactions as they were understood by the end of the 1900s. We know the century was well advanced before the word steelhead entered the fisheries management vocabulary. In spite of the ubiquitous neglect there were enough tidbits of information available to reveal what the aggregate Skeena summer steelhead stock size was and what happened to it, as well as the other five species of salmon, by the mid point of the century. To that point in time there can be no doubt it was the commercial fishing industry heavyweights that effectively controlled the fishery. There was no such thing as science in any aspect of the Skeena fishery until industry became desperate for help. First it was the Indian food fishery assessment, particularly at Moricetown, and the industry-inspired push to deal with that competition. Suffice to say the fix had little to do with the inland fishery. The first injection of science faded only to resurface when the Babine slide threatened the commercial fishery. Once again science rode over the horizon to address the problem. The solution of the day was enhancement. Its legacy was the sockeye spawning channels on the Babine Lake tributaries.

The problem of weaker stocks of every species being subjected to harvest rates beyond sustainable levels became worse but the post-enhancement supply of sockeye was all that really mattered to an industry oblivious to anything but straining every possible sockeye from the water and squeezing it into a can. The fishery managers couldn't have been unaware of the consequences of unleashing increasingly competitive and efficient fleets of gill-netters and seiners to target a single stock as relentlessly as they did. The only thing one can take from those circumstances is industry was still very much in control of the Skeena fishery. Any acknowledgement of problems of overharvest was accompanied by accusing fingers pointed at distant fisheries.

The conspicuous entry of steelhead into the Skeena commercial-fishery scenario came with the Salmonid Enhancement Program three quarters of the way through the century. One hundred years of commercial fishing were already in the rear-view mirror. The Province and its steelhead people naively believed there were better days ahead. As the surface layers of deception around catch reporting and harvest rates began to be peeled away the commercial industry dug in. The incestuous relationship between industry and the Federal managers, friends and neighbors all, in Prince Rupert was undeniable. Every attempt to alter the status quo with respect to where, when and how often gill nets and seines were deployed along known Skeena steelhead migration corridors met with failure. The mid-1980s coast-wide abundance of steelhead briefly anaesthetized the world to longer-term trends and consequences.

The polar opposite abundance of steelhead in 1991 was the harbinger. Seriously diminished steelhead supply in concert with growing angler expectations fertilized by the mid-80s abundance set the stage for conflict. The Province's steelhead management community and its constituency of supporters outside government could no longer be dismissed. The Richter Scale promise of a 50% reduction in steelhead harvest rates by the conclusion of the 1994 commercial-fishing season was the first ever acknowledgement of the problem the steelhead managers had been trumpeting for years. The first half of the immigrating steelhead population was being seriously overharvested. Conservation of fish was paramount but conservation of the fishing opportunity in upriver tributaries in the first half of the historic sportfishing season was equally important. Once again the pendulum of hope looked to be swinging favorably.

Hope faded. The central Federal figure who had promised the 50% harvest rate reduction was re-assigned. Any momentum that had been building was lost. Debate around translating the 50% promise into fishing plans was endless. The 50% reduction became 42%, the season divided into halves and the critically important first half of the aggregate Skeena steelhead population effectively sacrificed to accommodate the fishery for enhanced sockeye. DFO attempted to use some of the worst ever steelhead returns as the benchmark for judging the effectiveness of management actions akin to fiddling while Rome burned. Harvest rate ceilings became targets, irrespective of abundance. Accountability never entered the discussion when the harvest rate ceilings/targets were exceeded year after year. In 1996, five fishing seasons after the infamous 50% promise, the steelhead harvest rates substantially exceeded the 1985-91 base period average that was used as the benchmark for the promised reduction. That news drew nothing but yawns.

Industry and the DFO controllers of process relentlessly pushed their agenda of forcing MOE to prove to the satisfaction of the last critic standing the steelhead issue had a conservation component and wasn't all about stealing fish from real people for the benefit of undesirables upriver. In the eyes and minds of DFO and the industry a steelhead was a steelhead was a steelhead. There was never any management recognition of the demise of the early run steelhead through overharvest by sockeye-seeking nets. As long as the aggregate steelhead population was perceived to be adequate by salmon people who would move the goalposts to wherever it suited them there was no hope of altering the status quo. How does one go about proving a segment of a population

has been chronically overfished, depressed and, in some cases, probably extirpated? How does one convince the unconvinceable a mid-July steelhead does not beget a mid-September steelhead? How does one demonstrate the September component of the aggregate steelhead population today is stronger than it was historically because the commercial fishery has selected for stocks or components of stocks with that later time of return? The peak run timing of the enhanced Babine sockeye varies no more than a few days from year to year. The fisheries literature is replete with evidence and examples of the heritability of run timing. None of that was ever allowed on the DFO steelhead discussion table though.

How many times did we hear DFO repeat its hierarchy of priorities: conservation first, First Nations second and commercial and recreational fisheries third? How many times was the question asked, why don't those priorities apply equally to steelhead and most everything else but sockeye? Steadily emerging policies developed by the Federal shop's own research community in southern BC spoke to biodiversity and wild-stock conservation but Skeena steelhead were not about to be recognized in any such context. Industry, supported by DFO, contended they had an allocation of steelhead fully described by the harvest rate targets and they demanded their "right" to fish to those targets. The game of 'show us science we'll believe and then we'll talk about conservation' grew wearisome. No amount of science was ever enough, even if it was possible to bring forward. The federal folk's singular management tool for sockeye, the Skeena test fishery, was all the science they needed but the most black-and-white data on steelhead from their same test fishery was never met with anything but criticism and rejection unless the numbers favored their latest argument of convenience.

The three years over which the promised harvest rate reduction was to be delivered were lost while millions of dollars were spent re-inventing wheels. Looking back it is truly remarkable just how many monumentally useless studies were funded by the Federal government of the day. Industry even orchestrated its own "steelhead conservation and research program" claiming they would lead MOE out of the data wilderness and prove their gill nets did no harm. Credible technical reports from the professional community were already on the shelf proving beyond any reasonable doubt that industry's ideas of how to construct and deploy gill nets and solve the steelhead problem couldn't possibly achieve significant harvest rate reductions. Meanwhile the big thinkers in both DFO and MOE chose politics over fish and silence over leadership. Good money followed bad as the Federal coffers continued to underwrite a Skeena Watershed Committee that had lost sight of anything other than process.

Coho conservation was infinitely closer to the hearts or at least the mandate of Federal managers. When the coho equivalent of early run steelhead stock status finally entered the consciousness of those who open and closed fisheries, immediate conservation action was taken. Minister Anderson's 1998 fishery closures produced a night and day example of the impact the commercial fishery typically had on steelhead. Predictably, with no harvest pressure on July steelhead normally mixed with enhanced sockeye, the test-fishery index rose dramatically. The tributary fisheries beyond enjoyed the benefits. Decent fishing produced a return to the anaesthetized state of the mid-1980s. Steelhead and steelhead fishing conservation lost what little gains may have been

achieved after an intense decade of the combined efforts of steelhead managers and steelhead advocates. The issues that drove the steelhead symposium in Smithers in 1991, gave birth to the SWC and dominated the Skeena fisheries management agenda until coho seized the spotlight didn't disappear but they were not on the commercial-fishery management radar as the century wound down. Short years into the next millennium the suite of conditions that gave rise to so many of the events of the 1990s was back and another cycle of process and institutional inertia began.

Part 5: Anglers and Angling

Chapter 18
UPSTART COMPETITION

The early days of the steelhead sport fishery and the evolutionary pathway is lightweight business relative to the other two fisheries already discussed. That said the Skeena steelhead story would be sadly incomplete without some record of how the sport fishery unfolded. I'll offer that the sport-fishing history is more interesting to more people than either of the other two fisheries.

It took a lot of scratching to uncover any early references to sport fishing, let alone steelhead fishing, anywhere in the Skeena country. That isn't surprising given the remoteness of the country and the absence of anyone likely to be interested in a rod and reel until well into the 20th century. Large (1957) spoke of his personal experiences trout fishing on Babine Lake tributaries (Fulton and Morrison rivers as well as Pinkut Creek) and said they provided the finest of fishing for beautiful three-and-four pound rainbow trout. He made special mention of "millionaire's pool" on the Fulton and also commented that the finest of all fishing to be had was at the outlet of Babine Lake where the counting fence had been installed. Given that the fence was constructed in 1946 and his book was published in 1957 he was likely speaking of the late 1940s. The other sport-fishing reference of interest was also provided by Large in that same book. That was in the context of the early sternwheeler days on the Skeena when an anonymous passenger aboard one of those vessels in 1904 reported the captain had told him of catching between 25 and 50 trout in an hour on numerous occasions while fishing the Lakelse River.

A second reference to the productivity of the Lakelse system came from one of the Federal salmon biologists of the day (Bilton, 1952). He was a member of a team of researchers who were set to work as a result of the Skeena River Salmon Investigation program discussed earlier. Bilton and his colleagues were particularly interested in cutthroat trout and Dolly Varden char (provincially managed species) predation on their precious sockeye and coho smolts and pink salmon fry (federally managed species). Predation was known to be heavy in an area of the river near the lake outlet below which the Federal people had installed a fence to count the emigrating sockeye and coho smolts. No doubt the predation situation was aggravated by the mere existence of the fence and the concentration of smolts any such facility typically caused. Following three years of creel surveys of the river and lake sport fishery, as well as gill-netting in the lake the data indicated an abundance of cutthroat trout. Bilton surmised the number of cutthroat was so high that the food supply was insufficient to sustain their growth and individual fish size was therefore declining. He went on to recommend strongly that every effort be made to increase sportfishing pressure on the lake so that more cutthroat would be harvested and predation on juvenile salmon reduced. It is not clear whether there was ever any Provincial response to those recommendations. The priority accorded federally managed salmon relative to provincially managed trout and char is the thing to remember. The same thinking and actions prevailed for decades at Babine Lake as well but there were never any formal records kept as far as I could determine. The Federal Government's historic pre-occupation with commercially important species didn't disappear when the upstream boundary of tidal water was reached.

Retrievable records of steelhead angling on the Skeena tributaries are virtually non-existent until the 1950s. We can be reasonably sure the supply of fish and the timing of peak runs to all the tributaries had been influenced heavily by the 75 years of commercial fishing already on the record at that point. The full history of trends in abundance and timing will never be known with certainty but I'm of the opinion enough pieces can be put together to re-create a picture of at least the past 60 years. From the sportfishing perspective the critical issues have always been the cumulative total supply of fish available in the tributaries and when that supply reached threshold numbers sufficient to support a level of angling success that would sustain interest in fishing. How the timing and abundance is influenced by commercial fishing has been the primary focus of sportfishery management since the earliest days of Provincial Government involvement.

When considering the tributary fishing season an important point to remember is how short it is, even under ideal circumstances. River discharges are subject to late spring and summer snow packs and weather patterns. Flows subside to levels suitable for fishing sometime in August in most years. The first steelhead arrivals in preferred fishing areas probably never were until early August. Fennelly's descriptions of steelhead fishing at the outlet of Morice Lake in mid-August are instructive in that respect. As years wore by and the commercial fishery targeting enhanced Babine sockeye intensified we know the first half of the steelhead run timing curve was disproportionately negatively influenced. Peaks in the number of steelhead escaping the nets were pushed deeper into August. With that, fishable populations were generally not available in the tributaries until further and further into September. Weather and water conditions always constrained fishing opportunity and/or success in November and December. Today three or four weeks have been carved off the front end of the original twelve- or thirteen-week season when the cumulative total supply of fish was large enough to support reasonable steelhead fishing success and when weather and water conditions

and scenic amenities are at their annual best. The back end of the season is under Mother Nature's controls and slightly harder to manipulate. The objective for managing the steelhead sport fishery is to maximize steelhead abundance to create the highest possible encounter rates for the longest possible season. The commercial fishery, as it has been prosecuted since its inception, is the greatest obstacle to achieving that objective.

A couple of examples of altered steelhead run timing following disproportionate harvest of one segment of a run-timing curve serve as illustrations of what I'm convinced the commercial-fishery harvest had already done to the Skeena steelhead run timing curve before any of us arrived. In Washington State the Chambers Creek Hatchery has been the mainstay of consumptive winter steelhead fisheries all over the state for at least half a century. Chambers Creek fish were selected for a number of reasons, not the least of which was the early availability of brood stock. Over time the peak of the run timing for that stock was moved progressively earlier by selecting the earliest returning fish in the enhanced population as the brood stock. The problem that manifested itself in time was the swamping of the early returning wild steelhead in all the streams where the Chambers Creek hatchery stock was outplanted. The increased fishing pressure invited by the presence of large numbers of hatchery fish produced the same mixed-stock fishery circumstance so evident with Skeena. The less abundant wild fish were subjected to unsustainable harvest rates and were eliminated. Today the only self-sustaining wild steelhead left in any of the streams flooded with Chambers Creek hatchery steelhead return in late March and April, long after the fishery targeting the hatchery animals is over. The original mixed-stock fishery has been replaced by two discreet fisheries, one glutinous and focused purely on harvestable hatchery fish, the other ultra conservative (catch and release) and limited to the remnants of a run-timing curve once three months broader.

The other altered steelhead run-timing situation is Idaho's Clearwater River. The contemporary picture on that fishery comes from my long-time friend Steve Pettit who has lived streamside on the Clearwater for most of his adult life. Steve is a passionate steelhead angler who worked tirelessly on behalf of Clearwater steelhead during a long and distinguished career as a fisheries biologist with the Idaho Department of Fish and Game. In the Clearwater the stock of interest is the interior summer-run steelhead (commonly referred to as the B-run) not unlike the Skeena fish. Those fish were sealed off from their historic spawning areas by construction of Dworshak Dam on the north fork of the river around 1970. The compensation for loss of the wild-steelhead production was a massive hatchery program. In the pre-hatchery era the Clearwater fish exhibited a very pronounced bi-modal run-timing curve. About half the total annual return entered their natal river before mid-fall. The remainder of the annually returning stock came later and overwintered downstream in the impounded reservoir waters of the mainstem Snake River. They didn't enter the Clearwater until spring. Over time the front half of the run was subjected to increasing harvest pressure by anglers. The management agencies strongly encouraged harvest of as many steelhead as possible because they served no useful purpose otherwise. Between intensive and disproportionate angler harvest of the front half of the return and refusal of the hatchery managers to collect brood stock from that same run-timing component (because they died in hatchery holding facilities before they were ready to spawn) the selection for fish that returned late and/or overwintered in the downstream reservoirs and didn't enter the Clearwater until March and April was ever more pronounced. The Clearwater fishery for B-run steelhead today bears no resemblance to the one that created its reputation.

Back to the early Skeena sport fishery. The first of the Skeena tributary steelhead fisheries to climb into the spotlight was the Kispiox in the early 1950s. No doubt there are unpublished records out there somewhere that go back slightly further but there is no tangible evidence to suggest it wasn't the Kispiox fishery that vaulted Skeena steelhead onto the international stage. I clearly remember a discussion I had with a then member of the commercial-fishing industry caucus and, later, a prominent leader of the Tsimshian Tribal Council. This

was offline coffee talk at one of the many Prince Rupert meetings I attended in the early 1990s. The subject was the steelhead fishing his father had experienced in the Kispiox following his return from the Second World War. The war vet had arrived home with some state-of-the-art British-made sportfishing gear which he quickly put to use. The comment that stuck in my mind was "Bob, you have no idea what the fishing was like." I never doubted a single word of his story.

The circumstances that created instant notoriety for the Kispiox, and ultimately had much to do with all the other Skeena tributaries becoming so well known, tie directly to the annual fishing contest sponsored by *Field & Stream* magazine. Others have covered that in some detail (e.g. Lingren, 2004) making it unnecessary to repeat here. The main point of interest is that (arguably) the most prominent American sportfishing magazine which had been running an annual fishing contest since 1910 found its "Western Division, Trout" category dominated by entries from the Kispiox commencing in 1954. References to the Kispiox caught entries in that contest showed up in numerous places for the rest of the 1950s. To the sportfishing network already well established from Washington to California at the time goes credit for much of the early angling history of the Kispiox, as well as the pioneering of most of the other prominent tributary fisheries.

Chapter 19
RIVERS AND ACCESS

The primary reason for the lack of significant sportfishing activity on the Skeena tributaries until the 1950s had everything to do with access. The original modes of transportation of miners and settlers to the interior of the Skeena country were paddle wheelers that operated seasonally between the coast and Hazelton and/or pack trains along telegraph routes and old Indian trails. By 1909 wagon roads radiated out from Hazelton to Kispiox and as far east as a community known as Aldermere near the present village of Telkwa. The railroad paralleling the Bulkley from the Houston area, through Smithers to Hazelton and from there down the Skeena to Prince Rupert was completed in 1914. It had taken nine years to get from Prince Rupert to Fraser Lake where the east and west legs were finally linked. Communities such as Smithers and Hazelton weren't even named until the railway was a *fait accompli*. The first white settlers didn't arrive in the Terrace area until 1905. Construction of Prince Rupert didn't begin until 1906. Road access as we know it today was not available until fear of invasion by the Japanese during World War II prompted Canadian and American governments to establish a strong military presence in Prince Rupert. That required rapid construction of a road to reduce dependency on the only other access option, the railroad. It took only two years from the signing of the road-construction agreement between the two governments in 1942 until the road was officially opened. (With the influx of military and related personnel the population of the Prince Rupert to Port Edward area at the time rose to about 20,000 from its pre-war level of 6,000.) The airports in Smithers and Terrace were also a product of the military strategists. The Smithers strip was developed as an Air Force base in 1941. Terrace followed suit in 1943. Each was turned over to its respective local authorities by 1946 and both were accommodating regular airline passenger service by the early 1950s.

Following the war the logging industry in the Skeena drainage developed rapidly. There had been extensive high grading of spruce logs for airplane construction during WWI. and significant logging for railway ties and telegraph poles in the period between the two world wars. Spruce high grading was rekindled during WWII. However it wasn't until all the enlisted men returned from WWII that logging anywhere further than about five miles from the Skeena River itself cranked up. According to Large (1957) there were 180 sawmills operating along the Skeena corridor by 1954, three times the number in operation a decade earlier. The first (and only) pulp mill in the Skeena commenced production near Prince Rupert in 1951. Roads began to be pushed ever further into the sub-drainages as the supply of saw logs close to the mills was exhausted. The forest-harvesting history of the Skeena is remarkably similar to that of the fisheries. Rajala (2006) described it as a continuing liquidation project, unimpeded by governments more dedicated to promotion than regulation. Speaking of the 1945-70 period Rajala stated:

The forests were a source of profit and revenue needed to stimulate employment, community stability and the provision of social services. That the complacency and optimism these policies engendered rested on a thin foundation of scientific knowledge and management planning seemed inconsequential in a land of such abundance."

Exchange one word in that quote for a mirror image of the substance of a good part of this book.

The growth of the logging industry in the Skeena was a double-edged sword for steelhead and every other species inhabiting the same waters. Not only did it exact a toll in terms of fish-habitat alteration and outright destruction but it served to deliver anglers to places that had seldom, if ever, seen them before. The fish-habitat side of the story is a major volume and not one I intend to pursue in any detail here. Suffice to say the progression from horses to tractors to road-based logging reaching further and further into virgin landscapes was not without significant cost. Things unconscionable by today's standards were commonplace in my own lifetime. Consider the mid-1950s log drives on the Kalum River for example. There the forest-harvesting leaders of the day constructed wing dams and dikes to constrain river flows to a single channel and avoid stranding of their coast-destined logs in the multitude of highly productive off-channel fish-rearing areas. If scouring of river spawning beds and prime fish rearing habitat by log bundles driven downriver wasn't bad enough imagine using explosives and heavy equipment to dislodge log jams frequently created by logs and bundles. The lower Copper River almost became a repeat of the Kalum. There the loggers experimented with sending bundled logs down the lower river but the water license required to conduct operations on a continuing basis was refused. (A license had been obtained on the Kalum and was not about to be rescinded by the Provincial authorities of the day when the damage to fish habitat was revealed.) The same disregard for fish habitat also applied to the construction of the railroad and Highway 16, especially between Terrace and Prince Rupert. The further out of sight and out of mind the activity the worse the abuses.

The big push of logging roads into the major sub-basins of the Skeena began with the Kalum in 1950. Within eight years the roadwork extended all the way up the river and beyond into the Nass River watershed. The Zymoetz or Copper was not far behind. I have an old onionskin copy of a memo written by Terrace Game Warden D.B. Steuart in December, 1957 reporting that the Columbia Cellulose Corporation's road up the Copper extended only one half mile upstream from Highway 16 at the time.

Steelhead anglers were barely beginning to find their way beyond the Skeena/Copper confluence reaches. In 1968 when the original work on Skeena steelhead was being summarized by Provincial Government biologists the Copper River mainline logging road extended 20 miles upstream and the steelhead sport fishery was very much established. The same report that referenced the Copper River logging development indicated road access to the Kispiox extended 14 miles upstream in 1958, 40 miles a year later and 55 miles by 1966 (Taylor, 1968). It wasn't until the last decade of the century that the non-resident anglers began to make their presence felt in any significant way on the Copper. The first of the steelhead camps that became the nerve centers of the Kispiox fishery was developed shortly after Kispiox fish hit the international airwaves courtesy of the *Field & Stream* magazine revelations. Two other lodges followed in 1963 and 1965. The domination of the Kispiox angler population by non-residents, mostly American, was the hallmark of that fishery from its earliest days. That has never changed.

The Bulkley River was far more accessible than any of the other Skeena tributaries well before the post-WWII logging catalyzed so much activity elsewhere. The railroad and the highway were obviously major features in that respect. In spite of the head start in terms of development of the Bulkley corridor there is scant information to suggest that made any real difference in putting the river on the steelhead fishing radar before the sport fisheries elsewhere in the Skeena were developed. The Suskwa River was logged extensively in the decade of the 1970s. Once again the forest liquidators left their mark. Most of the Morice River was still virgin territory when John Fennelly's *Steelhead Paradise* experiences were unfolding between 1951 and 1955. The road from Houston to Morice Lake was constructed between 1954 and 1958. Roads into important steelhead-producing Morice sub-basins such at Thautil and Gosnell didn't come until long after. Unlike some of the other Skeena tributary fisheries, the Bulkley and Morice fisheries were resident-angler dominated at the outset. The non-resident competition that became a point of conflict with the locals emerged in the mid-1980s and grew steadily over the succeeding 15 years.

Before I dwell on the other two major Skeena steelhead tributaries not yet discussed in terms of access (Babine and Sustut) I should emphasize the fact there was no such thing as environmental protection planning or standards in the late 1940s through the 1960s when the first sustained rush of logging development was occurring in all the tributary watersheds downstream from Kispiox. We've seen already there was no Provincial Government fisheries presence anywhere west of Prince George until very near the end of that period. By the mid-1970s the environmental protection community inside and outside government had emerged and life became somewhat different for those whose purpose it was to convert wilderness into useful product. Therein lay the reason the latter-day history of resource development in the last of the great summer steelhead tributaries was much more convoluted and well documented than anything that went before.

Babine River was the second to last of the big-name Skeena steelhead tributaries to be visited by the logging industry. According to government forestry officials the first road access into the upper Babine River area wasn't developed until about 1966. The bridge that crosses the river just downstream from the DFO weir was constructed over the winter of 1971/72. The consummate historian of the Babine steelhead fishery, Bob Wickwire, provided the most complete information on the first arrival of anglers by road. Bob was deeply involved with the forestry people in the formative stages of access development to Babine River itself. Without his influence the bridge would have been built roughly one mile downstream of its present location. Bob knew full well how access at that point would have impacted his new Babine River Steelhead Lodge as well as the other lodge (Norlakes) that had commenced operation at almost the same time. An October 6, 1971 newspaper article Bob still has indicated a rough one-lane road could get trucks to the fisheries weir but regular use of that road by sport fishermen or their guides did not commence for at least another year or two. Bob added that creosote leaching from the original bridge pilings polluted the river and pervaded the surrounding air for years.

Prior to construction of the logging road and short spur from it to the fisheries weir the only options for anglers to reach Babine River were boat or float plane. As of 1956 the closest road and boat launch was at Smithers Landing. The fisheries weir just below the Nilkitkwa Lake outlet terminated boat access at that time and for many years after. It was 28 miles by water from the weir to Smithers Landing. At the other end of the Babine River the road that was constructed to deal with the 1951 rock slide was there but apparently rarely used because it was not maintained after the slide had been ameliorated. Fennelly (1963) wrote of hiring a taxi in Hazelton and traveling that road in 1955 but said it was "the most excruciatingly bad piece of road" he had ever attempted to travel in an ordinary automobile. His words brought to mind my first trip from Smithers to the Babine weir in early October, 1976. It was a four-hour white-knuckle trip through deeply rutted quagmire that somehow passed the test for logging-road status. My half-ton pickup got to the river only because climbing out of the ruts and turning around was impossible. Today a compact car will get you there in an hour and a half.

The evolution of the Babine fishery is instructive in its own right but also in terms of its connectivity to some of the other tributary fisheries that contributed to Skeena steelhead's position in the international sportfishing marketplace. Kispiox captured the early steelhead angling spotlight and developed its own evolutionary pathway. Interestingly, the Babine went quite a different direction even though there was fair overlap between the early anglers on both systems. The players that were central to the development of the Babine were not numerous. Some of the details of who they were and how they influenced so much of what happened there and elsewhere are worth putting on record.

The earliest of the Babine steelhead fishing activity was largely accounted for by one commercial operation. Norlakes Lodge located on the north east shore of Babine Lake about ten miles from the fisheries weir was the stepping off point. The first of the lodge buildings was constructed in either 1952 or 1953 depending on which source is referenced. Customers came in search of trout in the spring and summer and steelhead and coho in the fall. I have an early Norlakes Lodge brochure that includes a picture of one of the owners, Mac Anderson, with a 31-pound, 14-ounce Babine steelhead that won second prize in the 1954 *Field & Stream* magazine fishing contest. I also have a copy of a 1954 newsletter of San Francisco's Golden Gate Angling and Casting Club[24] that lists ten of its members who had already fished the Babine, although for trout rather than steelhead. In any case, Babine was on the map by then. The fall steelhead fishing remained the exclusive preserve of that first guide operation until well into the 1960s. Fennelly (1963) recounted daily floatplane excursions from Douglas Lodge on Stuart Lake to Fort Babine in early September, 1951 and renting an outboard motor equipped boat from the local Indians to travel to the outlet of Nilkitkwa Lake. From there he and his companion walked and waded downstream to the fisheries weir in search of trout. He wrote that he had heard rumors of steelhead in the area but never encountered any. On return to the area by float plane in 1961 he commented the only sign of encroaching civilization in the intervening decade was Norlakes Lodge. Fennelly and friends were hard after steelhead and camped at the fisheries weir site until cold weather prompted them to take up residence at Norlakes Lodge for the remainder of their stay. I have some personal letters exchanged between Cecil Brown, for a time one of the principles in Norlakes Lodge, and Fennelly dated 1964 and 1965 that evidence just how few the key players were and how strongly connected they were in the pioneer days of the Skeena steelhead sport fishery.

A journalist from San Francisco (more on him to follow) was a member of the first fishing party to ever travel down the Babine River to as far as the Nilkitkwa River confluence, a distance of about 2 miles. The date was November 2, 1955. The adventure was described in some detail in an article he wrote shortly afterward. He and his companions were Norlakes patrons. Standard fare of the day was to boat from the lodge to the weir and fish that immediate vicinity for steelhead and coho. Rainbow trout and Dolly Varden[25] were there in abundance but they weren't the preferred targets at that time of year. After several days of less than anticipated success one of the Norlakes proprietors (Tom Stewart) and a lodge

The road Right of Way to the proposed Babine River bridge site at the location known as "Lower Trail", one mile downstream from Norlakes Lodge. (August, 1987)

client ventured downstream to the Nilkitkwa confluence on foot. Their theory was the steelhead would be schooled up downstream from the first major tributary because the river was so low that year. They returned with tales of glory. The next day the other two Norlakes owners, Ejnar Madsen and Mac Anderson, arranged for two of the local Indians to take a boat from the weir downstream to the Nilkitkwa confluence. The boat carried all the required camping gear that couldn't be backpacked, as well as Anderson. At Nilkitkwa the three of them laid out a tent camp while a party of five Californians and Madsen hiked down river to join them. The writer described it as probably one of the wildest safaris the Canadian north woods had ever seen. The fishing had by those pioneer anglers over the following few days set the stage for development of the river-based lodge fishery to follow, albeit not on any sustained daily basis until about 14 years later. Those who know the upper Babine can appreciate what a task it must have been to get a heavily loaded, prop-driven, 20-foot, planked-hull boat through that water intact, especially at low river discharge. There was no discussion of the return voyage but it must have been even more impressive.

Wooden boats with outboard motors remained the only means of access to the Babine steelhead fishery through the late 1950s and 60s. The first rudimentary

lodge on the river, just downstream from the Nilkitkwa confluence, wasn't built until the mid-60s. Even then its use was limited to a single night of a one-week trip for anglers based at Norlakes on Babine Lake (Clegg and McMullen. 2010). Prop-driven boats and a foot trail along the right bank of the river downstream to the Nilkitkwa confluence were standard fare for the ever increasing numbers of anglers. They continued to arrive at Babine Lake by either road to Smithers Landing and boat thereafter or by float plane. It wasn't until 1972 or '73 that the forestry road to the Babine bridge precluded the necessity of the contorted combination of road and boat travel from Smithers to Smithers Landing to Norlakes Lodge to the fisheries weir to the river camp. A second lodge on the upper Babine (Wickwire's) slightly over six miles downstream from the fisheries weir, was under construction by 1967. A third along the helicopter-only access reaches of the middle section of the river, about 30 miles downstream from the weir, commenced operation in 1984. Its companion operation, seven miles upstream, opened its doors in 1988.[26]

The angler population of the Babine was almost exclusively non-residents initially. That was all about the original clients and their network centered in San Francisco. Non-resident domination has diminished somewhat although the guided-angler population that accounts for the large majority of the activity in all the best times and locations is still heavy to non-residents.

Forgive a bit more digression here but there is one piece of the Babine access history that I can't overlook. That deals with the logging-road access and bridge crossing proposal alluded to by Clegg and McMullen (2010). I first learned of the proposed crossing in a streamside conversation with the son of the Norlakes Steelhead Lodge builder, Karl Madsen, and one of his guide employees, Todd Stockner, during my tenth-annual

Silver Hilton, the furthest downstream of the three Babine River lodges. The photo was taken on August 11, 1987 when fixed-wing aircraft to the landing strip immediately behind the buildings was the primary mode of accessing the site.

The Sustut River looking toward the Skeena from a point mid-way between the Bear River confluence and the Skeena itself. The photo was taken in mid-September, 1991 when the upland areas were still in a relatively pristine state. The abandoned rail line was there on river right but only visible from the river in a few locations.

fishing trip to the Babine in 1985. I followed up the status of the proposal with an old friend and colleague who was the senior MOE fisheries authority in the Smithers office. I soon learned the bridge had been approved by MOE. I had serious trouble understanding how that could have occurred but I was in no position to do anything about it. My only recourse was to make two recommendations to try and salvage some semblance of a quality fishery following bridge construction. Foremost was to ensure there could be no jet boat launch opportunity at the bridge site. The other recommendation was to go to catch and release to try and minimize the impact of the buffalo hunters certain to descend as soon as the road to water's edge was completed. As fate would have it my colleague in Smithers became my boss in Nanaimo early in 1986. When his former position was posted I applied and won the competition. I assumed office in Smithers at the start of November and took on the Babine bridge issue as my highest priority. At that point a huge road right-of-way swath had been cleared to water's edge on one of the most productive runs on the upper river and one that was a major steelhead overwintering area. The contract for the bridge design was already in motion. The bridge site was exactly one mile downstream from Norlakes Lodge and the road leading to it a mere 1200 feet from its back door. Pierce and Debby Clegg were the new owners of Norlakes and were just through their first season on the

river. I had met them weeks earlier while on my annual fishing trip.

The cast of characters involved in the bridge dispute was substantially different than that described elsewhere. There were at least four more individuals who were pivotal in the strategy and process that ultimately saw the road and bridge proposal put to rest. One was Debby who, along with Pierce, spent many hours in my office being briefed on government process and communication lines. Another was Bob Wickwire who, at that point, had been guiding the Babine for 20 years. He was the one who brought grizzly bears into the equation. Bob had intimate knowledge of the entire Babine corridor and everything to be experienced along the way. He was astute enough to understand the public profile grizzlies had and how the Babine supporting cast could be expanded by emphasizing their contribution to the whitewater rafting and wildlife viewing constituency. The other two were Dave Narver (his name was at least mentioned), then the Director of the Province's Fisheries Program, and myself. Dr. Narver had worked for the Federal Government on the Babine sockeye stock in his early years as a fisheries professional. He was personally familiar with Babine steelhead from both his angling experiences while in the area and from his professional work examining their life history characteristics. The two of us clearly understood the value and profile of the Babine steelhead fishery and

The Sustut/Bear confluence as it appeared on September 23, 1989. The BC Rail crossing is clearly visible in the background. Bear River enters from river left on the downstream side of the trestle.

the importance of preserving it in as close to its natural state as possible.

Immediately following my arrival in Smithers I enlisted the assistance and influence of Dr. Narver in recommending to his headquarters counterparts in the Ministry of Forests that the entire bridge and logging access proposal be revisited. We are talking David and Goliath here. Just as the Province and steelhead had virtually no influence on DFO and sockeye, the forestry managers never allowed fish and wildlife interests to take priority over the quest for fiber. The prospect of a successful outcome was remote to say the least. The fact that the Smithers MOE office had already endorsed the proposal made a bad situation worse. Furthermore, there was absolutely no support from local anglers or the traditional sportfishing advocacy groups. Babine was steelhead mecca to them too but perceived as an opportunity denied by access limitations maintained for the exclusive benefit of guides and their high-roller foreign customers. Their chance had come and they weren't about to turn it down.

It took almost two years, an unprecedented amount of high-level discussion between the two Provincial Government agencies and steadily mounting public opposition to force decision-makers to do the right thing. The Cleggs were certainly a significant part of that but, had Dave Narver and I not launched the internal campaign to initiate and sustain pressure on the Ministry of Forests, the bridge would have been built before the 1987 fishing season. The quality of the Babine fishery would have been lost forever. Norlakes and Babine River Steelhead Lodge would have been finished just as they would have been 20 years earlier had Wickwire not intervened on the original bridge location. Killing the proposed bridge and decommissioning the road to it from its take-off point on the mainline logging road was anything but the one-man altruistic jihad it is made out to be elsewhere. The Smithers MOE staffer credited

by Clegg and McMullen wouldn't even qualify as a bit player on the Babine bridge stage.

The last Skeena tributary I'll discuss in the context of road access is the magnificent Sustut, in my opinion the prettiest of all the Skeena tributaries. That is, when I first saw it in 1972. It was a year when I was a newcomer working with the Province and headquartered in Victoria. They sent another rookie and myself to the Sustut to relieve two other Provincial employees who were partnered with DFO reps manning counting fences on the Sustut system The reason for the fisheries agency presence was a proposed hydro-electric development on the Skeena just upstream from the Babine River confluence. The hydro proponents knew they would never be able to dam the Skeena below the sockeye-rich Babine but it was postulated the fisheries values in systems beyond Babine would not be much of an impediment. We were helicoptered in to our respective base camps. My partner drew the lower camp on the Bear and I the upper, right in the middle of Fennelly's steelhead paradise at the confluence of the Sustut and Johanson. I thought I had died and gone to heaven.

The details of the time spent in the camps and the fish information collected was entirely secondary to what we experienced on September 28, the day we broke the camps down and departed for Smithers. As the helicopter circled to land at the Bear River camp we could plainly see an entire side hill across which BC Rail was constructing the rail bed for the extension of its line to Dease Lake had collapsed into the river, almost completely blocking the channel. A large Caterpillar tractor was in the middle of the slump. This was literally the bullseye of the richest chinook spawning habitat in the entire Skeena watershed and only days after the peak of spawning. MOE staff counted more than 3,000 steelhead (yes, that's right!) spawning in that immediate vicinity in the spring of 1971. The slide catalyzed a major investigation of the rail-construction procedures and a flurry of boardroom exchanges at the executive levels of two governments and the railway. In the end no charges were laid. Some minor concessions were made on the part of the railway's contractors but the construction continued. Natural forces were left to undo the mess left by the slide. The railway eventually crossed the mainstem Sustut immediately upstream from the Bear confluence, continued on down the Sustut and then turned up the Skeena. Five years later it became clear the railway construction and maintenance costs would never be offset by the promised mining development revenues and the railway was abandoned. I rank the BC Rail Dease Lake extension project as the single greatest environmental atrocity British Columbia has ever seen.

The Sustut steelhead fishery was changed forever by the access created by the rail line. First it was the construction crews who knew no boundaries when it came to fishing. It was impossible to police them in such a remote location. They were responsible for the

The original modes of access to the lower Sustut River steelhead lodges – fixed wing or rotary aircraft to air strips on the Skeena above Sustut (abandoned following the 1970s BC Rail debacle) and home-built speeders from there back to the lodges (September 23, 1989 photos) or float planes direct to the Sustut River itself.

entire Sustut from the Bear confluence upstream being permanently closed to fishing in 1973. Next came the adoption of the abandoned rail grade as a personal highway for an enterprising member of the Bear Lake Indian community. He developed a tidy little business using his own home-built speeder to transport anglers from their chartered float-plane terminus on Bear Lake down to the Bear/Sustut confluence. For several years in the late 1980s and 1990s some adventuresome entrepreneurs from Coeur d'Alene, Idaho flew groups of their friends into Bear Lake from Smithers at weekly intervals during the chinook salmon run. From there they traveled by speeder to a large camp set up at the Bear/Sustut confluence. They took their possession limits of everything they could transport and sometimes more and ferried them back for storage in freezers at the airport

in Smithers until they departed for home. I frequently heard about happenings from my next door neighbor who was the senior engineer for the airline involved. The tremendous Dolly Varden population that the fisheries crews encountered in the Bear/Sustut confluence area in 1972 diminished quickly at the hands of those who descended on that area and frequently discarded them while targeting chinook and the ever diminishing supply of early run timing steelhead (most of them likely bound for the upper Sustut area). Utilization of the abandoned rail line didn't end at the Bear/Sustut confluence. The two angling guide lodges that sprang to life on the lower Sustut River in the 1980s also became dependent on home-built speeders to get their clients to and from one of the abandoned air strips left over from the railway construction days. That was far less hazardous than the original business of float planes on the river. The abandoned BC Rail line came back to haunt the Sustut again in the mid-1990s. At that time the timber supply for high-tech sawmills in far-off Prince George that could eat a forest a day was exhausted. Jobs were at risk. All of a sudden Sustut timber was in demand. The rail line was refurbished to log haul standards and the onslaught began. Logging base camps were built and serviced by the upgraded rail line. Road networks radiated out from there. The lower Sustut was bridged half way between the Bear and the Skeena and the landscape forever altered. They're done with it for now but the fat lady isn't singing yet. Thankfully the railway (industrial use only) and aircraft will likely remain the only means of getting to the river. The current logging reprieve is all about the here and now mountain pine beetle infestations closer to Prince George and all the other mill sites in the central interior of the Province. The massive areas now affected

The upper Sustut River weir on August 26, 1996. The Omineca Mining Road can be seen in the background at center left. The weir at this site, approximately 2 miles downstream from Fennelly's revered Junction Pool, has been used annually since 1996 to count steelhead bound for Sustut and Johanson lakes.

Sustut Lake during a March 1999 radio-telemetry flight. At 56.35 north latitude and 4245 feet above sea level it isn't a very hospitable place for man and fish in winter.

command the enlistment of every available piece of road-building and logging machinery to deliver those trees so they can be sliced and diced before their relatively short merchantable life expires.

The upper Sustut system also succumbed to road access. This time it was mining. A road known as the Omineca Mining Road was extended further and further northwest from Fort St. James in the 1960s and early 1970s. Upgrading continued along with mining exploration and development beyond Sustut and Johanson lakes. By the mid-1980s there was regular vehicle traffic into the area and ten years later one could drive a car right to the upper Sustut River itself. Fishing had not been permitted anywhere beyond the Bear confluence since 1973 but that was no deterrent to First Nations members who descended on the area on a regular basis as soon as the road would take them there. There have since been some testy encounters during periods when salmon and steelhead were being enumerated at the weir on the Sustut. Of interest here is the reference of Gottesfeld and Rabnett (2008) to a 1948 report of the Skeena River Salmon Investigation which allegedly stated the Gitxsans maintained a fishing camp on the west bank of the outlet of Sustut Lake and harvested steelhead with gill nets in winter. I searched out that report at the Pacific Biological Station Library and found nary a word relating to the upper Sustut system. The First Nations people who we commonly encountered in that area in the 1980s and 1990s did not hail from the Skeena watershed and therefore were not Gitxsans. Other than the occasional reference to Indians acting as fishing guides as part of the Driftwood Lodge undertakings there was never the slightest hint of any Indian presence in these areas in any of the records I was able to obtain from the

anglers and pilots who frequented those areas from 1955 onward. That is awfully tough country to be maintaining a camp for the purpose of harvesting steelhead under that much snow and ice. Bear Lake was the closest settlement of any description. Even by aircraft it is more than 40 miles through rugged mountainous terrain between there and Sustut Lake. One can't help but wonder how anyone would have managed to get in there packing gill nets in days before aircraft and roads arrived. The fact that steelhead were much more readily available in the Bear River, a short distance away from historic Fort Connoly and the small Indian community that existed in that area before and since, only adds to the list of unanswered questions.

The logging-access story in the Skeena watershed will never be complete until the last merchantable log falls victim to a mechanical harvester. As goes the mountain pine beetle infestation so goes the Skeena logging. When the current rush to remove afflicted timber elsewhere runs its course we can be sure there will be renewed interest in the non-pine forests of the Skeena. The road systems that now cross the Babine at its confluence with the Skeena and the Skeena itself many miles upstream have opened up territory thought safe short years ago. Those roads will be longer. The hiatus up Sustut way will end. Expect to be able to drive to places heretofore accessible to only the most adventurous with pockets deep enough to charter helicopters. Steelhead will not be beneficiaries. Call up Google Earth and have a tour around the Babine, Sustut or upper Skeena country to see where we've arrived. While you're at it pay particular attention to that abandoned BC Rail line and the scars that remain 30 years after.

Next up in the steelhead fishing access discussion is aircraft. Their employment came at the same time as the post-war logging business went into overdrive. Float planes preceded helicopters by a good number of

Sustut pioneers (left to right) Charles McDermand, Mac Anderson and Ed Neal waiting out an October 5-6, 1956 snow storm at Johanson Lake. The float plane from Bear Lake Lodge picked them up later on October 6. Photo courtesy of Ed Neal.

years but their utilization for steelhead fishing purposes was much less further ahead. Float planes were relatively cheap and widely available but, of course, were only useful in situations that involved suitable landing and take-off sites. Generally speaking that meant lakes. I've already spoken about Babine. The Sustut and Johanson rivers where the best fishing could be found at the headwater lake outlets and downstream to the confluence of the two were the first to be highlighted. The initial exposure came from the same people who were on the ground floor of the Babine fishery. It occurred in the same year. A cherished collection of correspondence and photographs of early float-plane excursions into the upper Sustut country in 1955 and 1956 from Ed Neal, the outdoor columnist of the day for the *San Francisco News*, told the story. His accounts of those trips and the copies of his published daily columns reporting his party's fishing success make for gripping reading. Neal's fishing partners in 1955 were Norlakes co-owner Mac Anderson and Bob Engle. The latter was Anderson's partner in Driftwood Lodge constructed on the shores of Bear Lake by Anderson, his father and local Indians earlier that same year. Neal's inaugural visit to Driftwood Lodge was all about marketing the new hunting and fishing outpost

to the upper echelon of the well-established California outdoorsman community. The lodge served as the float-plane base camp for what can reasonably be assumed to be the first sustained steelhead sportfishing activity in the Sustut drainage.

Another valued piece of memorabilia is a 20-minute 16mm film ("Sportsmen's Paradise") of early fishing excursions out of Driftwood Lodge. That footage was professionally prepared and sponsored by Seagram's (as in whiskey). It begins with what was termed a warm-up for the real fishing to come. The warm-up was a fat 1- or 2-pound rainbow trout on every cast only minutes away in small outboard-driven boats from a very impressive lodge facility located on Stuart Lake near the Tachie River inlet. I could not determine the name of the lodge from the film but it may have been Douglas Lodge mentioned earlier in the context of Fennelly's original trips to Babine. The film's narrator stated it was a two-hour trip by float plane from the Stuart Lake base to Driftwood Lodge on Bear Lake. The host for the fishermen and film crew was Doug Robertson who apparently also had an interest in Driftwood Lodge. There is no date on the film but Mac Anderson was never mentioned suggesting it was shot after 1957, the year he drowned in Bear

River. Robertson flew the anglers being filmed from Bear Lake to the Sustut/Bear confluence in a helicopter. The Seagram's footage also covered both helicopter and float-plane flights from the Driftwood Lodge base to the Sustut Lake outlet after which Robertson helicoptered the crew around all the same areas first described by Ed Neal and later by John Fennelly. As stated previously, Neal was also a Driftwood Lodge patron but he had been deposited at Johanson Lake by float plane and walked downriver to the preferred fishing areas.

Neither of the two trips described by Fennelly in his 1963 *Steelhead Paradise* made mention of helicopters. In both 1959 and 1963 he and his party used float planes to arrive at Sustut Lake and move back and forth between Sustut and Johanson lakes. They walked from their camp at Sustut Lake to a second camp at the Sustut/Johanson confluence. Buzz Fiorini, a Seattle-based entrepreneur with ties to Driftwood Lodge, served as a guide/outfitter for the Fennelly party in both years. Fiorini made all the arrangements to accommodate Fennelly. He ferried full camp equipment and provisions from Driftwood Lodge to Sustut Lake in his own float-equipped Cessna. In 1988 Fiorini kindly forwarded copies of his personal photographs of the 1963 Fennelly trip to the Smithers MOE office. (*See page 125*)

Whereas helicopters had been used for a variety of non-fish—related purposes in and around the Skeena watershed since the early 1950s and were reported to have been used to count spawning salmon in 1956, the Driftwood Lodge excursions highlighted in the Seagram's film probably represented the first time they were used to guide steelhead fishermen. The date cannot be determined precisely at this point but it was probably after 1963. Otherwise Fennelly and others who were guided on the upper Sustut system would have been using them.

Final comments on the early Sustut days: Doug Robertson was the first of the guides on the lower Sustut. He built what is now Suskeena Lodge in 1969. Helicopters provided the only access to the lodge in the short period between its construction and the arrival of the railway. Lastly, during the 1972 fisheries investigations alluded to previously, I saw no evidence of any angler activity in the Sustut/Johanson area.

Aircraft use to transport steelhead anglers expanded to new frontiers as the Skeena steelhead sport fishery developed but disappeared in the areas where it all began. Following the early years (late 1980s) of the lower Babine lodge operation, when fixed-wing aircraft were utilized, helicopters became the access option of choice. The angling closure on the upper Sustut system terminated any airplane facilitated fishing there. Logging roads into the upper Babine replaced the need for float planes. A Terrace-based lodge added the upper Copper to the heli-fishing list in the mid-80s and a guide from Smithers followed suit in the early 90s. Kluatantan is another delicate little stream now subject to regular commercial use. Apart from the commercial operations

the past 15 years has seen a steady increase in the number of private individuals chartering helicopters to deposit and/or retrieve them on excursions into both Babine and Copper rivers and occasionally the upper Skeena itself. The lowermost lodge on the Sustut River was probably the last operation to utilize float planes to any extent but only briefly between its construction in the early 80s and the owners' switch to fixed-wing aircraft strips and speeders and, eventually to conventional vehicles. The speeders used by both the Sustut operations are now retired thanks to the road system developed following the arrival of the loggers.

Before I move on to later developments in the steelhead fishing access business I want to make mention of messages that scream at me from the pages of so much of the early sportfishing history material I researched in preparing this book. This seems an appropriate place to do that. The abundance of fish and game in the upper Skeena country was staggering by anything imaginable today. Those who were among the first to fish Babine's Rainbow Alley and the weir area of the river below spoke to catching 50 trout on days that started mid-morning and ended mid-afternoon. The fish were much larger then. Dolly Varden were far less sought after but equally abundant in the upper end of the Babine River. The Sustut anywhere near the Bear confluence was the same. Dollys were huge by present standards. There were accounts of individual anglers catching 30 coho in a day on the Babine. Coho were not only abundant and commonly caught in the Bear River but they were easily found spawning in Bear Lake inlet streams. In many days I spent fishing the Babine and Sustut rivers between 1976 and 2009 I can count on one hand the number of coho I caught. My angling diary entries on the Babine in 1976 show there were still lots of 1-pound rainbow in the weir vicinity at the time but nothing like what had been there years before a road. I never saw a single 2-pound fish, let alone the common 3-pounders spoken of 20 years earlier. By 1950s standards Dollys were all but absent anywhere near the weir and downstream too. Commercial fisheries and/or habitat degradation were not the culprits. The Morice fishing described by Fennelly was every bit as amazing as Babine. Rainbow, early steelhead and Dollys were there in abundance that will never be seen again. All the early records for the upper Sustut and Johanson were consistent. They spoke of schools of steelhead circling about the lower bays of those lakes and fish moving on into the main body of the lakes, replaced daily by new arrivals from downstream. Remember the file note about the 3000 steelhead spawners observed in Bear River in 1971? Then were the second-hand reports of Fennelly stemming from conversations with Fisheries Officers who told him there were rivers beyond Babine and Sustut that had far more steelhead than either of those. One officer stated he had seen large schools of steelhead in one of them. It could only have been Kluatantan, a small unproductive river not unlike the upper Sustut, lake headed and capable of sustaining overwintering steelhead. My money says there hasn't been more than a few dozen steelhead and even less coho in that pretty little stream for at least 20 years. That situation had nothing to do with angling either.

There is a perplexing side to those early written accounts of anglers, guides, pilots and anyone else who wouldn't pass today's test as a qualified professional. Their records carry no weight in either the fisheries-management boardrooms or the courtrooms of the land. Contrast that with the oral history of the First Nations community which is frequently accepted as sacrosanct in either of those forums. I mean no disrespect to First Nations people but the rules that apply to them are fundamentally different than those applied to anyone else, especially lowly sport fishermen.

Jet boats are next on the list of access developments. We can thank logging and road building for the first major round of pushing back the frontier for Skeena steelhead chasers. The introduction of jet units for outboard motors was round two. I corresponded with the outboard jet manufacturers and patent holders to try and establish the year when the jets arrived in Skeena country. Company president and inventor Dick Stallman advised their first units were produced in 1960 but they weren't commercially sold until 1962. The first river they appeared on was Oregon's Rogue that same year. The early experiments with their application are well described by Arman and Wooldridge (1982). Stallman said the earliest jet units wouldn't have been sold in Canada until at least the mid-1960s. Once again any uncertainty was put to rest by Bob Wickwire. Bob purchased his first jet unit directly from Stallman in the spring of 1966, the year before he started building Babine River Steelhead Lodge. He also said Ejnar Madsen had a jet unit one year earlier, although it was not used on the river on a regular basis until the Norlakes steelhead camp near the Nilkitkwa River confluence began full-time operation in 1967. Babine was the first of the Skeena tributaries but not the first river in the province to see this innovation. Personal correspondence with Dean River guiding pioneer Rob Stewart indicated his father's camp began using Dick Stallman's jets no later than 1964 and all their 50 HP Mercury-driven riverboats were jet equipped by 1965.

In thirty years, about five steelhead generations, the sport fishery on all the larger Skeena tributaries and the mainstem Skeena itself was revolutionized by jet boats. It wasn't just the fact that they facilitated access to areas previously untouched or only lightly so. Rather, they increased the efficiency of anyone who owned them. Think about the historic gill-net fishery at the mouth of the Skeena and how it changed dramatically with the conversion from sails and oars to gasoline engines. This was no different. Miles of river could be covered and anglers deposited on the best side of the best pieces of steelhead holding water every day of a season. An angling population once comprised of those who could only drive to specific access points and walk from there to fish not more than a few locations on any given day was progressively dominated by one that put new and relentless pressure on every piece of steelhead holding water on every day water conditions suited. The commercial fishery closed for several days each week for the past 50 years and never opened at all in some years. The prime sportfishing season never closed regardless of the strength of the steelhead return. Of course not all the Skeena tributaries are large enough or navigable enough to accommodate jet boats. Those that aren't see flotillas of drift-craft such as never before. Some rivers, notably the Bulkley and Morice and, during the best times, even Babine, see waves of both. The only steelhead tributaries of consequence that aren't subjected to relentless boat traffic are too small or too access limited to feel the squeeze. That list would include Suskwa, Kitseguecla, and Kitwanga. Arguably, none of them support enough steelhead to invite much angling interest even if they weren't access limited. A few canyon sections of the Copper and Kalum rivers exempt them as well but anglers are now all over the reaches above and below.

For most of its sportfishing history Mother Skeena was relatively lightly fished other than along the bars between Terrace and the head of tide. There too, however, power boats became ever more frequent all through the late 1980s and 1990s. A burgeoning guiding industry had much to do with escalating effort there. Today's ever more aggressive boating fraternity is reaching out and focusing steadily, increasing pressure on obvious migration corridors and tributary confluence areas all along the Skeena from Terrace to Kispiox. Even the uppermost reaches of the Skeena around the Sustut confluence and beyond are now in anglers' crosshairs. Guides and boats frequent all the best places in September and early October whenever mainstem flows are suitable. Virtually no one runs the wooden boats with 40 or 50 HP outboards that initiated the jet-boat era. Now there is an industry cranking out custom-made aluminum jet boats ever more capable of negotiating whatever flows might be encountered. Triple-digit horsepower outboards or inboard equivalents of pick-up truck motors are commonplace. There is no end in sight and no regulatory mechanism to control or limit any of that. There is no government will to try and address it either. Seldom considered in the fact diminishing supplies of fish are easily masked when increased angler efficiency results in a higher and higher proportion of those present being caught. Commercial and recreational fisheries share that feature equally. The difference is the number of commercial-fishing vessels has been capped for many years.

The bottom line on access is it took not more than 30-40 years for anglers to be able to reach every piece of steelhead-bearing water in every Skeena tributary. River after river that never saw an angler before the greybeards among us were born is now on the fast-food menu. We're

Steelhead Paradise author John Fennelly approaching Fiorini's Cessna on Sustut Lake.

a long way past the time when a steelhead passing the last commercial gill net or one deployed near a First Nations community lived unmolested for the rest of its freshwater residence. Seldom considered is the additional cost to the resource that evolutionary pathway exacted. The search for new frontiers is long over. All that remains is the inevitable competition for time and space in the conquered territory.

There is one more feature of the changing steelhead fishing landscape that has had as much bearing on angling traffic and distribution and angler efficiency as roads, helicopters and jet boats ever did. I'm talking www here. The internet offers up instant updates on water and weather conditions, fish supply, latest and greatest equipment and techniques, where when and how to "get 'em", who to hire to guarantee success, yada, yada, yada. A digital equivalent of a fishing Super Store provides up-to-the-minute fishing reports on rivers from Smithers to Prince Rupert and the news and availability on anything between rubber worms and riparian real estate to both neophytes and veterans. Nothing is left to chance or self discovery any more. Odds have been shortened dramatically. What took years for an entry-level angler to learn a generation ago is mere mouse clicks away. No apprenticeship necessary. Fish porn proliferates at a steadily accelerating pace on bulletin boards, blogs and YouTube. Addicts inflate their egos with kiss-and-tell and hero worshippers thrive on their every word and video clip. Then, when they show up and find competition around every bend of the river, they complain about crowding. In the near term the internet may be the best thing that ever happened in the eyes of many fishermen. They'll learn otherwise in the longer term as the object of their affection bears the cost.

Fennelly with a fish taken at the infamous Junction Pool (Sustut/Johanson confluence).

Chapter 20
OFFENSE AND DEFENSE

Regulations that govern sport fisheries demonstrate a consistent pattern. They are the stuff of rear-view mirrors. In the case of the Skeena the progression of restrictions surrounding where, when and how steelhead could be harvested and what the daily, possession and seasonal catch limits were paralleled the development of access. There was no such thing as anticipation nor was there ever a climate or appetite for adjusting regulations in advance of the inevitable opening up of the country. The defense was always developed after the offense necessitated it.

When sportfishing regulations in the Province of BC first appeared in 1931 the Skeena country was not treated any differently than any other part of the province. All streams were closed to fishing from November 15 until May 23 and the catch limit for steelhead was the same as it was for any other "trout" over 8" long—15 fish per day! There was no season limit. Residents of BC didn't even require a fishing license until 1938 and only if they fished south of 52 degrees north latitude (the Skeena watershed is well north of that boundary). Such liberal regulations made no difference given the fact there was virtually no one fishing for steelhead anywhere in the Skeena at the time. In 1941 the November through May closure was rescinded but the catch and size limits remained. One year later a three-fish daily catch limit for steelhead was imposed but it took until 1946 for a possession limit of three days' catch limit to arrive. This would have been around the time steelhead angling in the Skeena was entering its discovery phase. In the 1945-46 regulations the Bulkley and Lakelse rivers were again closed to fishing between November 15 and May 23. These measures likely arrived as a result of the information being compiled by the Fisheries Research Board scientists who were very active at the time studying sockeye at both Lakelse Lake and Moricetown (the Skeena River Salmon Investigations described earlier).

An annual limit of 40 steelhead was instituted in 1958. The steelhead fishery was obviously well known by then and the inevitable restrictions that accompanied its development kept on coming. The steelhead license or punchcard that became the basis for the steelhead angler questionnaire which provided the ongoing angling effort and catch statistics came into effect in 1966 after three years of preliminary experimentation. In 1967 the 3/day catch limit was reduced to 2/day although the three-day possession limit remained until 1976 when it was dropped to two. The annual limit for steelhead became 20 in 1974 but two 20-fish punchcards could still be purchased until 1975. Other notable measures of those earlier years included no angling from boats on the Kispiox River or on the Bulkley at Moricetown (1961), roe bans on Kispiox and Morice (1956) and later Babine (1970) and fly-fishing-only upstream from the Babine weir (1970). Winter angling closures that had been imposed on the Bulkley and Lakelse disappeared by the mid-1950s. Others were imposed on the upper Morice (1965), the Babine (1970) and the upper Zymoetz (1971).

As knowledge of Skeena steelhead and steelhead fishing activity accumulated through investigations supported by the early Salmonid Enhancement Program the volume and complexity of the steelhead sportfishing regulations increased commensurately. The details of the river-and time-specific rules around daily, possession and seasonal catch limits that descended over the space of about two steelhead generations are secondary to the broader measures that came in the decade of the 1990s. That was the decade that began with three successive years of some of the lowest ever returns of Skeena summer steelhead as estimated from test fishery catches. It also marked the first time ever that in-season measures were taken to try and connect steelhead abundance and angling harvest. Anglers were already voluntarily releasing a large majority of their total steelhead catch by then but conservation and the political optics of the day demanded more. These were the Skeena Watershed Committee days when reducing harvest by commercial and First Nations fishermen was perceived to be nothing more than reallocation of their rights to steelhead to undeserving anglers.

The end point of the in-season measures that began with a Fisheries Public Notice (the legal instrument for delivery) issued August 1, 1991 was the adoption of catch and release as a license year opening measure under the formal BC Sport Fishing Regulations which came into effect on April 1, 1997. I dealt with some of the issues around that business earlier. At that point there was nothing left for Skeena steelhead anglers or MOE to give. The sport fishery was regulated on a single barbless hook, artificial lure, zero harvest basis and every tributary fishery was closed from January 1 through June 15. That suite of restrictions remains the most conservative, forward-looking steelhead sportfishery management regime anywhere in the animal's North American range. I'm proud to have been part of that.

Besides the lingering displeasure among a small number of mostly Bulkley Valley resident anglers over the fact there is no longer any connection between abundance and harvest there is more to the steelhead catch-and-release story. Precise quantification is impossible so, like so many other elements of fisheries management, interpretations tend to be a matter of religious persuasion as much as anything else. I'll try and explain.

The most striking feature of the steelhead catch-and-release era in the Skeena tributaries, as well as everywhere else in British Columbia, was the immediate escalation in the estimated catches derived from the long-standing mailed survey questionnaires sent to anglers following the conclusion of the license year. Some of that is related to a well-understood problem inherent in questionnaire surveys. The technical term is positive response bias and it has been well documented a number of times in BC. For background and examples there are two excellent reports available (De Gisi, 1999 and Ahrens, 2006). Successful steelhead anglers responding to questionnaires at a higher rate than unsuccessful anglers is the source of the bias and inflated catch estimates. Multiple captures of individual fish also serves to create the illusion of more fish present than there actually are. Anglers who embellish their report of how many fish they caught increase the bias. (I love that old outdoor writer Ed Zern's words, "fishermen are born honest, but they get over it.") There are several situations in southern BC where streams under heavy fishing pressure end up with catch estimates that far exceed the most liberal estimate of the steelhead population that could have been present. How much of the catch inflation is due to questionnaire response bias and how much due to repeat captures of the same fish is impossible to determine. Taken without qualification the trends in estimated steelhead catch create the illusion of expanding steelhead populations. Aggravating that is the steady increase in angling efficiency that results in an increasing proportion of the total fish available being caught one or more times. Boats are a big part of that. There are commonalities between the published figures on commercial catches of steelhead and those for the sport catch accept that the bias for the latter is in the opposite direction. In both cases the qualifications that should be applied when publishing the figures aren't.

The rebound in steelhead abundance and the increased catch rates enjoyed by the angling community immediately following the coho conservation measures imposed in 1998 had a very clear relationship with the virtual elimination of commercial fishing. I don't think anyone would argue that year and every other one with reduced commercial-fishing pressure produced similar results. What wasn't and still isn't credited for improving the fishing in any of those years is the catch-and-release regulations. The science community, the armchair biologists and all the biostitutes out there seem unable to agree on the business of whether or not more steelhead spawners ever produced or ever will produce more recruits. Federal people are quick to seize credit for the slightest evidence of coho stocks rebounding pursuant to the 1998 measures but when was the last time anyone acknowledged steelhead in the same context? That would be an admission there was a steelhead conservation problem. Don't hold your breath. One thing is certain. The steelhead spawning populations between 1991 and 1997 were significantly larger than they would have been if a kill fishery had remained in place. That result came not just from terminating recreational harvest but also from the markedly reduced fishing pressure that followed implementation of catch and release.[27] Continuation of the zero-harvest policy is the best possible scenario for a sportfishing community dominated by those abhorred at the thought of killing a wild steelhead. Given that the steelhead sportfishery management objective is to maximize the encounter rate what better way to achieve it than to eliminate as much mortality as possible?

Chapter 21
SUPPLY AND DEMAND

ood fishing is not always good news. The years 1984, '85 and '86 saw some of the highest ever returns of summer steelhead to the Skeena River. Those years were unprecedented in the life of the test fishery to that point in its history. Despite the heavy toll taken by the river mouth net fishery there were still lots of steelhead getting past to support the sport fishery upstream. These were the years that benefitted from the highest steelhead smolt to adult survivals experienced in decades all along the Pacific. Good fishing quickly dulled the memory of those who had been around for any length of time. Newer arrivals didn't know any better. Three successive years was all it took to catalyze an explosion of interest in guiding. Those already in the business expanded while first-time applicants for guide licenses lined up to capitalize on this wonderful new opportunity to partake of a perceived lucrative green industry. Advertisements and promotional literature extolling the virtues of Skeena flooded the sportfishing networks. There were no limitations on entry to the guiding business other than having to be of legal age (19), a BC resident, free of any fish-or wildlife-related contravention of regulations and vaguely familiar with the sportfishing regulations. Caution was never in anyone's thoughts.

The rapid expansion of guiding became a major focus of local residents who were displeased with the competition they began to encounter in their favored haunts. Rumblings of discontent over the influx of non-guided non-resident anglers began to surface. Residents demanded priority. Guides demanded insulation from foreigners who didn't need or want to be guided. The tourism sector that relied on those same foreign anglers demanded their piece of the pie be protected. Then there was the ubiquitous perception that many of the foreigners were guiding illegally. No one was happy and everyone looked to government to fix their problem. In the classic embodiment of the cliché be careful what you wish for MOE took bold steps to do exactly that. That was the beginning of the process that culminated in the classified-waters legislation that came into effect in 1990. Call it demand management.

If there is any subject anglers will get exercised about above all else it is someone messing with their fishing opportunity. Even the net fisheries in the Skeena River approaches removing half the steelhead run in a poor return year never generated the passion demonstrated by anglers who demanded government fix the angling conflict problems but stay out of their face and their pocket. To use another well worn but perfectly appropriate cliché, everyone wanted to go to heaven but no one wanted to die.

The dominant issues of the 1988 through 1990 period, when the circular debates around managing steelhead angling effort were all-consuming, were crowding and deterioration of the quality of the fishing experience. Unfortunately those at the center of the debates could never agree on definitions or boundaries around either of those concepts. None of the three groups of anglers involved—residents, guides and non-guided non residents—accepted any responsibility for contributing to perceived problems. Residents blamed guides and non-guided foreigners. Guides blamed all the foreigners that weren't their clients for stealing their business opportunities. The foreigners blamed the guides, many of whom had far less experience on the rivers than they had. The excellent fishing of the years leading into the debates dominated consciousness. Expectations were high. Volumes of material, including two major discussion papers, extensive notes from exhaustive public meetings, written submissions and cards and letters from near and far, had to be weighed and incorporated into the decision-making process. The product that emerged, legislation known as the Angling and Scientific Collection Regulations, established a benchmark, but for angling-guide activity only. In spite of the firm convictions of so many vocal participants in the processes leading to the legislation there was no agreement on limiting the effort of any of the other licensee groups, not even the much maligned foreign, non-guided anglers. The strategy was to freeze guiding at not more than the average of the three years any existing guide had reported used in the period leading up to the impending restrictions. No new licenses would be issued and no expansion of the existing licensed operations would be allowed. A reasonable system of monitoring was in place to assess the results of the new rules.

The limitation of commercial sportfishing activity that was intended with implementation of the new regulations in 1990 was sound in principle but short on reality. The windfall profits for guides who were grandfathered rod-day quotas and the instant wealth created by those quotas were predictable, although no one really appreciated how valuable the quotas would become. Questions are still asked about why a tiny minority should have profited so handsomely at the expense of the majority? The grandfathering process itself was where the implementation of the well-intentioned regulations failed miserably. The most glaring examples were the Bulkley and lower Skeena rivers which had been at the center of the angst that precipitated the classified-waters legislation. There were others that were less obvious at the time but predicted to become contentious. That list included the Kispiox, the Zymoetz and the Babine.

MOE's statutory authority for issuing angling-guide licenses and their accompanying rod-day quotas made serious errors in application of his discretion when he assigned those quotas. Not only did he use the highest year rather than the average of the three reference years but he used the flimsiest of evidence to generate numbers which became carved in stone. In those cases the mandatory reports from guides on daily, water-specific guiding activity that were supposed to be the basis for establishing rod-day quotas were absent or highly deficient. Instead of placing any responsibility on delinquent guides to provide acceptable evidence of their level of activity the statutory authority arbitrarily assigned numbers he deemed acceptable. Advice from informed staff about the dangers of issuing unrealistic and indefensible rod-day quotas was brushed aside on the basis the initial quotas were readily adjustable through the "use it or lose it" provisions of the new legislations. Worst fears were realized. The delinquent and/or unscrupulous guides were rewarded with quotas substantially in excess of any previous level of guiding activity and the promised adjustment based on the "use it or lose it" clause in the regulations never occurred. In a very few years all those overzealous rod-day allocations became redistributed among existing licensees who had small quotas initially or to new guides who purchased the quotas from the original owners and promptly put them to use with real business plans. The analogy between the once-sanctioned practice of old and decrepit commercial-fishing vessels being bought up and their tonnages pyramided and applied to large, new, technologically sophisticated vessels with fishing power that vastly outstripped the cumulative total of the vessels replaced is striking. The level of guiding activity was very substantially increased, especially on those two rivers nearest and dearest to the resident-angler community. To this day there has never been a single rod day removed from any of the river-specific rod-day quotas assigned to guides in the 1990 processes.

While all the demand-management business was unfolding steelhead abundance went south. No sooner had the ink dried on the new regulations and the initial implementation proceeded than the fishing activity it was premised on began to evaporate. Angling demand was eclipsed by fish supply. All the attention of the managers shifted away from peace in the angling valley to the Palestinians versus Israelis conflict at the mouth of the Skeena. The irony of the preoccupation with fishing while fish were disappearing was lost on most people at the time.

The angling-demand-management fish-supply oscillations lived on through the remainder of the 1990s and are still with us today. All the original debates around what constitutes a quality angling experience, what constitutes crowding, who contributes how much, what measures should be implemented, who is responsible for administering them and how they will be evaluated linger on. Processes intended to address those points have consumed millions of dollars in direct and indirect costs and inordinate amounts of time and energy. The similarities between them and, for example, the Skeena Watershed Committee and all its spinoffs are quite remarkable. To those of us fully conversant with the various river fisheries and closest to the art of the possible in terms of regulations the course corrections that could have and should have been applied in the first five or so years following the classified-waters legislation were lost in the same institutional inertia that befell virtually all fisheries issues then and since.

Those with a masochistic bent or in need of more background on what I'm referring to can find it readily enough.[28] Fish supply over the same period has been up and down depending on the vagaries of environment and commercial-fishery impacts. New strategies to address some of the angler-demand circumstances have been recommended and accepted by government but promises of implementation have proven to be worthless.[29] The climate within the current Provincial Government is unaltered from the one that has pervaded the past 20 years of Skeena steelhead management. If there is a hint of controversy the prescription is process. Few have the resources and stamina to endure the expectations of the architects. Too often the issues that create process are diluted beyond recognition long before they are addressed.

The stark reality is the only thing that has changed in 20 years of managing angling on the blue-ribbon steelhead waters of the Skeena is the price of admission, especially for a non-resident angler. The lower Skeena is as crowded with guided and non-guided non-residents as it ever was, the residents are no less squeezed and illegal guiding allegations are still rampant. The prime weeks on the Bulkley have been far more crowded and competitive in the past five years than they ever were in the first five of the classified-waters era. A fly-fishing school became another full-fledged guiding operation. The angler population that once walked the Bulkley's bars has been largely replaced by jet boats and float boats but no one wants to address the difference between 100 pedestrians and 100 boaters. The Kispiox is still dominated by non-guided non-residents and the valley people are as divided as they ever were over the definition of guiding and who is or isn't or should or shouldn't be allowed. Bed and breakfast and shuttle services that never existed twenty years ago are prominent. Some have web sites. Riparian property purchases by non-Canadians escalated dramatically post 1990 (as they did on the Bulkley). The underground economy centered on the Kispiox fishery assumed new proportions. During the best five or six weeks the upper Babine was oversubscribed with anglers when almost all of them were guide clients. Now, with the addition of all the new kids with their jets and rafts it is far from the quality experience and the reputation the regulations were intended to preserve. Europeans bent on exploiting every crack in the regulation armor are far more prevalent on the Zymoetz today than ever before. The Kalum and Lakelse are not far behind. The guides who were known and, in some cases, proven to be chronic offenders in terms of adherence to rod-day quotas and other conditions associated with their licenses and revenue remittance are still in operation.

Rod days that were originally unlimited and carried no fee cost the guide owner a whopping $1.00 each in 1990 when regulations were imposed. The sky fell in when government increased the price to $10.00 a few years later. Meanwhile each one of those rod days commanded hundreds of dollars from the end-use angler

even without accommodation as part of the guiding service package. Look up the web site of any guide on any Skeena classified water and see for yourself what you'll pay for a day of their services on public waters. Guides may pay more for their rod-day quotas than they once did but that never even began to address the windfalls that many of them enjoyed at the outset nor did it consider, then or now, the market value of those days when sold, sometimes for as much as $1000.00 each. Publicly owned resources were given to a favored few. The owners were never compensated originally or at any juncture since as days escalated in value and were sold and resold. There is no turning back on that but that doesn't mean it isn't worth remembering.

Rod-day quotas allocated to classified-waters guides only applied to the most preferred weeks of the fishing season, generally September and October. There were no restrictions on the shoulder seasons before and after. Before was unimportant because the supply of August-returning fish was no longer sufficient to market fishing that early. Zymoetz was the only possible exception. November, however, became instantly valuable. With no restrictions on the number of guided rod days and no fees for any of those days the door was open to add to the pressure on fish at times where that pressure had no precedent. By November the steelhead are in overwintering mode. The water is cold and the fish lethargic. They concentrate in predictable places where they are highly vulnerable to capture. The Babine became the primary illustration of the quest for profit usurping all else. Selling the "secret season" when anglers prepared to endure the chill were promised double-digit days of "ripping on 'em" was hardly a demonstration of the respect for the fish at least one prominent guide espoused.

Comparatively, resident anglers still get their classified-waters cake for cheap. And, of course, they still expect government to supply fishing opportunity that now exists only in memories and dreams. Implementing and administering an effective system for manipulating the number of anglers on any specific water at any specific time would cost money, lots of it. Credible data on which it should be based is enormously expensive to collect. If anyone thinks government is going to front those costs out of the goodness of its heart they haven't been paying attention. User pay is the only game in town but the license fees required to underwrite the management desired and expected would never be accepted by the participants. Of that we can be sure. What's left to govern who shows up is some unknown and completely unpredictable combination of fish supply, gas prices, foreign currency exchange rates and international economic circumstances.

There is one more aspect of the classified/quality-waters management financing story that deserves to be highlighted. That involves the revenue that accrues from the several different licenses involved (daily licenses for non-residents, season licenses for residents, angling-guide and assistant guide licenses). Most people seem to believe those funds are applied to the waters from which they originate. That is not the case. Provincial classified-waters license revenue is largely attributable to the Skeena because most of the classified waters of any consequence are in that watershed. Yet, the majority of that revenue flows to a non-profit society (Freshwater Fisheries Society of British Columbia) carved out of MOE in the mid-1990s to manage the provincial trout-stocking program. That program is focused heavily on productive central and southern interior lakes distantly removed from Skeena country. Why lake-stocking programs continue to be allowed to consume any funds, let alone the majority, derived from licenses that relate purely to steelhead rivers and steelhead fishing is a policy question those in command are uninterested in confronting.

Part 6: Into the Future

Chapter 22
CYCLIC PHENOMENA

We all know that the technical definition of insanity is to repeat the same actions while expecting a different outcome; yet, we persist in making the same mistakes over and over, often in parallel redundant processes.[30]

The first few years of century 21 were less than dynamic in terms of steelhead and steelhead advocacy. Coho conservation measures that severely curtailed fishing along migration corridors leading to the Skeena and in the traditional gill-netting areas in and around the estuary did wonders for steelhead passage. The 1998 bonanza was never repeated but fishing in the upriver tributaries was good enough to maintain the illusion the clock would not be turned back. Two years later the momentum built a decade before was a distant memory and the commercial-fishery door that had closed was starting to re-open. Steelhead were no longer a consideration because the harvest-rate ceilings discussed previously were never going to be reached given the measures imposed that promised to protect them. To refresh, those were things like mandatory non-possession non-retention, recovery boxes, weed lines, daylight-only fishing and, eventually, half-length nets soaked for shorter periods. The infamous steelhead model said there was no problem and everyone lined up on the commercial-fishing side of the fence marched to that drummer. Coho conservation had usurped any steelhead concerns but convenient ways of avoiding that problem showed up almost immediately.

The agenda for the DFO managers who controlled the commercial fishery was always more about sustaining gill-netting than conserving fish. That was the reason for dabbling at the fringes of the problem. None of them will ever admit that but history speaks for itself. Why else would a conservation problem as starkly evident as it was for coho be addressed by manipulating net configurations and pretending license conditions around recovery boxes and shorter set times that were never enforced actually accomplished what model outputs predicted? How could tinkering with a fleet of gill nets possibly adequately address the fact that only 10 of 68 middle and upper Skeena coho stocks were not at risk (Morrell, 2000)? The same question could be asked of sockeye (30 of 65 not threatened), chinook (11 of 48 not threatened) or lowly chum salmon (6 of 26 stocks not threatened). Who left an office to evaluate the worth of model outputs that said all was good out there on those 68 coho streams?

Previously I said moving the net-fishing fleet inside the river to avoid the areas where coho encounter rates were high was a worst-case scenario for steelhead. DFO couldn't possibly have been unaware of that when it concentrated all the gill nets in the innermost commercial-fishing areas where steelhead encounter rates were known for a century to be higher than anywhere else. The addition of seiners to those same waters in the intervening periods when gill-netters were not fishing magnified the deception around reducing steelhead impacts. Meanwhile the model outputs said the harvest-rate offsets afforded by tweaking gill nets and their deployment and pretending seiners were in perfect compliance with steelhead and coho protection measures were more than adequate to mitigate any impacts from more vessels and more days in critical times and places. How those measures passed the red-face test and escaped broad exposure of their impotence by the steelhead fraternity remains another distressing bit of history.

All of this coho conservation kept steelhead off the political radar for the first five years of the new century. In 2006 however, another tipping point was reached. That year was classic in terms of putting DFO squarely in the cross hairs of steelhead sport fishers for a perceived return to the bad old days. The Babine sockeye run which had been bad enough to seriously reduce the number of openings for gill-netters in 2003 and 2004, and eliminate them altogether in 2005, rebounded. Industry argued strenuously that coho stocks were well along the rebuilding path and would receive all the protection necessary with all the net tweaking and license conditions that were then in place. Harvest-rate model outputs for steelhead had been so far below the supposed accepted targets for so long there was never a thought given to any consequences from harvesting all those enhanced Babine sockeye at rates not seen for years.

The 2006 commercial-fishing season impact on steelhead is crystal clear from the figures on the following page. There it can be seen the gill-net fleet fished for 15 days between July 10 and August 10, the timing window for the highly prized first half of the summer steelhead return. Gill nets fished another nine days on the back half of the run, although with considerably fewer boats per day. To add insult to steelhead injury the seine fleet was called in to help avoid the worst of all worlds for the commercial industry, over-escapement. Seiners fished another 13 days during that critical first half of the steelhead run and nine more days later. Collectively the two fleets fished 11 consecutive days at one point (August 16-26). Anyone who believed a sophisticated harvest-rate model was required to judge the impact of such a fishery on steelhead was mentally deficient. No matter how innovative the test-fishery critics were at attempting to discredit the steelhead figures and pretend the steelhead run was late there was no escaping the fact the number of steelhead getting past the nets was pathetically small. This was the classic manifestation of the position that

harvest rate was a useless and meaningless metric when the run size was so far below the accepted minimum conservation requirement. What does it take to appreciate the relationship between blue and purple in the figures? How could it be more obvious?

Just to translate the gravity of this situation into some readily understandable numbers consider this. The conservation requirement for steelhead had been established as 35,000 fish getting past the last commercial-fishing net. As of the long-term mid-point of the annual steelhead return (August 7) there were about 6200 fish safely in the Skeena. Call it 18% of the conservation minimum. Did that ring any alarm bells with DFO or the commercial-fishing industry? Obviously not. They just kept on fishing at a level unprecedented in decades—11 consecutive days! In the final analysis, the only time when any significant number of steelhead escaped the nets was in the one-week closed window before the 11 consecutive days began and the two weeks following the end of that string. That shows clearly in the figures.

The 2006 combination of the intensity of commercial fishing and the low test-fishery estimates of steelhead escapement did not go unnoticed by the DFO managers. One of their own broke ranks and shared his frustration in a confidential message sent to me in mid-August. To this day I have never divulged any of the information in our exchanges because it was mutually understood how his position would be jeopardized if his message went public. I applauded him for having a conscience. Months later the same information surfaced elsewhere. For that reason I have less difficulty today disguising messages and sources. Look no further for the smoking gun that evidenced the DFO commitment toward steelhead. The clip that follows wasn't from some trivial message between office mates. It was formal notification from a stock-assessment expert to the top gun in the Prince Rupert office clearly enunciating the circumstances at hand.

"Further to our discussions. With the most recent opening down here (today, tomorrow and this weekend), I now expect to see the old SWC steelhead guidelines exceeded in the post-season review. The area 3-4 fishery this year has been quite aggressive and given the complete relaxation of selective fishing requirements this year (no short nets, no short sets, low effective compliance for attempting to revive fish, few weedlines, etc) I doubt there will be anything technical I can provide that will show we (DFO) implemented any of the selective fishery objectives for steelhead as outlined in section 3.1.6 of the 2006 IFMP."

The IFMP acronym refers to the Integrated Fisheries Management Plan, a pre-season document that was supposed to have been forged and endorsed by First Nations, commercial- and recreational-fishery sector representatives, as well as both DFO and MOE. I refreshed myself on those pre-season documents recently. The six pages taken to list the "key" government contacts

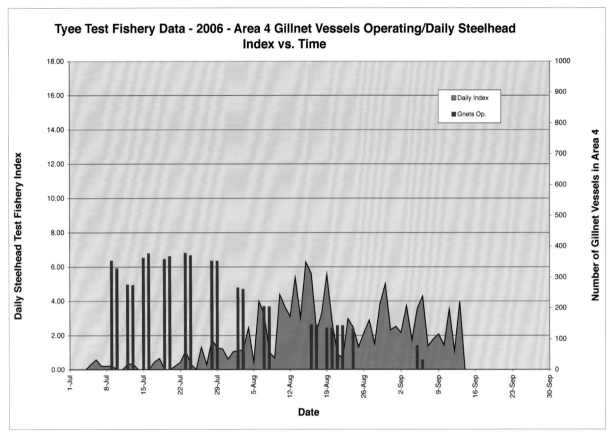

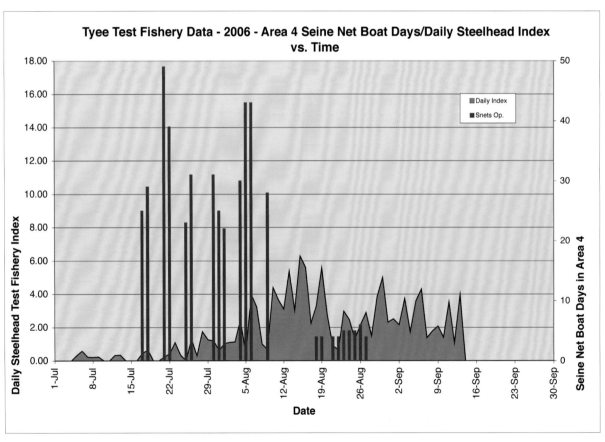

and web sites central to the plan was a bit intimidating. More institutional inertia?! The escape door for the Federal people was the same old same old-harvest rate ceiling come target. As long as the modeling exercise outputs didn't produce harvest-rate figures substantially in excess of those they contended everyone endorsed in the mid-1990s there wasn't a problem. Keep in mind, though, the harvest rates were supposed to be reduced substantially by the selective fishing measures noted in the above quote...except all those measures were being ignored and no one but a whistleblower ever acknowledged that reality. The fact that less than one fifth of the minimum steelhead-escapement target had been reached by the mid-point of the return had a snowball in purgatory chance of any influence. The consequences for upriver sport fishing had even less bearing, or so they thought. The truly remarkable outcome of the entire charade was the consistent post-season denial by the DFO overseer of the in-season commercial fishing that any of the circumstances alluded to in the quote above ever occurred.

There was another twist to the 2006 season that added a bit more flavor to the stew. The Provincial Government's tourism people provided three tourism associations, including Prince Rupert, substantial awards to promote local tourism opportunities. Rupert chose to use its award to sponsor a season-long coho salmon derby with prize money of $200,000.00. Presumably this was all part of some plan to inject a bit of life into a local economy reeling from the sinking of the BC Ferries Queen of the North, forest-industry collapse and three successive poor commercial-fishing seasons. The derby began at about the same time the net fleets were readying for the surge of Babine sockeye. So, we had commercial fishermen forbidden from retaining or possessing coho (I didn't say they didn't kill any) plying the same waters at the same time sport fishermen were actively encouraged to bring in as many as they legally could for prize money.[31] The same Provincial Government, albeit a different branch, that had been making gill-netter's lives miserable with all the pressure brought to bear by steelhead champions was now seen to be promoting and inviting exploitation of that other species similarly responsible for their problems of the day. By the time the news of the coho derby reached the MOE steelhead managers it was too late for a heart-to-heart discussion with the tourism promoters.

The commercial-industry response to the coho derby was open hostility toward the Province. They took it out on steelhead and let the world know they were doing so. DFO turned a blind eye, thus the preceding quote about complete relaxation of selective fishing requirements. Many months later, after a long string of e-mails from a persistent upriver steelhead angling guide, confirmation of the enforcement void finally arrived. The 2006 enforcement program roll up for the entire Skeena commercial fishery indicated a grand total of four "warnings" had been issued. That alone was a remarkable

contrast to the denial by the same people of the situation described in the in-season quote from their man in the stock-assessment office down the hall. Still later, multi-year data on enforcement actions out of DFO's Prince Rupert office indicated there were more charges laid against sport fishermen for barbless-hook violations than there ever were for the ubiquitous non-compliance with conditions of commercial-fishing licenses.

The year was 2006. There we were with 30 years of continuous hammering on the evils of mixed-stock fisheries under our collective belts, a promise of 50% reduction in steelhead harvest rate come and gone, thousands of pages of rhetoric about conservation, sustainability, stewardship and wild-stock preservation on the shelf, commitments to fishery restructuring and improved decision-making, a sea of consultation, shiny new allocation policies, widely publicized endorsements of United Nations resolutions on sustainable fisheries and biological diversity plus a code of conduct for responsible fisheries, promises of implementation of a Wild Salmon Policy replete with the contemporary, politically correct buzz about conservation and bio-diversity, etc. etc. Then a few extra Babine sockeye showed up.

Needless to say the steelhead fishing was poor in 2006, poor enough to rouse the sleeping dog. The upriver steelhead fraternity was angry and they were up for another run at DFO and industry. The circumstances were entirely parallel with those of the early 1990s with the exception of the communications options. The world was now digital and everyone was wired to play. Within a few short months the sportfishing community organized itself to lead another campaign for significant reform. The 2007 season proceeded under intense scrutiny from all sides. A repeat of 2006 was not in the cards. The steelhead return in 2007 was the worst since the 1991-93 seasons that gave rise to the harvest-rate reduction promise, the Wild Steelhead Campaign, the Skeena Watershed Committee and all the related events covered previously. The sockeye return was as good as it had been in many previous years and would have been sufficient to justify an average commercial-fishing season had other forces not combined to exert enough influence to force a more precautionary approach. Steelhead didn't matter but the status of weaker sockeye stocks (Kitwanga and Nanika especially), ongoing coho concerns, the embarrassing gap between DFO's Wild Salmon Policy and how fisheries had been prosecuted and the mounting threat of First Nations legal action for destroying their historic fisheries certainly did. Throw in the fact the value of pink salmon had declined to a level insufficient to justify net-fleets pursuing them. Reduced gill-netting time for sockeye in July and early August and no one showing up in August was the only thing that got any of the desperately small steelhead return of 2007 safely into the river.

Steelhead fishing success hit its lowest point in 15 years in 2007. The dog that woke up in '06 was rabid by the time '07 was done. As was the case in the early 1990s, steelhead was the driver. No one, not even the First Nations, was putting the pressure on DFO to address the perceived commercial-fishery management atrocities that the steelhead fraternity was. The response to the political heat that developed was more process. First there had to be a technical review of all the circumstances surrounding management of the Skeena fisheries. Second, there had to be a body of stakeholders to deal with the recommendations arising from the review. In the words of an old New York Yankee catcher, it was déjà vu all over again.

To be clear, the momentum that had developed by the conclusion of the disastrous 2007 steelhead fishing season was unlike anything before it. The level of organization, the knowledge base, the communication networks, the funding available to sustain it and the unrelenting commitment of key participants was big-league stuff. It was impossible to make these people go away on the strength of chronically undeliverable promises of selective fisheries prosecuted with gill nets that couldn't and wouldn't ever discriminate between sockeye and steelhead... and coho... and chum... and chinook. Sport fishermen were out to fundamentally change the way the commercial fishery had been managed for well over a century. Anyone needing evidence of the level of organization and connectivity of the community supporting modification of the status quo might want to look up a few web sites. Among them are Ecotrust, the Wild Salmon Center, the Gordon and Betty Moore Foundation, Skeena Wild Conservation Trust, the North Coast Steelhead Alliance and the Skeena Watershed Conservation Coalition.[32] None of this firepower was in the arsenal of those involved in the 1990s Skeena steelhead scenario.

The group of scientists that undertook the mandatory scientific review process was labeled the Independent Scientific Review Panel (ISRP). The Panel undertook its assignment between January and April, 2008. Its cost was underwritten by the Gordon and Betty Moore Foundation of San Francisco, California. The Moore Foundation support resulted solely from the connections between the steelhead advocacy community and key associates of the Foundation. The objective of the ISRP's work is worth remembering... and comparing to those from any number of other processes that consumed so much time, energy and public resources over the previous two decades.

"The objective of the Panel was to use the best available science to review the current management of anadromous salmonids in the Skeena watershed, to recommend a renewed approach to fisheries management, and identify what additional monitoring and data collection would be needed to implement Canada's Wild Salmon Policy (WSP). The Panel was to take into consideration the WSP, respect for the interests of First Nations people, and the sustainability of commercial and recreational fisheries for the people of Canada."

The report of the ISRP was tabled on May 15, 2008 (Walters et al. 2008). The overriding impression I took from it was it fell well short of independent. It read as though its real purpose was not to critique DFO management of the Skeena fishery but to exonerate it. Review of the terms of reference for the Panel was all the evidence I needed. They stated a consulting firm had been assigned the role of technical support. That firm and the DFO staff intimately involved with the Panel throughout its assignment have a long history of contract relationships. No doubt all of them would reel in righteous indignation at any suggestion of bias or conflict of interest but, frankly, the report reeked of it. I'm not alone in that interpretation. Many of the recommendations appearing in the report smacked of setting the table for more lucrative contracts. I'm advised one of the report's authors lost his cool in one of the public sessions that occurred along the way and blurted out that anyone who said there was a steelhead conservation problem was a liar. Those were pretty strong words for an independent scientist supposedly listening to public input.

What troubled me most about the report was the complete lack of acknowledgement of most of the work that had been done on Skeena steelhead. Panel members obviously made no significant effort to familiarize themselves with dozens of published reports readily available from MOE staff in the Smithers office. There were four reports on Skeena steelhead radio telemetry projects already on the shelf. (Actually there were several more but four were directly associated with steelhead in either the Skeena approach waters or the lower Skeena itself.) One of the four, by far the most costly, was prepared by the same consultants advising the Panel. Collectively those reports supplied overwhelming evidence of the limitations of radio telemetry involving steelhead captured in the immediate Skeena approaches and the lower river itself. How then does it happen that the Panel's report includes among its principle steelhead-related recommendations a massive radio telemetry program to document stock-specific steelhead migration patterns, timing, exploitation rates, etc?[33] That is just a mite too self serving for me to swallow. If the learned Panel had spent five minutes looking at the immediately available steelhead data from the Skeena test fishery alone it would have had a hard time calling itself credible in producing that and related recommendations. Ignorance is no excuse but it does provide an explanation for how the Panel could be led to include proposals for more radio telemetry. Other than a few inside MOE, who among the remaining audience for the ISRP report would know that wasn't a good idea?

The ultimate ISRP eye poke was taking one report from the MOE Research Section staff at the University of British Columbia completely out of context and stating that MOE had determined there was only one conservation unit (CU) for Skeena summer steelhead. The Panel accepted there were 32 sockeye CUs. The significance of one CU was probably lost on most but certainly not on DFO or those with influence in the commercial industry. With only one summer steelhead CU there isn't and wouldn't ever be any conservation problem. No commercial-fishery manager need ever distinguish between those upper Sustut or Morice fish and those bound for Kispiox or Babine. There are no strong stocks or weak stocks or early or late-run timing stocks to worry about. There is just one big homogenate of steelhead. It wouldn't matter if the entire front half of the steelhead run-timing curve was extirpated as long as there were still some fish left from the back half. (Perhaps the one CU interpretation was the root cause of the "liar" outburst of the Panel member.) In one breath the Panel spoke of (salmon) biodiversity and how one third of it had been destroyed before 1950. In the next it confirmed its lack of concern for any such principle relative to steelhead. If this wasn't a dream come true for anti-steelhead industrialists bent on straining every possible Babine sockeye from the mouth of the Skeena I can't imagine what would be. How such information ever managed to get out in a final report speaks volumes about the attention paid to steelhead data by the Panel. [34]

The Panel eye-pokes did not end at CUs, unfortunately. Their report effectively indicted MOE for negligence in terms of accurately estimating stock-specific abundance of steelhead, failure to monitor angler and guide catches, stonewalling analysis of data emanating from the Moricetown tagging exercises, inability to connect Tyee test-fishery data with commercial-fishing exploitation any time after 1980 (heaven knows why they picked that year), impotence with respect to Alaskan interception of steelhead, failure to estimate accurately the efficacy of practices used to reduce interceptions and mortality rates of net-caught steelhead, etc., etc. Once again, every one of these claims is more evidence of just how little effort was made to investigate the realities of the Skeena steelhead scenario and the extensive material already available. A process that was catalyzed by steelhead morphed into a template for managing commercially valuable salmon under a Wild Salmon Policy that steelhead were conveniently configured to conform with. Steelhead being lost in the shuffle was all too reminiscent of the coho eclipse exactly ten years earlier.

I mustn't overlook some inclusions in the ISRP report that steelhead folk were pleased to see. Despite the inherent contradictions they presented when compared to so much of the remainder of the report and its recommendations they were welcome confirmations. Topping the list was dismissal of the notion gill nets could be managed as a selective fishing tool and that captured fish can be released with high survival rates. Close behind was rejection of DFO's steelhead harvest-rate model as a reliable predictor of any commercial-fishery outcome. Those I could agree with. Unfortunately, however, the Panel failed to connect its pronouncements on the efficacy of gill nets with spending another million dollars a year

to radio-tag steelhead so their harvest rates and survival could be documented with appropriate scientific rigor.

At the risk of losing people in technical intricacies of CUs and the direction set by the esteemed scientists who produced the ISRP report I need to dwell briefly on the connection between CUs and the Wild Salmon Policy (WSP) (Anon. 2005).[35] They are inseparable in terms of how DFO promised to manage fisheries when the WSP was published in 2005. Remember that year. It pre-dates the conflict around Skeena steelhead and commercial fishing that re-surfaced in 2006 and snowballed through 2007 until it was put on hold by the ISRP process in 2008.

Make no mistake the WSP is a good document but implementation is the key and that isn't going so well. The interrelationship between it and CUs is clearly enunciated as follows:

"Wild salmon will be maintained by identifying and managing Conservation Units that reflect their geographic and genetic diversity. A CU is a group of wild salmon sufficiently isolated from other groups that, if lost, is very unlikely to recolonize naturally within an acceptable timeframe (e.g., a human lifetime or a specified number of salmon generations)."

When the ISRP report pronounced there was one Skeena summer steelhead CU it eliminated any need to accommodate the geographic, genetic and life history diversity so abundantly clear to anyone with even the most basic familiarity with those fish. Needless to say, MOE was taken aback over the single CU pronouncement. But, guess what, the only way the mistake could be corrected was to pile on more science. Closing in on three years later the long and contorted process of proving what never should have been necessary is nearing completion. Thank you ISRP. I'm left to wonder though. When the steelhead CU report hits the table and provides all the science demanded to demonstrate there are eleven Skeena summer steelhead CUs to deal with under the WSP policy, how is that going to play out? If a gill net can't discriminate between a sockeye and a steelhead how is it going to tell the difference between steelhead from different CUs? Is anyone really prepared to implement the WSP provisions for steelhead? Does anyone believe a gill-net fishery can ever be managed with the surgical precision necessary to achieve that?

Three commercial-fishing seasons after a report that was supposed to mould the future of the Skeena fishery ought to be sufficient to gauge progress. The status quo prevailed in 2008 on the basis that there was insufficient time between the release of the report and the start of the commercial-fishing season. Thus, the abundance of Babine sockeye largely determined the extent of fishing. The steelhead harvest-rate model, in all its glorious impotence, was still in use and the gill-netters and seiners were still doing their catch-and-release thing largely unmonitored. Thankfully the sockeye run was not large and commercial-fishing time was only half of what it was two years earlier

when the most recent round of discontent began. The 2008 steelhead escapement was double the 2007 estimate. The 2009 and 2010 commercial-fishing openings focused on Skeena sockeye were negligible due to poor returns in both those years. Once again the steelhead escapements were good. So, three years deep, a truck load of money, and process at levels never before seen, nothing had really changed. Babine sockeye abundance was still the only thing that mattered in the grand scheme of things. Think of the opportunity cost of all that money and time. To anyone who wanted to look, the parallels with the Skeena Watershed Committee of the 1990s were quite amazing.

Those at the center of processes they designed or endorsed and those who participate because they are left with no alternative tend to view them differently than do those on the outside. I'm satisfied that, in itself, is part of the agenda. I also think I've seen enough from both sides to understand how momentum is diffused and lost. The standard excuse for lack of any significant action is not enough science. If something can't be proven it can't be accepted as justification for change. I've said it before but it bears repeating, no data = no problem. Now, if it was a case of a freeze on anyone going fishing until the science was on the table (otherwise known as the precautionary principle) something might actually be accomplished. That never happens. All the problems that created the process live on while the energy of those who inspired it is sucked out of them through all the obligatory discussion about terms of reference, representation, protocol, priorities, funding, responsibilities, communication, and so on and so on. Then, one year's worth of even the best of data is never enough. Two or even three years must be compiled, analyzed, debated and sold to widely divergent interests before any change is even contemplated. When cash-strapped governments whose political aspirations are completely unaffected by any fish, let alone Skeena steelhead, are lobbied for funding to support the science demanded to alter the status quo, what do we think the odds on success are? Even if the science happens, change requires consensus. Peace in the Middle East is as likely. The specter of institutional inertia looms once again. The 2009 and 2010 fishing seasons were two more in strong support of failed sockeye runs being the salvation of steelhead and steelhead fishing.

More evidence of how impenetrable the DFO armor is with respect to steelhead surfaced in the very late stages of preparing this book. Unknown to me until late January, 2011, lawyers representing the North Coast Steelhead Alliance (their web site was footnoted earlier) attempted to instill some accountability into DFO by filing a complaint with a tripartite international body known as the Commission on Environmental Cooperation (CEC).[36] The NCSA asserted that beginning in 2006 Canada was failing to effectively enforce its own regulations pertaining to conditions of commercial-fishing licenses. Those conditions were all described earlier (short nets, short sets, mandatory brailing, recovery tanks supplied with circulating water,

non-retention/non-possession, etc.). We need to remember that for several years prior to the 2006 commercial-fishing season DFO and industry had been aggressively selling those measures as the solution to steelhead mortality in gill nets and the zero-cost justification for continued fishing in times and places where steelhead encounters were significant. The response to the NCSA submission was prepared jointly by DFO and Environment Canada (EC). It is dated July 2010. Unfortunately it hasn't attracted the attention it deserves.

What the respondents came back with was an unprecedented level of distortion of truth and reality. It weaved together everything from the rationale for DFO's Pacific Region enforcement policy, Interim Fisheries Management Plans (IFMP), the origin and history of results of the steelhead harvest-rate model and carefully selected statements from the ISRP's four wise men into dismissal of any validity to any aspect of the NCAS submission. They polished it off with the claim none of the perceived 2006 in-season transgressions were important anyway because the post-season review confirmed the steelhead harvest rate met but did not exceed the 24% level alleged to have been negotiated and endorsed by the sportfishing community ever since 1997. DFO had fully met its obligations and therefore complaints about failure to enforce regulations were irrelevant.

I must be missing something here. In 2010 the harvest-rate model that was declared useless in a report sponsored by the federal government (i.e. the ISRP report) in 2008 emerges as the foundation of the same government's case that the model calculations prove no harm was done in 2006. Brushed aside was the fact not a single DFO officer visited the Skeena's steelhead killing fields in 2006. All those high-level government folk who undoubtedly reviewed these findings before the DFO/EC response to the NCSA complaint was sent to CEC failed to acknowledge the existence of their own staff's e-mails indicating they had relaxed all those conditions of license in 2006 and crossed their fingers the season-end harvest-rate modeling results could be shown to come in at 24% or less. The DFO/EC response makes no mention of the ISRP's condemnation of the model but it conveniently cherry picked other sentences from the same report to justify its actions (I warned of the potential for the ISRP pronouncements to be used in such fashion). For example:

"It is not true that steelhead escapement is higher on average when the Area 3-5 commercial fisheries are substantially reduced."

I can accept the four wise men may have been shielded from or unaware of the data appearing in the gill-net versus test-fishery index figures presented earlier in this chapter but for DFO/EC to selectively use ISRP outputs in a fabricated defense of itself fits my interpretation of malfeasance. It gets worse. The response stated DFO shut down the commercial fishery for eight consecutive days in 2006 because the in-season harvest-rate model outputs indicated the target 24% had been reached. The truth is DFO knew it had already seriously contravened its pre-season commitments as described in its IFMP. They deliberately fished their way into a worst-case scenario in splendid isolation of any consultation with the steelhead advocacy community it purported to embrace in its IFMP processes. The reason: the enhanced Babine sockeye run was stronger and its timing more protracted than expected. The contrived explanation given the NCSA might have passed the red-face test if that damned unexpected late pulse of sockeye hadn't shown up. When it did DFO bowed to the pressure of industry and called the fleet back in. That's when the job of rationalizing and justifying the steelhead harvest rate got a lot harder and that's when the smoking gun DFO e-mail warning senior staff of the consequences of more fishing surfaced. The bottom line is the most black-and-white circumstances involving the absence of an enforcement presence in 2006, together with DFO's own internal acknowledgement of that and its deliberate avoidance of even promoting, let alone enforcing compliance, still wasn't enough for the Federal Government (i.e. DFO) to eat the tiniest piece of humble pie and admit it should have done better.

The process-related inertia that stifles change doesn't rest solely with the outfall from the ISRP report. Woven in is another process that thickens the glue. On surface it gives the appearance of painting DFO into shrinking corner but digging beneath exposes a more likely outcome. Enter the Marine Stewardship Council (MSC) certification process. Tired of acronyms yet?

MSC certification is another of the long and contorted processes that makes silk purses from sow's ears. It's the commercial-fishing industry's game plan to convince concerned consumers that the products they purchase originate from fisheries (in this case Skeena) that have been placed under an appropriate microscope and deemed to have been conducted sustainably. The entire MSC process as it relates to Skeena steelhead is one steeped in conflict of interest and pure unadulterated politics. Anyone with a month of spare time and a masochistic bent can wade through the MSC web site material on certification of British Columbia sockeye salmon fisheries and draw their own conclusions.[37] I'll try and capture the essence of almost a decade of process in my own executive summary. I think it worth the ink because it adds a fair bit of clarity to the picture of what fisheries management has become and how it relates to Skeena steelhead in the foreseeable future.

MSC certification is all about maintaining access to foreign markets where BC sockeye salmon have been sold for decades. For Skeena sockeye that means Europe. Threat of boycott by local consumers forced major retailers to deal only in products that were "eco friendly". That demanded certification by the MSC, a London-based, worldwide organization that seems to have monopolized all such certification. Their web site leads one to believe the European marketplace has been conditioned to reject

seafood products that do not bear their now familiar blue MSC eco label. Certification of the BC sockeye fisheries (Skeena is/was one of four) was forced by certification of the Alaskan sockeye fishery in 2000. That was seen as giving Alaska a competitive advantage in a marketplace that was becoming greener by the year. The BC processors initiated their certification application in 2001. My impression is the Alaska certification process was a walk in the park relative to that endured as the years wore on in BC.

The MSC is in business to service clients. There is a lot of money involved. In British Columbia client means the commercial fishing industry or, more specifically, the British Columbia Salmon Marketing Council (BCSMC... and abject apologies for the continuing stream of acronyms). The BCSMC represents the harvesters and processors of commercially caught BC salmon and promotes the quality, availability and value of BC wild salmon in national and international markets. The MSC has set out standards and principles that only MSC accredited third parties qualify to pursue on behalf of client applicants. Those standards and principles are motherhood sorts of things no one ever disagrees with nor can they quantify to the extent that they qualify as an objection sufficient to reject a certification application. Here's an example taken directly from the MSC web site:

"These principles reflect a recognition that a sustainable fishery should be based upon the development and maintenance of effective fisheries management systems taking into account all relevant biological, technological, economic, social, environmental and commercial aspects."

Ultimately the Skeena sockeye-fishery certification process became a tug of war between those whose interests were purely economic and those who saw it as an avenue to fundamentally change the focus of the Skeena fishery on the enhanced Babine sockeye to the exclusion of somewhere between 30 and 50 other sockeye stocks, as well as all the stocks of all the other species that formerly graced Skeena tributaries. How the term sustainable could even be contemplated, let alone be promoted as justifiable, with the overwhelming evidence of the consequences of more than a century of gill nets targeting Babine sockeye staring everyone in the face is a phenomenon to behold. Needless to say the field where the tug of war is played out is not exactly level. The resources available from the client applicants are orders of magnitude greater than those that can be cobbled together by the conservationists and the rules around time given to respond to the staged outputs of the MSC accredited third-party application reviewers are ridiculously short. Voluminous highly technical documents that take the hired guns many months to produce are made available to those outside the process for 30 days. Comments must be returned within that time frame to be considered. Objections are dealt with in a quasi-judicial process that I can only describe as purposely designed to ensure failure of any opposition.

Tracking the tremendous amount of material generated by the MSC certification process revealed more about who's who in the zoo. The BC sockeye-fishery certification application was originally handled by California-based Scientific Certification Systems (SCS). That's another interesting web site for a walkabout. As noted, SCS acted on behalf of the BC processors. Eventually SCS was replaced by another of the MSC-accredited organizations known as Tavel. That one was based in Halifax, Nova Scotia. In January of 2010 came an announcement that Tavel had been bought up by Moody International and turned over to its subsidiary Moody Marine. Moody International is owned by a Bahrain-based private equity firm. Their web site boasts of the many corporate takeovers they have orchestrated in recent years. The pockets of those pursuing the sustainable-fishery blessing are obviously a touch deeper than those of any sport fishermen trying to stand in front of their bulldozer. The original client, the BCSMC, was replaced by a newly formed society, the Canadian Pacific Sustainable Fisheries Society, also in 2010. This new Society lists all the significant BC fish processors (20) as its members. The news there seems to be the BCSMC could no longer afford the cost of participation.

As in all things fisheries, nothing happened fast on the certification front. That had everything to do with the heroic efforts of the conservation community that wasn't about to stand by and do nothing while a green stamp was put on the Skeena net fisheries so clearly in need of drastic change. DFO certainly couldn't be trusted to protect the interests of steelhead or the steelhead anglers that had made its life miserable for so much of the past 20 years. The Provincial shop was nowhere to be found, other than through its obscure little group that operated in isolation of any public input while ensuring the interests of the fish processors it licensed were accommodated. Did I mention that group was comprised mostly of former DFO employees?! Functionally it was (still is) the latter-day edition of the new kids on the block that I spoke of earlier in relation to their entry into the Skeena Watershed Committee processes. Remember, the processors were the applicants for MSC certification. While the certification was grinding away in the background along came the 2006 and 2007 fisheries and the ISRP process the events of those two fishing seasons catalyzed. That was a very untimely and unwelcome speed bump for certification seekers. If ever there was evidence of the impact of the Skeena sockeye fishery on non-target stocks and how far off the acceptable MSC standards the conduct of the Skeena net fisheries were, those were the years to demonstrate it. The certification process stalled while a progressively larger, more informed and more aggressive conservation community worked tirelessly to mount an anti-certification case.

The black and white of the 2006 and 2007 fisheries faded to shades of grey as the MSC-certification process continued over subsequent years. The only real debate left became not whether certification would arrive but when? Moody International announced its blessing in July 2010 and issued a certificate stating the Skeena sockeye salmon fishery had been assessed and conformed with the requirements of the MSC principles and criteria for sustainable fishing. A certificate of registration was issued to the Canadian Pacific Sustainable Fisheries Society on July 2, 2010. It is valid for a period of five years. No one seems able to provide direction on what happens after that.

The MSC certification carried with it several conditions specific to steelhead that are now the subject of much confusion. Those conditions were interwoven with some of DFO's Wild Salmon Policy pronouncements and material contained in the Independent Science Review Panel report. For example, one condition states:

"Certification is conditional until the management agencies implement a scientifically defensible program for estimating steelhead catch in the Skeena sockeye fisheries and escapement and stock status for Skeena steelhead stocks."

All the conditions in the MSC-certification documents use precisely the same clause, "certification is conditional...". Further, every condition specifies a time frame for implementation. In the case of the condition quoted above the implementation date is 2011. The question I have posed to several participants in the MSC processes is what does the "certification is conditional" clause mean? Does it mean certification will be withdrawn if one or more conditions are not met? The closest I have come to an answer to that question is a sentence buried in one of the documents filed on the MSC web site. It states that failure to comply with a condition within the timeframe required by the condition *may* result in loss of certification. That same document also says the MSC procedure contemplates various forms of audits to monitor compliance with the conditions so that MSC can demonstrate its process encourages and requires good stewardship of a fishery. I know industry is nervous about the consequences of failure to meet several of the conditional conditions listed by the MSC but I have little faith that the language used has any teeth. The other confidence killer is the escape clause in the WSP that underlies all of the ISRP and MSC inspired recommendations and commitments. Try this:

"Where an assessment concludes that conservation measures will be ineffective or the social or economic costs to rebuild a CU are extreme, the Minister of Fisheries and Oceans may decide to limit the range of measures taken. Such a decision will be made openly and transparently."

The governance process created in accordance with the ISRP recommendations is going nowhere fast. The Moore Foundation that has been underwriting most of its cost for three years is looking hard for evidence of progress, and well it should. Its glasses are probably more rose tinted than my own but I can't see that lasting much longer. Moore is demanding linkage between all the projects it is funding and decision-making around harvest-management commitments inherent in the WSP. Meanwhile a DFO document labeled "An Action Plan to Address Conditions for Marine Stewardship Certification of British Columbia Sockeye Fisheries" assumes there will be no requirement for additional departmental resources but warns that if the assumption is flawed it would have to be re-evaluated. Does DFO really think the conservation community is going to keep writing cheques or that industry bears no responsibility for ensuring MSC certification standards are being met? How long will the shifting burden of responsibility game continue? If the sockeye-certification process hasn't been enough to kill any enthusiasm for a better tomorrow perhaps the pink-salmon certification currently in motion will finish the job.

I see long and rancorous debate about what qualifies as *scientifically defensible*. I see consultants who have been intimately involved in so much of the background to the ISRP and the MSC certification continuing to attract large sums of money to pursue recommendations they helped to craft. I see those who feed off the commercial fishery continuing to ignore and discredit work already done because they can. I see benchmarks set at years and circumstances distantly removed from where they should be. I see agencies opting out of MSC evaluation on the strength of escape clauses in the WSP and/or insufficient resources. Finally, I see nothing that gives me comfort anything other than the abundance of enhanced Babine sockeye is going to have any measurable effect on the Skeena summer steelhead. The challenge facing the sportfishing and conservation communities to stay in the game of holding agencies' feet to the fire to avoid losing any more wild-fish and wild fish habitat has never been greater.

Chapter 23

REQUIEM?

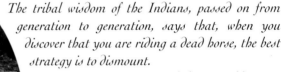

In 2003 I was a participant in a steelhead management policy discussion attended by people who fancied themselves as influential players. Through a series of rather strange circumstances one of them was the man who promised the 50% steelhead harvest-rate reduction twelve years earlier. Somewhere along the course of events in that 2003 session he passed along a piece I squirreled away in a digital file I labeled quotable quotes. It struck me I might have use for it one day. I have no idea who wrote this, when, or why but it describes more than a few situations in the world of the present. In relation to Skeena fisheries management the fit was too good to pass up. Here it is.

The tribal wisdom of the Indians, passed on from generation to generation, says that, when you discover that you are riding a dead horse, the best strategy is to dismount.

However, in governments, a whole range of far more advanced strategies is often employed, such as:

Buying a stronger whip.

Changing riders.

Appointing a committee to study the horse.

Arranging to visit other countries to see how other cultures ride dead horses.

Lowering the standards so that dead horses can be included.

Reclassifying the dead horse as living impaired.

Hiring outside contractors to ride the dead horse.

Harnessing several dead horses together to increase speed.

Providing additional funding and/or training to increase dead horse's performance.

Doing a productivity study to see if lighter riders would improve the dead horse's performance.

Declaring that as the dead horse does not have to be fed, it is less costly, carries lower overhead and therefore contributes substantially more to the bottom line of the economy than do some other horses.

Rewriting the expected performance requirements for all horses.

Promoting the dead horse to a supervisory position.

So much for scary funny.

One hundred and thirty four years of commercial-fishing influence on Skeena summer steelhead stocks are behind us. Meaningful oversight of the fisheries by DFO and its predecessors has existed for perhaps half of that period. The steelhead sport fishery is no more than 60 years old. MOE or its precursor have presided over it for about two thirds of that time. Underlying both of those fisheries is the historic Indian fishery. No one knows for certain how long it has existed but it clearly predates the others by centuries. So, where does that get us?

The commercial-fishing industry or, more particularly, the gill-netting component of it, is now in the crossairs of almost everyone except the commercial-fishermen's union and an increasingly influential First Nations network. DFO is in the hopelessly conflicted position of applying its own policies on management of fish right along with mutually exclusive policies intended to increase the number of First Nations participants. Judges compound the difficulties through successive court decisions that atone for perceived sins of our forefathers but bear no resemblance to the capacity of fish resources to accommodate the demands they create. More dollars to increase the number and proportion of First Nations participants in commercial fishing and to increase the First Nations capacity to manage fisheries in replacement or isolation of DFO and MOE is hardly the solution to depressed and declining stocks. The same governments that purport to manage publicly owned fish resources are also the ones who license and promote virtually all the development that continues to erode the productive capacity of fish habitat. No one has stopped the habitat onslaught, much less reversed it, and Mother Nature isn't producing as many fish from the remaining habitat, whether river or marine, as once seen. Who connects all these dots?

While the First Nations component of the commercial-fishing industry is being strengthened and enhanced the rest of the commercial fleet isn't going away. The gill-netter's position is as entrenched as it ever was. Seiners and gill-netters continue to fight over who gets to play and how much. Neither will back down, especially when they can see the competition up there at the top of the Skeena funnel safely on the other side of an international boundary. It is awfully hard to imagine the Wild Salmon Policy commitments will not have progressively greater influence on at least the non-First Nations gill-net fishery as the years unfold, but don't expect concessions focused on steelhead. After all there just isn't proof of need. The ISRP said so. The union voice (and the upriver First Nations fishermen) will be trumpeting that in the face of steelhead folk until hell freezes over. Weak stocks of every species are going to be caught in the middle of the competition for survival.

MOE finds itself in a position no more enviable than that of DFO. It was intimately involved with the players that were responsible for creation of the ISRP and it couldn't do anything other than endorse it. After all, once again, this was motherhood. Unfortunately, by design or default, the steelhead focus that catalyzed the initiative was obfuscated by the time the Panel report and its recommendations were tabled. MOE was trapped. The process the steelhead advocacy community thought would finally set the stage for enlightened management of the net fishery served only to create more roadblocks. More science, please! Good people now spend their professional lives buried in the stifling administrivia surrounding applications for funding, requests for proposal, proposal evaluations, terms of reference, budget monitoring, mandatory submission of quarterly reports to funding organizations on the status of the few projects that survive the ever more rigorous application screening process and meetings on meetings to deal with all of the above. In their leftover hours they get to attend plenary and technical sessions of the multi-stakeholder governance bodies set up in the wake of a Panel long over the horizon. Ask any of them how they feel about the efficacy of the process three years on. Ask also if the science quest they are mired in has put any extra steelhead up the river or if they think it ever will. Then there is the all-consuming latest round of re-organization of MOE that has yet to settle out. That will really benefit the fish and the habitat from whence they came.

Sport fishermen suffer under the illusion they are exempt from any accountability. Armed mostly with fly rods and prohibited from harvesting a Skeena steelhead for almost two decades how could they ever be part of the problem? Think again. The commercial fishery has been comparatively far more regulated and controlled over the history of the Skeena steelhead sport fishery than has the recreational fishery. A gill net today is remarkably similar to a gill net of a century ago. That is a good part of the reason for the problems of the present. Boats used to deploy one have changed dramatically but the number of those boats and the times, places and conditions under which they fish have been increasingly constrained and justifiably so. In all commercial fisheries there is at least some connection between fish supply and fishing effort. We can argue there isn't enough or that its too little too late but we can't argue there isn't any. Seines are obviously in a different orbit in terms of technological advancement and fishing power. But, there too, the vessels involved are heavily restricted in terms of where and when they go fishing. Contrast that with the sport fishery that now subjects every productive piece of steelhead stream to equipment and technology increasingly capable of exploiting every fish. Then factor in the instantaneous communication systems that leave nothing to chance and invite more of all of that. With no connection between fish supply, fishing effort and fish catching power or efficiency the sport fishery is in its own special class. Exemption from regulations that link fish supply to effort and technology is no more supportable for sport fishermen than for any other user. The position there is no footprint is ripe for challenge. The religious conviction that catch-and-release fisheries can be prosecuted without limit is not going to stand the test of time. It's all about attitude. Renowned author Tom McGuane, another of the Skeena steelhead angler aficionados, captured it perfectly in a passage in his 1999 *The Longest Silence: A Life in Fishing*.

"The sport of angling used to be a genteel business, at least in the world of ideals, a world of ladies and gentlemen. These have been replaced by a new set of paradigms: the bum, the addict, and the maniac. I'm afraid that this says much about the times we live in. The fisherman now is one who defies society, who rips lips, who drains the pool, who takes no prisoners, who is not to

be confused with the sissy with the creel and the bamboo rod. Granted, he releases that which he catches, but in some cases, he strips the quarry of its perilous soul before tossing it back in the water. What was once a trout – cold, hard, spotted, and beautiful – becomes number seven."

Don't ever think there aren't any bad guys out there with fishing rods either. For every commercial netter who deliberately kills a steelhead there's an angler sneaking around using forbidden bait to catch more fish to kill for bait to catch more fish. The difference is DFO turns a blind eye with respect to commercial fishers while the MOE enforcement guys are just too few and under-resourced to catch the often-known recreational fishery offenders in the act. Either way steelhead die.

The future of the First Nations fisheries of the Skeena is exceedingly unlikely to be anything but bigger and broader. I'll dare to suggest it won't be with any overall plan or accountability. The boardroom and podium speeches will say otherwise. They always have. Those who buy that storyline need to go and look for themselves. Moricetown is as far as anyone need travel to appreciate what I'm saying. The FSC fisheries can't help but expand given the demographics of the First Nations community of the Skeena. ESSR fisheries or economic opportunity fisheries or those to come under some other yet-to-be announced acronym will carry on over and above the FSC fisheries. They'll catch steelhead. Who is going to monitor those fisheries and document credibly what happens? The four wise men of the ISRP were highly critical of MOE monitoring of recreational catches. Did they offer any comment or advice on the First Nations fisheries catch? Did they even ask about them? Will DFO do anything to accommodate steelhead in the First Nations fishery planning meetings they hold in isolation of any MOE participation? Does anyone have jam enough to question the veracity of the steelhead catch estimates cobbled together from various First Nations sources in recent times? Would they have a job on Monday morning if they did?

Why the continued investment in pretending to derive ever more accurate estimates of steelhead abundance at Moricetown? Even if population estimates acceptable to all could be circulated within a reasonable time period following the conclusion of the fish marking and recapture exercise, what purpose would that serve? Who would benefit and how? Who should be paying for more of this enlightened management? The high-priced consultants who oversee the data still haven't acknowledged important questions, the answers to which should have been basic elements of annual reports for a decade. For example, how many steelhead tagged in years other than the current year were recaptured or how many fish tagged at the test fishery were recovered at Moricetown or what was the distribution of tag recoveries upstream and downstream from the tagging location or what have we learned about the time and distance between tagging and recapture?

Why not a moratorium on the fish abuse and, instead, spend a fraction of the money on a thorough analysis of what we already know (or should) or, if not, why not? Call it a course correction founded on the precautionary principle. Who will dare push for such an approach other than a few enlightened angling advocates?

Dateline January 17, 2011. My oft-made comment that uncertainty is fertile ground for those whose purpose is to exploit it manifests itself again. A proposal to conduct another mark/recapture population estimate based on the tags applied to steelhead by the Wet'suwet'en project staff at Moricetown in 2010 is now in circulation. It calls for an angling-based recapture effort throughout the Bulkley and Morice rivers in the upcoming March through May period.[38] The rationale includes statements that shouldn't pass unnoticed. Consider the following direct from the project proposal:

"This particular program, and any like it which have the recovery component in the immediate vicinity of the tagging operation, are very likely to severely violate assumptions of the Petersen mark-recapture methodology."

No credible fisheries professional familiar with the Moricetown methodology ever disagreed. The problem is the project proponent is "Wet'suwet'en Fisheries". That would be the same group responsible for the annual Moricetown projects from the outset and the people who turned a blind eye to the same issues when Welch, et al published their report on the sonic tagging experiments done under their watchful eye in 2008 and 2009. Are they now telling us the work they have aggressively promoted as technically valid from day one is of questionable value? Before there is even a draft report of their own 2010 tagging project and population estimate available they are claiming its inherent uncertainties are justification for spending more public money ($55,000.00) to generate more uncertainty? So, the public should finance another project to produce another report, this time by August 2011, to enlighten us on how many steelhead some contractor thinks went through Moricetown one year earlier. And the value of that would be? One would hope this Wet'suwet'en acknowledgement of the deficiencies of its own mega-project might signal an end to "science"-ustified fish abuse rather than more.

Out on the coast we can be sure there will be as many or more First Nations owned or operated commercial-fishing vessels catching FSC fish as there ever has been. How will violation of MSC certification standards and transgression of WSP commitments stand up against constitutional rights? Surely there isn't anyone in a position of any knowledge on those fisheries naïve enough to believe steelhead are ever going to have any influence or even that catches will be reported. What governance model is going to change that? DFO has another in its tsunami of draft discussion papers out there in the public domain as I speak.[39] It talks about well-known catch

reporting deficiencies (for salmon) that prevailed from 1951 until 1998 before there was even formal recognition of the problem. Twelve years later all the tiresome verbiage about guiding principles, challenges and opportunities and strategic approaches is in our faces for the umpteenth time. What magic potion is this latest process going to concoct that will alter decades and even century-old collective mindsets and behavior of commercial and First Nations fishers such that every salmon and steelhead caught will suddenly appear on a ledger?

No one ever seriously contemplates the basic economics of commercial fisheries anywhere in British Columbia. Someday they probably will but history teaches us fisheries never collapse economically until it is far too late to reverse the ecological consequences. For as long as I can remember, people familiar with the west coast BC salmon fisheries have talked about the management costs exceeding the landed value of the catch. I suppose it all depends on what is included in the definition of management but I have no difficulty believing there is truth to that. If the net benefit (pardon the pun) of sending a fleet of gill-netters out to do damage to everything other than a single stock of enhanced fish is negative would it not make more sense to pay fishermen to stay home? If the average annual earnings of a Skeena River gill-netter are as low as we're told they are, the entire fleet could be bought off with a fraction of what is being spent on process, science, capacity building, transfer of licenses, and so on. How about just a week or two of no fishing at peak steelhead migration times? How much would it cost to buy that? The same logic applies to Moricetown. I'm reminded of Dr. Peter Larkin's assessment of the Salmonid Enhancement Program when it was still in the planning stages in the mid-1970s. Dr. Larkin said the $250 million being talked about would be better spent in buying out the commercial-fishing fleet for ten years and calling that the enhancement program.

While I'm on the subject of economics, who pays attention to the value of the recreational fishery? It continues to grow while the returns on commercial fishing spiral downward. The latest analysis from a study funded by the Moore Foundation and conducted on behalf of the Pacific Salmon Foundation (Counterpoint Consulting, 2008) revealed the net worth of the recreational fisheries focused on Skeena salmon and steelhead exceeded that of the commercial fisheries by a factor of 3.5. If one was to tease out of that study the management costs for steelhead relative to the direct and indirect dollar benefit accruing from the sport fishery that factor would increase substantially. Show me evidence that has influenced any decision-making. Instead of favoring one ethnic group over another through an Allocation Transfer Program that does absolutely nothing for fish why not reallocate the same boats and licenses to the same user group to build capacity for low-cost high-return recreational fishery development? I need the explanation on why that would not be a better investment.

Twenty-one years ago Jim Vincent wrote an article for the Early Fall issue of *Gray's Sporting Journal*. Its title was "The Steelhead Bums – Destruction of a Sacred Reliquary". It was an emotionally charged personal lament for the changing times and proposed angling regulations that threatened the Kispiox steelhead fishery beloved by he and a few of his respected veteran angler friends. Exactly one year later Tom Pero, editor of Trout Unlimited's quarterly magazine, *Trout*, wrote and published a milestone article titled "Splendid Skeena". That one was a penetrating contemporary snapshot of management of the Skeena First Nations, commercial and recreational fisheries. The most striking feature of those articles is they could have been written yesterday. If one was to black out the dates and pass them around to the current collection of players in the Skeena fisheries-management arena I'm betting most of them wouldn't know they weren't. That is a statement on how little progress has been made on altering a course set long ago. Outside the arena, individuals will acknowledge their contribution to the problems but, when in front of microphones and cameras, they retreat to their silos. No sector will give ground to another. We've seen the results of a Skeena Watershed Committee and we're mired in another far more expensive and convoluted Skeena Watershed Initiative process predictably going nowhere. The volume of material spewing forth from judges and treaty negotiators, from policy wonks and planners and from processes so numerous no one can even remember them all is beyond anyone's ability to integrate and apply. Fish and fishing, the intended beneficiaries, become the victims. If you love Skeena steelhead your only real hope is bad sockeye years.

If all of the above isn't depressing enough we can talk about habitat. We should. We aren't making any more and looking after what we had isn't a big success story. Holding the line would be a highly desirable outcome but that is not going to happen just because a few fish lovers wish it to be so. The Pacific Ocean is not always the happy home for salmon and steelhead it was assumed to be for most of the last 100 years. Fluctuations in sea surface temperature regimes, upwelling and nutrient supply are increasingly understood to be major factors in the inter-annual abundance of all Pacific salmonids. Skeena fish, steelhead included, have fared better than those originating from rivers to the south. No one knows where to from here except that climate change is highly unlikely to produce more favorable circumstances for salmon and steelhead over any longer term. In fresh water, where habitat quality and quantity can be measured comparatively easily, the picture is no prettier. I'll reiterate what I said in speaking to rivers and access. It's worth a tour on Google Earth to see how far roads and clear-cuts and railway rights of way have penetrated into parts of the Skeena drainage that were virgin territory as little as ten and twenty years ago. Scare yourself into appreciating what is left and how sensitive and vulnerable it is.

The only piece of the watershed that remains largely intact today has come to be known as "the Sacred Headwaters". It is the line in the sand for First Nations and an environmentalist community determined to prevent the assault of profit-seeking miners and pipeline builders encouraged by near-sighted governments hell bent on economic development and jobs, jobs, jobs. Those who man the blockades to save the habitat that produces the treasures for others to enjoy and profit from deserve a lot more recognition and support than they're receiving. Their problem is our problem. Edward Hoagland's 1969 words in *Notes from the Century Before* say it much more eloquently than I can.

"It's as though the last bit of ocean were about to become more dry land, planted and paved. The loss would not be to us who have already sailed it, who would wish to be seamen, and who can always go back and relive in our minds what we've experienced. The loss is to people unborn who might have turned into seamen, or who might have seen it and loved it as we, alive now and not seamen, have seen and loved it."

It hasn't taken long to irreversibly alter a lot of fish habitat in the Skeena watershed. Neither has it taken long to depress and even extirpate fish stocks that people alive today remember well. We ought to have learned a few lessons along the way. Unfortunately, as my friend Pete Broomhall once told me, us humans learn what's bad for us at a much faster rate than we learn what's good. Color me pessimistic if you like but color me realistic. I'm glad I was fortunate enough to spend the time I did on rivers like Sustut and Babine and witness the magic of the upper Skeena watershed when people were scarce and viewscapes unaltered from what they had been centuries before. I'm glad too that I met and knew a few of the pioneers who shaped a sport fishery predicated on preserving fish and experiences that represent the best of the best. Their stories and advice were never forgotten. Their treasures are mine too. Thankfully there was still a bit of what I was so fortunate to experience to share with my son before it was managed beyond recognition. Saturdays when morning hockey could be followed by afternoons on your home river, when you could easily find virgin water, when you knew and waved at everyone encountered and when fish caught rarely bore evidence of human contact is an experience my grandson will struggle to comprehend.

Endnotes

Introduction

A comment by Salman Rushdie in a televised interview aired on CTV, October 2010.

Chapter 2

[2] The area referred to as "the Gap" is actually the innermost part of Sub-Area 4-12.

Chapter 3

[3] This is the successor to the Pacific Stock Assessment Review Committee mentioned in Chapter 1.

Chapter 4

[4] Page 192 of Gottesfeld and Rabnett's 2008 "Skeena River Fish and Their Habitat".

[5] The "Fisheries Inspector" was officer Helgesen's boss. He was the first ever Inspector for the entire BC coast north of Bute Inlet and assumed office in Port Essington in 1904, the year this statement was made.

Chapter 5

[6] The IANC term that is used to accurately reflect the population of those who meet the criteria for Indian status.

Chapter 6

[7] Genetic analysis of all steelhead sampled at the Skeena River test fishery between 2000 and 2008 inclusive revealed between 30 and 40 percent of those fish were Bulkley/Morice origin. The Bulkley/Morice contribution estimated by habitat capability modeling is similar.

[8]The hatchery program operated between 1960 and 1966 but was abandoned when it became evident the blasting at Hagwilget fishways at Moricetown and three days per week of fishing closures were far more successful in attempts to rebuild Nanika sockeye.

[9]Steelhead and, especially, chinook generally preferred their historic migration routes over the falls rather than the fishway route. Sockeye and pink salmon were the primary beneficiaries of the fishways.

[10]When the report based on 2008 and 2009 sonic tagging finally surfaced (Welch et al. 2010) it confirmed in spades all previous observations and predictions and clearly highlighted the population inflation potential inherent in failing to account for dropback, mortality, tag loss, etc.

[11] I'm advised recently that both fresh and smoked pink salmon were sold at Moricetown in 2010.

Chapter 7

[12] A former colleague advised me that 1000 individuals from three separate (non-Skeena) First Nations held a "jamboree" in the area in 2010 to gill net and snag salmon and steelhead.

[13] The Kispiox and all the other summer steelhead tributaries of the Skeena are closed to fishing from January 1 until June 15. Enforcement authorities choose not to charge First Nations anglers with contravention of angling regulations because all such charges have a history of being dismissed by the courts.

Chapter 8

[14] Years later (October 23, 2001) a government fisheries inspector intimately familiar with the north coast fish plants, and the number of steelhead laundered through one of them in particular, contacted me in frustration over what he was surrounded by. Among other things he told me that First Nations fishers were adamant they didn't threaten steelhead, rather that steelhead threatened them.

Chapter 9

[15] Tides commonly reduced fishing time to something less than 24 hours per day but it was still legal to fish.

Chapter 10

[16] From the earliest days of commercial fishing the landings were referred to as "pieces".

Chapter 12

[17] The steadily diminishing number of canneries was due in part to technological innovations and consolidation but also to diminishing fish supply. Today there is only one cannery still operating in the Prince Rupert vicinity and it processes more Alaskan-caught pink salmon than anything else.

Chapter 13

[18] The test fishery data for all species are now readily available at http://www.pac.dfo-mpo.gc.ca/northcoast/webdocs/Tyee%20Test/Internet%20Tyee%20Test.htm

[19]This pattern was far more evident in the 1980s and before when weekly openings were usually four days or more. In most years after 1991, openings rarely went for more than two successive days.

[20] If the Skeena River afforded fishwheel opportunities anywhere near comparable to the Nass no one would ever have employed nets to capture steelhead for tagging purposes.

[21] The sonic tags were applied externally, a less invasive process than internally applied radio tags.

[22] Years later the Federal managers were trading sockeye from Rupert for foregone fishing at Moricetown to conserve Nanika sockeye but, by then, steelhead were far more valuable as a political and employment commodity than a food item or a reminder of constitutional rights.

Chapter 17

[23] Crutchfield, James A., and Giulio Pontecorvo. 1969. "The Pacific Salmon Fisheries: A Study in Irrational Conservation". The Johns Hopkins Press, Baltimore, Maryland, 220 pp.

Chapter 19

[24] That club was considered by many the center of the mid-1900s universe of steelhead sportfishing knowledge and expertise.

[25] All the early accounts of fishing in the Skeena refer to Dolly Varden. In reality these were/are bull trout.

[26] The third lodge and satellite camp was also constructed by Bob Wickwire several years after he had sold his original lodge on the upper river.

Chapter 20

[27] There are numerous examples from elsewhere in British Columbia where imposition of catch-and-release regulations for steelhead resulted in a sharp decline in angler participation followed by a slow but steady recovery to former levels within one or two steelhead generations.

Chapter 21

[28] The complete history of the several Classified Waters/Quality Waters processes and documents is available at http://www.env.gov.bc.ca/skeena/qws/.

[29] On March 7, 2011 the Provincial Government issued a news release indicating the measures it committed to enacting by April 1, 2011 had been shelved indefinitely.

Chapter 22

[30] Bailey, Larry L. and Michelle L. Boshard. 2006. Follow the money. Pages 99-124 in R. T. Lackey, D. H. Lach, and S. L. Duncan, editors. "Salmon 2100; the future of wild Pacific salmon." American Fisheries Society, Bethesda, Maryland.

[31] Commercial industry champions must have been embarrassed mightily when one of the prize-winning coho (good for a shiny new pickup truck) was later determined to have been caught by a gill-netter!

[32] The respective web sites are: http://www.ecotrust.org/, http://www.wildsalmoncenter.org/, http://www.moore.org/, http://skeenawild.org/, http://www.ncsteelheadalliance.ca/ and http://www.skeenawatershed.com/.

[33] The ISRP report suggested radio tagging several hundred steelhead on the outside edge of Area 4 and monitoring their fate. The suggested cost was "possibly $1M per year".

[34] Shortly after the ISRP report was released I wrote a long personal message concerning problems and deficiencies to each of its authors and their consultant facilitator. None of them ever responded.

[35] The Wild Salmon Policy is available at http://www.pac.dfo-mpo.gc.ca/publications/pdfs/wsp-eng.pdf.

[36] Details on the Commission can be found at http://www.cec.org/.

[37] http://www.msc.org/track-a-fishery/certified/pacific/british-columbia-sockeye-salmon/assessment-downloads-2

Chapter 23

[38] The author of the proposal has played the system similarly three times previously. The science community dismissed the efficacy of the undertaking on all occasions but politics prevailed. We're still waiting for evidence of anything of substance added to the management scenario.

[39] Strategic Framework for Fishery Monitoring and Catch Reporting in the Pacific Fisheries, November 2010.

REFERENCES

Ahrens, R. 2006. "Utility of the Steelhead Harvest Analysis in Determining Population Trends and Estimating Escapement." Ministry of Environment, University of British Columbia, Vancouver, B.C.

Andrew, T.F. and H. McShefrey. 1976. "Commercial interceptions of steelhead trout in British Columbia." *Fish. Mgmt. Bull. 1*, Marine Resources Branch, Victoria, B.C.

Anonymous. 1962. Fisheries Research Board of Canada Annual Report 1960-61. Biological Station, Nanaimo, B.C.

Anonymous. 1970. *Skeena Digest*, Volume 2, Number 1, Spring 1970. Provincial Archives of British Columbia, Victoria, B.C.

Anonymous. 1976. *Skeena Country. Sound Heritage*, Volume V, Number 1. Provincial Archives of British Columbia, Victoria, B.C

Anonymous. 2005. "Canada's Policy for Conservation of Wild Pacific Salmon". Fisheries and Oceans Canada, Vancouver, B.C.

Arman, Florence and Glen Wooldridge. 1982. *The Rogue: A River to Run*. Wildwood Press, Grants Pass, OR.

Asante, Nadine. 1972. *The History of Terrace, British Columbia*. Totem Press Limited. Terrace.

Barbeau, M. "An Indian Paradise Lost". *Canadian Geographic Journal*, V.2, June, 1930.

Beere, M.C. 1991. "Steelhead migration and timing as evaluated at the Skeena River test fishery, 1989". Skeena Fisheries Report SK#69. Ministry of Environment, Smithers, B.C.

Bilton, T.H. 1952. "The creel census of cut-throat trout at Lakelse Lake", 1952. Progress Reports of the Pacific Coast Stations of the Fisheries Research Board of Canada, Issue No. 92, pp. 18-20.

Blyth, Gladys Young. 1991. *Salmon Canneries: British Columbia North Coast*. Oolichan Books, Lantzville, B.C. 180pp.

Bouchard and Kennedy Research Consultants. 2007. "A Literature Review of First Nations in the Environs of the KSL Pipeline Looping Project." Prepared for Westland Resource Group, Victoria, B.C.

Campbell, K. Mack. 2004. *Cannery Village: Company Town. A history of British Columbia's Outlying Salmon Canneries*. Trafford Publishing, Victoria, B.C.

Coates, Ken. 2001. "The Past, Present, and Future of Northern British Columbia in an Age of Globalization". *In, Writing Off the Rural West: Globalization, Governments and the Transformation of Rural Communities*. Edited by Roger Epp and Dave Whitson. University of Alberta Press, Edmonton, Alberta.

Colt, Steve. 2000. "Salmon Fish Traps in Alaska: An Economic Perspective". Version 1.1, ISER Working Paper 2000.2. www.Alaskool.org.

Counterpoint Consulting. 2008. Economic Dimensions of Skeena Watershed Salmonid Fisheries. A report prepared for the Pacific Salmon Foundation, Vancouver, B.C.

De Gisi, Joseph S. 1999. Precision and Bias of the British Columbia Steelhead Harvest Analysis. Skeena Fisheries Report SK122. Smithers, B.C.

DFO. 2003. Skeena River Sockeye Salmon (update) DFO. Can. Sci. Advis. Sec. Stock Status Rep. 2003/047.

Duff, Wilson. 1964. The Indian History of British Columbia – The Impact of the White Man. Royal British Columbia Museum. Victoria, B.C.

Garner, K. and B. Parfitt. 2006. First Nations, Salmon Fisheries and the Rising Importance of Conservation. Report to the Pacific Fisheries Resource Conservation Council. 37 pp.

Fennelly, John F. 1963. Steelhead Paradise. Mitchell Press, Vancouver, Canada.

Gladstone, P. 1953. Native Indians and the fishing industry of British Columbia. The Canadian Journal of Economic and Political Science: 19(1):20-34.

Godfrey, H, W.R. Hourston, J.W. Stokes and F.C. Withler. 1954. Effects of a rock slide on Babine River salmon. Bulletin No. 101, Fisheries Research Board of Canada, Ottawa.

Gottesfeld, Allen S. and Ken A. Rabnett. 2008. Skeena River Fish and their Habitat. Ecotrust, Portland, Oregon.

Harding, D.R. 1969. The Status of the Nanika-Morice Sockeye Salmon Population and the Moricetown Native Food Fishery in 1967 and 1968. Department of Fisheries of Canada, Vancouver BC, 16p.

Harris, Douglas C. 2001. Fish Law and Colonialism: The Legal Capture of Salmon in British Columbia. University of Toronto Press. 306 pp.

Harris, Douglas C. 2008. Landing Native Fisheries, Indian Reserves and Fishing Rights in British Columbia, 1849-1925. University of British Columbia Press. 256 pp.

Hoaglund, Edward. 1969. Notes from the Century Before. Random House, New York.

Jones, R., Shepert, M. and Sterritt, N.J., 2004. "Our Place at the Table: First Nations in the B.C. Fishery: A Report by the First Nation Panel on Fisheries". Prepared for Aboriginal Fisheries Commission and First Nations Summit. Available online at www.bcafc.org/documents/FNFishPanelReport0604.pdf (last accessed Oct 20, 2005)

Large, R.G. 1957. The Skeena: River of Destiny. Mitchell Press Ltd., Vancouver.

Lewis, Adam. 2000. Skeena Steelhead and Salmon: A Report to the Stakeholders. Steelhead Society of British Columbia, Bulkley Valley Branch, Smithers, B.C.

Lingren, Art. 2004. Kispiox River. Frank Amato Publications, Inc. Portland, Oregon.

Lyons, Cicely. 1969. Salmon Our Heritage. Mitchell Press. Vancouver, B.C.

McGuane, Thomas. !999. The Longest Silence : A Life in Fishing. Random House. New York.

McRae, Donald M. and Peter H. Pearce. 2004. Treaties and Transition:
Towards a Sustainable Fishery on Canada's Pacific Coast (DFO web site)

Meggs, Geoff. 1991. Salmon - The Decline of the British Columbia Fishery. Douglas and McIntyre, Vancouver BC.

Meggs, Geoff and Duncan Stacey. 1992 Cork Lines and Cannery Lines: The Glory Years of Fishing on the West Coast. Douglas and McIntyre, Vancouver BC.

Milne, D.J. 1948. Skeena River salmon investigation, interim report, appendix no.1 : History and trends of the Skeena River salmon fishery. Fisheries Research Board of Canada, Nanaimo, British Columbia, 60p.

Milne, D.J. 1948. Skeena River salmon investigation, interim report, appendix no.3 : The effect of the Indian fishery on the Skeena River salmon runs. Fisheries Research Board of Canada, Nanaimo, British Columbia, 29p

Milne, D.J. 1948. Skeena River salmon investigations, interim report, appendix no. 4: Major Obstruction – Moricetown Falls. Fisheries Research Board of Canada, Nanaimo, British Columbia, 21p.

Milne, D.J. 1949. Salmon tagging off the Skeena River in 1948. Fish. Res. Bd. Canada, Pacific Prog. Rept., No. 80, pp. 50-51

Milne, D.J. 1950. Moricetown Falls as a hazard to salmon migration. Bull. Fish. Res. Bd. Canada, 86: 1-16.

Milne, D.J. 1955. The Skeena River salmon fishery with special reference to sockeye salmon. J. Fish. Res Bd. Can. 12:451-485.

Morrell, Mike. 1985. The Gitksan and Wet'suwet'en Fishery in the Skeena River System. Gitksan-Wet'suwet'en Tribal Council, Hazelton, B.C.

Morrell, Mike. 2000. Status of salmon spawning stocks of the Skeena River system. Northwest Institute for Biological Research, Smithers, B.C.

Newell, Dianne. 1989. The Development of the Pacific Salmon Canning Industry: A Grown Man's Game. McGill-Queen's Press. 303 pp.

Oguss, E. and T.R. Andrews. 1977. Incidental catches of steelhead trout in the commercial salmon fisheries of the Fraser River, Skeena River and Juan de Fuca Strait. Fish. Mgmt. Bull. 7, Marine Resources Branch, Victoria, B.C.

Oguss, E. and L.K. Evans. 1978. Incidental catches of steelhead trout in the commercial salmon fisheries of Barkely Sound, Johnstone Strait, and the Skeena and Fraser rivers. Fish. Mgmt. Rpt. No. 14, Marine Resources Branch, Victoria, B.C.

Palmer, R.N. 1967. An assessment of salmon migration and the native food fishery at Moricetown Falls in 1966. Department of Fisheries of Canada, Vancouver, B.C.

Palmer, R.N. 1966. An assessment of the native food fishery at Moricetown Falls in 1965. Department of Fisheries of Canada, Vancouver, B.C.

Palmer, R.N. 1964. A re-assessment of Moricetown Falls as an obstruction to salmon migration. Department of Fisheries of Canada, Vancouver, B.C.

Palmer, R.N. 1986. The Status of the Nanika River Sockeye Rehabilitation Program 1960-65. Department of Fisheries and Oceans of Canada, Vancouver, B.C.

Pauly, D. 1995. Anecdotes and the shifting baseline syndrome of fisheries. Trends in Ecology and Evolution, Vol. 10, No. 10, October 1995, p. 430. (See page 157 in Rose's Who Killed the Grand Banks?)

Pritchard, A. L. 1948. Interim Report: Skeena River Salmon Investigations. Fish. Res. Bd. Can., Pacific Biological Station, Nanaimo: 30p. + Appendices.

Pritchard, A.L. 1948. Salmon tagging off the Skeena River in 1947. Fish. Res. Bd. Canada, Pacific Prog. Rept., No. 75, pp. 40-42.

Rabnett, K. 2005. Morice-Nanika sockeye recovery plan: backgrounder, Skeena Fisheries Commission, Hazelton, BC, 44p.

Rajala, Richard A. 2006. Up-Coast: Forests and Industry on British Columbia's North Coast, 1870-2005. Royal British Columbia Museum, Victoria B.C. 294 pp.

Rutledge, Leo. 1989. That Some May Follow. The history of guide outfitting in British Columbia. (MOE Library, Smithers)

Sigurdson, G., B. Stuart and P. Gallaugher. 2008. Summary of the Skeena Watershed Committee debriefing session, Terrace, B.C. Department of Fisheries and Oceans, Vancouver, B.C.

Spence, C.R. and R.S. Hooton. 1991. Run timing and target escapements for summer-run steelhead trout (Oncorhynchus mykiss) stocks in the Skeena River system. PSARC Working Paper S91-07. BC Ministry of Environment, Smithers, B.C.

Sprout, P. E., and R. K. Kadowaki. 1987. Managing the Skeena River sockeye salmon (Oncorhynchus nerka) fishery - the process and the problems. Pages 385-395, in H. D. Smith, L. Margolis, and C. C. Wood (Eds.). Sockeye salmon (Oncorhynchus nerka) population biology and future management. Canadian Special Publication of Fisheries and Aquatic Sciences 96.

Taylor, G.D. 1968. Report on the preliminary survey of steelhead of the Skeena River drainage streams. Unpublished MS provided from personal collection of the author.

Thomas, J.O. 1993. Catch sampling and tag recovery involving steelhead caught in the 1993 northern British Columbia net fishery. Unpublished report prepared by J.O. Thomas and Associates Ltd. for the Ministry of Environment, Lands and Parks, Smithers, B.C. 108 pp.

Walters, C.J., J.A. Lichatowich., R.M. Peterman and J.D.Reynolds. 2008. Report of the Skeena Independent Science Review Panel. A report to the Canadian Department of Fisheries and Oceans and the British Columbia Ministry of the Environment. May 15, 2008, 144p.

Welch, D.W., Jacobs, M.J., Lydersen, H., Porter, A.D., Williams, S., and Muirhead, Y. (2009). Acoustic Telemetry Measurements of Survival and Movements of Adult Steelhead (Oncorhynchus mykiss) within the Skeena and Bulkley Rivers, 2008. Kintama Research Corporation, Final Report to the B.C. Ministry of the Environment, 50 p.

Welch, D.W., Lydersen, H., Porter, A.D., Neaga, L., and Muirhead, Y. 2009. Acoustic Telemetry Measurements of Survival and Movements of Adult Steelhead (Oncorhynchus mykiss) within the Bulkley River, 2009. Kintama Research Corporation, Final Report to the B.C. Ministry of the Environment, 47p.

Withler, F.C. 1960. Skeena Salmon Management Committee Annual Report 1959. Manuscript Report, Fisheries Research Board of Canada, Biological Station, Nanaimo, B.C.

Wood, C.C. 2001. Managing biodiversity in Pacific Salmon: the evolution of the Skeena River sockeye salmon fishery in British Columbia chapter in: B. Harvey and D. Duthie (ed.). Blue Millennium: Managing Global Fisheries for Biodiversity

Wright, Miriam. 2008. Building the Great Lucrative Fishing Industry: Aboriginal Gillnet Fishers and Protests over Salmon Fishery Regulations for the Nass and Skeena Rivers, 1950s-1960s. Lavour/Le Travail, 61.

ABOUT THE AUTHOR

Bob Hooton was born in Vancouver, raised in the suburb of South Burnaby and resident in that heavily populated part of British Columbia long enough to obtain a BSc from Simon Fraser University. The magnetism of steelhead came naturally to him. A successful angling apprenticeship was served on the highly competitive streams within striking distance of Vancouver before the university degree and before a neighbor fisheries biologist arranged an introduction with a high-ranking colleague in the Provincial Government headquarters in Victoria. So began a 37-year career that included an MSc session at the University of Idaho. Most of Bob's career was focused on steelhead management, first on Vancouver Island and later in the Skeena country. The most challenging and rewarding years, between 1986 and 1999, were spent in Smithers as the senior fisheries authority for the then Ministry of Environment's Skeena Region (the spatial equivalent of Oregon plus almost half of Washington). Bob's career bracketed the good, the bad and the ugly of steelhead management in British Columbia. The author was honored by both his peers and the sportfishing community with the Steelhead Society of British Columbia's Cal Woods Award (1993), the Ministry of Environment's Fisheries Professional of the Year (1994), the Totem Flyfishers' Roderick Haig-Brown Conservation Award (1997) and the Gilly Award from the British Columbia Federation of Fly Fishers (1999). The Skeena steelhead story could never be told until after the author retired in 2008.